Solidarity

Other works by Alain Touraine

published by Editions du Seuil

Le Pays contre l'Etat (with François Dubet, Michel Wieviorka and Zsuzsa Hegedus), 1981
La Prophétie anti-nucléaire (with François Dubet, Michel Wieviorka and Zsuzsa Hegedus), 1980
Lutte étudiante (with François Dubet, Michel Wieviorka and Zsuzsa Hegedus), 1978
La Voix et le regard, 1978
La Société invisible, 1976
Au-delà de la crise (under the author's supervision), 1976
Lettres à une étudiante, 1974
Pour la sociologie, 1974
Vie et mort du Chili populaire, 1973
Production de la société, 1973
Université et Société aux Etats-Unis, 1972
Le Mouvement de Mai ou le communisme utopique, 1968
La Conscience ouvrière, 1966
Sociologie de l'action, 1965
Ouvriers d'origine agricole, 1961

by other publishers

Mouvements sociaux d'aujourd'hui (edited by Alain Touraine), Editions Ouvrières, 1982
L'Après-Socialisme, Grasset, 1980
Un désir d'histoire, Stock, 1977
Les Sociétés dépendantes, Duculot, 1976
La Société post-industrielle, Denoël, 1969
L'Evolution du travail ouvrier aux Usines Renault, CNRS, 1955

Solidarity

The Analysis of a Social Movement: Poland 1980–1981

ALAIN TOURAINE

FRANÇOIS DUBET   MICHEL WIEVIORKA

JAN STRZELECKI

in collaboration with

GRAŻYNA GĘSICKA   ANNA MATUCHNIAK
TADEUSZ CHABIERA   MALGORZATA MELCHIOR
ANNA KRUCZKOWSKA   KRZYSZTOF NOWAK
IRENEUSZ KRZEMIŃSKI   WŁODZIMIERZ PAŃKOW
PAWEŁ KUCZYŃSKI   DOROTA RECZEK

translated by

DAVID DENBY

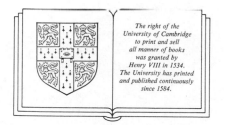

The right of the
University of Cambridge
to print and sell
all manner of books
was granted by
Henry VIII in 1534.
The University has printed
and published continuously
since 1584.

CAMBRIDGE UNIVERSITY PRESS

Cambridge

London   New York   New Rochelle   Melbourne   Sydney

EDITIONS DE LA MAISON DES SCIENCES DE L'HOMME

Paris

Published by the Press Syndicate of the University of Cambridge
The Pitt Building, Trumpington Street, Cambridge CB2 1RP
32 East 57th Street, New York, NY 10022, USA
296 Beaconsfield Parade, Middle Park, Melbourne 3206, Australia
and Editions de la Maison des Sciences de l'Homme
54 Boulevard Raspail, 75270 Paris Cedex 06

Originally published in French as *Solidarité* by Librairie Arthème
Fayard, Paris, 1982 and © Librairie Arthème Fayard 1982

First published in English by Editions de la Maison des Sciences de l'Homme
and Cambridge University Press 1983 as *Solidarity*
English translation © Maison des Sciences de l'Homme and Cambridge University Press
1983
Reprinted 1984

Printed in Great Britain at the University Press, Cambridge

Library of Congress catalogue card number: 83-1859

British Library Cataloguing in Publication Data
Solidarity.
1. Solidarność
I. Touraine, Alain   II. Solidarité. English
331.88′092′4   HD6735.7

ISBN 0 521 25407 8 hard covers
ISBN 0 521 27595 4 paperback
ISBN 2 7351 0058 8 hard covers (France only)
ISBN 2 7351 0059 6 paperback (France only)

To

Bogusław, Jan, Janusz, Krystyna, Marian, Mirosław, Paweł, Teresa,
Zbigniew and Zenon,
in GDAŃSK.

Franciszek, Henryk, Jan, Józef, Karol, Krystian, Mirosław, Stanisław,
Stanisław, Władysław,
in KATOWICE.

Andrzej, Eugeniusz, Grzegorz, Jerzy, Kazimierz, Krystyna, Stanisław,
Starszek, Tadeusz, Teresa and Wacław,
in WARSAW.

Bozena, Ewa, Jan, Jan, Kazimierz, Luiza, Krzysztof, Mieczysław, Tadeusz
and Wiesław,
in SZCZECIN.

Alojzy, Andrzej, Anna, Anna, Ewa, Genowefa, Kazimierz and Ryszard,
in ŁÓDŹ.

Andrzej, Bogumiła, Edmund, Henryk, Józef, Roman, Ryszard, Tomasz and
Zdzisława,
in WROCŁAW,

workers and technicians
members of SOLIDARNOŚĆ
who worked with us

Contents

Contents

Contents

Acknowledgements

When Michel Wieviorka and François Dubet left for Poland in April 1981 to set up our research project, with the help of Richard Stawiarski of the CFDT, Solidarity immediately gave us the warmest support. We owe a great debt of gratitude to Bronisław Geremek and Andrzej Wiełowiejski, Solidarity advisers in charge of the Centre for Socio-Professional Research. Lech Wałęsa agreed to see us, and greatly encouraged us in our work. At the same time the University of Warsaw, its President, Professor Samsonowicz, the Dean of the Faculty of Social Sciences, Professor Szacki, and our colleagues from the Institute of Sociology, signed an agreement with the Ecole des Hautes Etudes en Sciences Sociales which was of the utmost importance for the conduct of our research. Professor Szczepański, a member of the Sejm and of the Council of State, was a constant source of advice. Of course, none of these individuals is in any way responsible for the presentation of our findings, of which they knew nothing before publication.

The Polish research team, led by Jan Strzelecki, was involved in every stage of the research. Their names appear on the title page, and we wish to express our gratitude to them. Above all we hope that this project, connected as it is with an exceptional period in their country's history, will help them in their personal and professional lives.

The research was organised with remarkable efficiency by Dorota Reczek; without her, nothing would have been possible. The French researchers were aided by a team of very competent interpreters, in particular Joanna Rutkowska, Wojtek Maczkowski, Ewa Kołodziejczyk and Marek Siwakowski.

The work of the research groups was made possible by the help of many trade-union leaders and factory managers. Many people, from the Party, the Church, industry, the press and Rural Solidarity, came to take part in discussions with the groups of militants which we had brought together. We thank them heartily for their cooperation. The leaders of Solidarity also gave a lot of time to our research groups. In view of recent developments, we are particularly keen to express our gratitude to Zbigniew Bujak, Andrzej

Gwiazda, Adam Michnik, Professor Kukołowicz, Mr Bałenkowski and Mr Kropiwnicki, and to members of the political opposition such as Mr Moczulski and Mr Czuma.

On the French side, this project was made possible by a research grant from the Délégation Générale à la Recherche Scientifique et Technique which was awarded with exceptional speed thanks to Mr Pierre Aigrain, then Secretary of State for Research. The Ecole des Hautes Etudes en Sciences Sociales and the Maison des Sciences de l'Homme allowed us to hold a seminar in Paris in July 1981 bringing together the Polish and French researchers. Krzysztof Pomain, Alexander Smolar, Jurek Strzelecki and Bernard Guetta, as well as the journalists of the Agence France-Presse and the Italian press agency ANSA, allowed us to draw on their remarkable knowledge of the Polish situation.

Danièle Monmarte, Jacqueline Salouadji, Claire Lusson, Monique Mathieu and Béatrice Prunaux-Cazer took on the heavy administrative burden which this study represented for more than a year.

This study is a sociological intervention: it is the result of a dialogue between the self-analysis of militants and the interpretations proposed by the researchers. The members of Solidarity, shop-floor and office workers, technicians and engineers, who took part, are therefore much more the authors than the objects of this book. It is not enough simply to thank them. Their first names are printed at the beginning of the book, and it is to them that it is dedicated. They understood from the very first day that this research could be both a source of understanding and an aid to action, by giving them time and space for thought and free discussion. Some of them are now living through dramatic moments in their lives; all their hearts are full of sadness, bitterness and anger. Our hope is that, in spite of it all, this book, whenever and however it reaches them, will help them, and we can say to them today that they are the pride of the working class, brave children of Poland whose action is a great symbol of democracy. Whatever their present trials, their example will continue to inspire those who, as a worker in the Ursus factory used to say, wish to see men and women no longer a mass, but the subjects of their own history.

Note: The French authors of this book wish to stress that their Polish colleagues were unable to see the text before publication, and that they cannot therefore be considered responsible for the opinions which it expresses.

Vocabulary and abbreviations

AK	Home Army, linked to the Polish government in exile in London; responsible for the Warsaw Rising
AL	People's Army
AS	Solidarity press agency
CFDT	Confédération française démocratique du travail; one of the two main trade-union confederations in France, enjoying some links with the Socialist Party [Tr.]
DiP	'Experience and Future', a discussion group of Party and opposition intellectuals
Grunwald	A Nationalist and anti-Semitic group, close to the Party
KIK	Club of Catholic Intellectuals
KKP	Solidarity's National Coordinating Committee, replaced by the KK (National Committee) after the Congress
KOR	Workers' Defence Committee. Set up to support those arrested in the disturbances of June 1976. Expanded to include broader elements in 1977 and re-named KSS-KOR (Committee for Social Self-Defence and Workers' Defence) but referred to as KOR.
KPN	Confederation for an Independent Poland, a nationalist party
KWZZ	Founding Committee of the Baltic free trade unions
KZ	Factory committee of the union
MKS	Inter-Factory Strike Committee (summer 1980); forerunner of Solidarity
MKZ	Inter-Factory Founding Committee; regional organisation of Solidarity

Vocabulary and abbreviations

NSZZ	Independent self-governing trade union; the title adopted in the early days of the movement by certain groups of workers before they affiliated to Solidarity
OPS-Z	Solidarity's Centre for Socio-Professional Research
PAX	Catholic party; collaborated with the regime, but began to move away from it after 1980
PUWP (PZPR)	Polish United Workers' Party; the Polish Communist Party
RMP	Young Poland Movement
ROPCiO	Movement for the Defence of Civil and Citizens' Rights
Samorząd	Workers' self-management
Sejm	Polish Parliament
Sieć	Self-management network
Strajk	Strike
TKN	Society for Academic Courses; 'flying university' organised by opposition intellectuals
województwo	One of the forty-nine administrative districts into which Poland is divided, under the authority of the *wojewoda*
Zjednoczenie	Union of industrial enterprises
ZR	Regional Council of Solidarity
Związek Zawodowy	Trade union

Glossary of names

EDMUND BAŁUKA Led the Szczecin strike in 1970

KAZIMIERZ BARCIKOWSKI Member of the Politburo

BOGDAN BORUSEWICZ Member of the KOR, organiser of the free trade unions in Gdańsk

STEFAN BRATKOWSKI President of the Journalists' Association, founder of DiP, expelled from the Party in 1981

RYSZARD BUGAJ Solidarity economist

ZBIGNIEW BUJAK President of the Masovia MKZ

BOGDAN CYWIŃSKI Solidarity adviser close to the Church

TADEUSZ FISZBACH First Secretary of the PUWP in the Gdańsk district, member of the Politburo from December 1980 to July 1981

WŁADYSŁAW FRASYNIUK President of the MKZ of Lower Silesia, aged 27

BRONISŁAW GEREMEK Historian, a leading Solidarity adviser, chairman of the Centre for Socio-Professional Research

EDWARD GIEREK First Secretary of the PUWP, 1970–80

MIECZYSŁAW GIL Solidarity leader at the Lenin steelworks

JÓZEF GLEMP Primate of Poland, successor to Cardinal Wyszyński

WŁADYSŁAW GOMUŁKA First Secretary of the PUWP, 1956–70

TADEUSZ GRABSKI Member of the Politburo until 1981

ANDRZEJ GWIAZDA Gdańsk leader of Solidary, Vice-President of the National Committee

ZBIGNIEW IWANÓW Initiated the 'horizontal structures' movement within the Party

MIECZYSŁAW JAGIELSKI Member of the Politburo since 1971, Deputy Prime Minister, government negotiator for the Gdańsk Agreement

ZBIGNIEW JANAS Solidarity leader at the Ursus factory

WOJCIECH JARUZELSKI General, Prime Minister since 9 February 1981, First Secretary of the PUWP since 18 October 1981

SEWERYN JAWORSKI Vice-President of the Masovia MKZ

MARIAN JURCZYK President of the Szczecin MKZ, leading figure in the 1970 strike

STANISŁAW KANIA First Secretary of the PUWP from September 1980 to October 1981

Glossary of names

LESZEK KOŁAKOWSKI Philosopher, expelled from Warsaw University in 1968, now teaches at All Souls College, Oxford

ANDRZEJ KOŁODZIEJ Leader of the strike at the Paris Commune shipyard in Gdynia, aged 20

ROMUALD KUKOŁOWICZ The Primate's representative with Solidarity

JACEK KUROŃ Co-author of the *Open Letter to the Party* in 1964, imprisoned, member of the KOR, Solidarity adviser

STEFAN KUROWSKI Economist, Solidarity adviser

EDWARD LIPIŃSKI Economist, member of the KOR

BOGDAN LIS Vice-President of the Gdańsk MKZ, and member of the National Committee

JAN LITYŃSKI Member of the KOR, editor of *Robotnik*

ANTONI MACIEREWICZ Member of the KOR, with nationalist sympathies

TADEUSZ MAZOWIECKI Formerly a member of Parliament and of the Znak group; editor of the periodical *Więź*, president of the committee of advisers to the Gdańsk MKS, editor of the weekly *Solidarność*

ADAM MICHNIK Historian, expelled from the University in 1968, member of the KOR and an adviser to Solidarity

MIECZYSŁAW MOCZAR General, Minister of the Interior 1964–8; left the Politburo after the workers' rebellion of 1970, and returned to it 2 December 1980

LESZEK MOCZULSKI Historian, founder of the KPN

KAROL MODZELEWSKI Historian, author, with Kuroń, of the *Open Letter to the Party* (1964), imprisoned; member of Solidarity's National Committee and of the Presidium of the Wrocław MKZ

STEFAN OLSZOWSKI Member of the Politburo since September 1970, considered the leader of the 'hard-line' faction

KRZYSZTOF POMIAN Historian, student leader in 1956, opposition intellectual living in France

MIECZYSŁAW RAKOWSKI Deputy Prime Minister, in charge of relations with the trade unions

JAN RULEWSKI President of the Bydgoszcz MKZ, victim of police brutality in March 1981

ANDRZEJ SŁOWIK President of the Łódź MKZ

ALEXANDER SMOLAR Economist, representative of the KOR in France

JADWIGA STANISZKIS Imprisoned, then expelled from the University, for her part in the events of 1968; Solidarity adviser

KAZIMIERZ ŚWITOŃ Organiser of independent trade unions in Silesia in 1978

JAN SZCZEPAŃSKI Sociologist, member of Parliament and of the Council of State

FATHER TISCHNER Theologian close to Pope John Paul II

Glossary of names

ANNA WALENTYNOWICZ   Militant at the Lenin shipyard whose dismissal was one of the causes of the strike in August 1980

LECH WAŁĘSA   President of Solidarity, born in 1943

ANDRZEJ WIEŁOWIEJSKI   Founder of the Warsaw KIK, Solidarity adviser

HENRYK WUJEC   Member of the KOR, active at the Ursus factory

STEFAN WYSZYŃSKI   Primate of Poland, died 28 May 1981

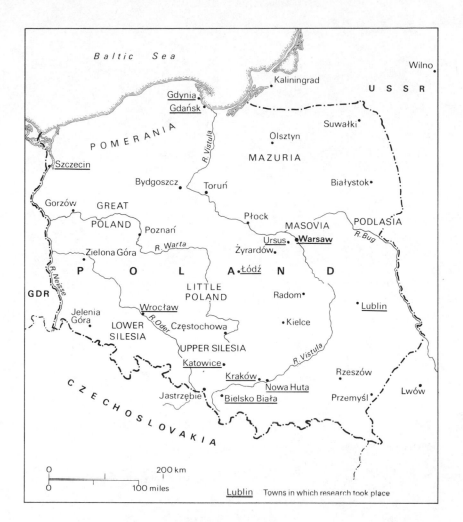

Figure 1. Poland

Introduction

1. This book appeared a few months after the declaration of martial law on 13 December 1981, the arrest of thousands of members of Solidarity and the first acts of resistance by Polish workers to the outlawing of their liberation movement. As we wrote it, all those who had worked on it with us, Polish researchers and workers of whom we now had no direct news, were present in our thoughts.

As a mark of friendship and admiration, we should perhaps simply have expressed our disapproval at the destruction of so many hopes and so much courage, our condemnation of martial law. We have instead chosen to maintain the tone and the content which the whole research team, Polish and French, had chosen to give to the book. We must do more than protest at the repression which is now taking place: our task is to promote a better understanding of this movement which the military authorities are trying to destroy.

There are two reasons for this. Firstly, our team is the only one which has been able to conduct an in-depth sociological study of Solidarity with the agreement and active participation of its members. Our method, sociological intervention, makes the actors and interlocutors the analysts of their own action, and our findings therefore have a historical value which makes it essential that we analyse them as thoroughly as possible. Secondly, it is not enough simply to mark one's solidarity with those who are being attacked today; we must do this in full knowledge of what it is that is being attacked, constantly respecting the ideas and feelings of those we seek to defend. We inevitably project our own categories onto others, but this belief in the universality of our actions and opinions leads to conclusions which are at best surprising and, more often than not, simply wrong. Is it possible to support the action of Solidarity if one confuses the Polish national consciousness with the forms which nationalism takes in France, or if one is reluctant to admit that the attachment to Catholicism is an essential component of working-class struggles in Poland? We want this book to make the voice of Solidarity heard, not only in its most solemn declarations, but through an examination of the work of analysis and discussion which active members of Solidarity undertook with us close to their workplaces.

2. This book has no pretensions to being a history of those sixteen months of social ferment in Poland. Its aim is to understand the nature, the internal workings and the evolution of Solidarity, one of the biggest social movements to have stirred a country at the end of the twentieth century.

Three essential questions arose during the research:

The most important concerns the nature of the movement: Solidarity is a trade union but, obviously, more than a trade union. It is a workers' movement, born in the factories where it is now fighting against repression, but it is also a national movement and a struggle for the democratisation of society. Outside Poland, many observers try to reduce it to only one of its dimensions: for some, it is a purely working-class movement animated by socialist ideals which were deformed or destroyed by regimes having their origins in Stalinism; for others, it is above all a struggle for national liberation in the tradition of the uprisings of the eighteenth and nineteenth centuries and the Warsaw Rising of 1944. Finally, there are those who maintain that Solidarity is of particular concern to us because it appeals openly to the values of Western democracy, human rights and political pluralism. The difficulty is that all these images are in themselves correct: working-class consciousness is just as strong in Solidarity as the attachment to the figure of the Pope, and this is a national liberation movement which has sought to establish the most highly developed forms of representative democracy. Our aim must therefore be to discover why and how these three levels of action – trade-union, democratic and national – combine in Solidarity to form what may be called a total social movement aiming to change all aspects of public life.

The second question is less obvious, but is a greater challenge to received notions. Is Solidarity a movement, an upsurge of collective will, with all the richness which we have just suggested, or is it in fact the instrument for the reconstruction of a whole society, for the renewal of social institutions and even of those economic and social forces which may eventually enter into conflict with Solidarity itself? Our tradition has encouraged us to see the two terms *movement* and *institution* as radically opposed, to see every great social movement as necessarily revolutionary, by which we understand a movement whose objective is the seizure of power and even the imposition of absolute rule, considered essential if privileges are to be destroyed, the interests of the people defended, and enemies at home and abroad resisted. Consequently, we can only think of attachment to institutions and legality as a sign of moderate, not to say conservative, political tendencies. Solidarity was indeed an immense social movement which in the space of a few months succeeded in bringing together nearly ten million members. But it never sought to seize power: on the contrary, it concerned itself with

institutional reforms, trying to install competent and hard-working managers in industry and wanting to see the freedom of the press respected and
censorship abolished. It also helped the peasants to organise, at a time when
food shortages threatened to set peasants' and workers' interests against
each other. Here was a popular movement which behaved like a legislative
assembly infinitely anxious to respect legal procedures. How is it that these
two types of action are brought together in Solidarity?

The third question follows from the brutal rupture of December 1981. At
the beginning, Solidarity managed to limit itself and its demands to such an
extent that the agreements signed after the strikes of August 1980
acknowledged the Party's leading role in the state and the sanctity of
Poland's international alliances. But was the movement not gradually
drawn into a struggle for power itself? Is it true to say that the workers,
whose demands at the outset were of a predominantly trade-union nature,
were led by radical intellectuals – denounced by the Party as anti-socialist
elements – towards an increasingly far-reaching questioning of the
legitimacy of the regime itself, and therefore towards inevitable rupture?
Some would maintain that it was the confrontation between the union and
the government which paralysed the country, and that Solidarity thus
bears a share of the responsibility for the worsening economic crisis which
could not but lead to political rupture. This kind of criticism has been made
often enough of the Popular Unity government in Chile to deserve closer
examination in the case of Poland. But it must be rejected. The military
interests of the Soviet Union in Poland were never directly threatened
during the Solidarity period; there was no civil disturbance, not even mass
demonstrations outside official buildings; the daily press, radio and
television remained throughout under the control of the Party, as did
Parliament, the economic administration and, of course, the army, the
militia and the secret police. If the power of the Party weakened and even
disintegrated, then it was through its own impotence and decay rather than
any direct pressure from the masses, who never went beyond short national
warning strikes.

3. This book takes as its field the factory and the Solidarity activists within
it. Its main purpose is to present the findings of six research groups, each
made up of union militants at factory level.

Why did we choose to work at rank-and-file level, when Solidarity has
produced a huge amount of written material, factory and regional news-
sheets, statements made by the press agency AS and in the weekly
newspaper *Solidarność*? Why did we not interview all the national and
regional leaders of Solidarity, instead of a selected group of them? Because,
in a social movement, the participants are far more than just a base
prompted by questions of immediate self-interest which it is the leaders' job

to transform into a programme and a set of political strategies. Solidarity's enemies have often claimed that its worker members were straightforward trade unionists, whereas the leaders were political agitators. If one listens for a moment to the rank and file, it very quickly becomes apparent that this accusation is groundless, that in each of our research groups just as in every enterprise we visited, the big questions – political freedoms, national independence, industrial management, social justice – are as constantly present as they are in the debates of Solidarity's National Committee. We can even say that, at the base, protest and questioning are more direct, since at the top the need to negotiate and awareness of external threats lead to greater caution.

At a deeper level, the example of Solidarity is a striking demonstration of how false it is to believe that the most exploited and dependent groups in society can only reveal and aggravate the contradictions of the system which dominates them, without for a moment being able to escape from their chains, to conceive and organise for themselves their own liberation. This old idea, popularised by Lenin's *What is to be done?*, and moreover quickly refuted by the formation of the soviets in St Petersburg in 1905, serves to justify the dominance of ideologists and political leaders over the social base. It is rejected by Solidarity, rank and file and leadership alike, and their example shows how mistaken and dangerous it can be. The members of Solidarity are not only conscious of being downtrodden; they have a positive awareness of themselves and of their rights. As producers they oppose the incompetence and corruption of the managers of industry; in the name of the national consciousness and the history of Poland they seek to reject foreign domination; in the name of truth they demand freedom of expression and information. Their movement is not a mechanical reaction to oppression which has become unbearable; it manifests ideas, choices, a collective will.

The shipyard workers of the Baltic coast and the miners of Upper Silesia are better paid than most Polish wage-earners. They are not a lumpen-proletariat, but highly educated workers, eager for information, concerned about economic problems and well disposed towards the modernisation of production plant and methods. They are close to the technicians and young production engineers, whose wages are often lower than theirs. They are not carried away by sudden fits of anger, they do not behave like a mob, they do not blindly follow a leader or calls to strike. They belong, and consciously so, in the great trade-union tradition of workers attached to their trade and to a working-class culture, proud of their work and of the banner of their union branch, which has been blessed by a priest and around which they mount a guard of honour on special occasions. In the same way, they do not experience national dependence as colonisation, as a destruction of their roots, even in the case of the large numbers of Poles who had to leave their homes in the Eastern areas occupied by the Soviet Union to settle in the parts of Western Poland which were previously German. Their national state is dependent and constantly under threat, but their sense of national identity is just as strong as it was when the peasants of Poznań managed to hold on to and even extend their lands in the face of Prussian measures to dispossess and Germanise them. The militants of Solidarity do not simply overturn obstacles; they affirm principles and values, their will and their consciousness make them actors in their own history and, without singing the praises of their movement, they are convinced of its exceptional importance and know that the world is watching them. They realise that they can only rely on their own strength, and at the same time they know that theirs is an exemplary struggle.

Familiarity with Solidarity should convince us – and one of the aims of this book is to help establish this belief – that men and women are not subject to historical laws and material necessity, that they produce their own history through their cultural creations and social struggles, by fighting for the control of those changes which will affect their collective and in particular their national life.

From some quarters we shall perhaps be accused of identifying too closely with the people whose actions we are seeking to understand, of not being sufficiently objective and distanced. This criticism must be categorically rejected. Firstly, the reader will observe that we have enough respect for Solidarity to show its weaknesses and negative aspects as well as its greatness and its liberating drive. Above all we hope that the reader will understand that it is precisely those who speak of a social movement without trying to enter into the ideas and feelings of the participants, who lack objectivity, for they cannot even see the object which they claim to be analysing.

Solidarity was not simply a social and political force which modified the course of Polish history. It was, and is, a movement, a collective will, and its significance goes far beyond the results it has obtained. When the dominated protest and seek liberation, their hopes are never entirely realised: the shadows cast by history remain. But great upsurges like Solidarity bring with them at least the certainty that the behaviour of the dominated is never totally determined by the dominant forces.

Humanity remembers the dazzling movements which break through the darkness of oppression. The light of Solidarity shines on us all.

Should we use the past tense to speak of Solidarity? In a quarter of a century, will young Poles know as little of Solidarity as young Hungarians today know of the revolution which set their country alight in October 1956? Is it not true that every uprising in Communist Central Europe, in Poland, Czechoslovakia or Hungary, is a battle lost before it is even fought, because the enslaved society and its all-powerful masters are such unequal adversaries? The military coup of 13 December may seem to suggest this, but the life and work of Solidarity prove the opposite. Recent events in Poland have constituted not an insurrection, but the reconstruction of democratic society. Solidarity did not launch itself impetuously at the walls imprisoning Poland; it sought to change Polish society from the inside, by imposing certain limits on itself. This was not a popular movement which burned itself out in an impossible dream; for many months, it allowed Poles to live in a new way, to speak, to look for the truth, within the economy and within history. We thought that societies living under regimes of totalitarian inspiration had become a shadow of their former selves, but Solidarity showed that Poland was alive, its imagination and its memory intact. Nothing can now hide the obvious truth: a society may be hidden by the apparatus of domination, but its real, living language is of a different order to the wooden language of its rulers. The society's national consciousness contradicts official interpretations, and in its search for truth it discards an ideology which claims to be scientific and which no longer even believes in itself. The totalitarian regime's ambition of imposing its phrases and its ideas on a whole society has failed. Even in defeat, Solidarity still demonstrates that the Party-state and its successor the Party-as-police are more foreign than ever to the preoccupations and the hopes of the people which, for a time, they may rule by force of arms.

4. This book is the product of a *sociological intervention*, a piece of research conducted according to a method designed for the study of social movements. Let us recall its main principles. Sociology, when it studies behaviour which may be considered as a response to a situation, uses the method of the survey. Consumers choose between different products and electors between different candidates, residents in an area, or workers, state their degree of satisfaction or dissatisfaction with the situation in which they find themselves. At this point, the sociologist's task is to group together individual responses on a statistical basis so as to establish correlations between a certain type of behaviour, opinion or attitude on the one hand and, on the other, a particular position in the organisation and especially the stratification of society. The sociological survey is therefore particularly suited to certain types of behaviour; but social movements are as far removed as it is possible to be from this category. A social movement is not a response to a situation, precisely because its specificity is to challenge that situation. The workers in a factory make judgements on the exercise of authority in the workplace, but the trade union exerts pressure in order to change these authority relations according to its vision of conflicts of interest and workers' rights. What was needed, then, was a method just as well suited to these conflictual forms of behaviour which challenge a situation as the survey is to forms of behaviour which have more to do with

consumption. The primary principle of this method is that it works with a number of collective actors organised in groups; and these groups, rather than being centred on themselves, consciously represent some collective action. Since a social movement is a collective action, the study of it should clearly concentrate on a collective body of individuals.

The most immediately apparent feature of sociological intervention is that it seeks to define the meaning which the actors themselves attribute to their action. Because a social movement challenges a situation, it is always the bearer of normative values and orientations. Rather than enclosing the group in a reflexion upon itself, the technique involves opening it up so that it can experience, in conditions which one might describe as experimental, the practices of the social group or movement to which it sees itself as belonging. To this end the group invites interlocutors, both sympathetic and hostile, to participate in its discussions, in order to produce a corpus of responses which the group will then confront, and on the basis of which it will embark on a process of self-analysis which is impossible in ordinary circumstances because of the pressure of decisions to be taken and, indeed, the pressure of the organisation itself. In this context, the researchers are not only refusing to take as the object of their study a situation; they start from the position that the behaviour being observed must be considered inseparable from the body of meanings which the actors attribute to that behaviour.

This work of self-analysis does, however, have its limits. Every actor is an ideologist, in the sense that he produces a representation of the situation in which he finds himself, and that that representation corresponds to his own interests. No actor can become a disinterested analyst. The researcher must therefore intervene more directly. But at this point a double difficulty arises. On the one hand, if he adopts the attitude of a remote and objective observer, he cannot reach the very thing which he seeks to understand: the coldness of objectivity will hold him back from the heat of the social movement. Conversely, if he identifies with the actors' struggle, he ceases to be an analyst and becomes nothing more than a doctrinaire ideologist; in this case, his role becomes entirely negative. The method's response to this difficulty is to say that the researcher must identify not with the actors' struggle in itself, but with the highest possible meaning of that struggle, which is nothing other than the social movement: the element in a struggle which challenges the general orientations of a society and of the social systems for controlling the use of the main resources, cultural and in particular economic. In this way the researcher is neither external to the group, nor identified with it; it is through him that the group will attempt to isolate, amongst the various meanings of its action, the one which challenges the central core of the society.

Sociological intervention, then, has two phases: the direct intervention of the researchers, during which they help the militants to move towards self-analysis; and the corollary of this, which we have called the 'conversion' of the group, the moment at which it moves on to analyse its own practices and those of the movement of which it is a part on the basis of the hypotheses introduced by the researchers, which may, of course, be accepted or rejected. Two researchers are therefore needed to take charge of the work: one, whom we call the interpreter, is the agent of self-analysis; the other, the analyst, introduces the hypotheses elaborated by the researchers, tries to ensure their acceptance by the group, and observes their effects on the workings of the group. These effects are, indeed, the main test of the relevance of the hypotheses. A false hypothesis can only cause disorder, noise, unstable or inconsistent responses. A hypothesis which gains acceptance, on the other hand, increases intelligibility and clarifies relationships between members of the group. But a second test must be added to the first. A hypothesis may be judged satisfactory if the group can use it to return to action, to understand both its own initiatives and the responses of its partners. This return towards social practice we have called permanent sociology.

This method supposes protracted work with each group. Whereas a survey is extensive in operation, intervention proceeds intensively. The researchers spend tens of hours with a group of about ten people. Moreover it is important to set up several intervention groups, and each intervention must include two phases with an interval of several months in between. All this produces a corpus of written material of several thousand pages which the research team must integrate into its conclusions.[1]

In the case of the research carried out in Poland, this method was followed very closely, thanks to the constant support which we received from Solidarity militants at local and national level. Groups of militants, as diverse as possible in composition, were formed in the spring of 1981 in Gdańsk, Katowice and Warsaw, and in the autumn in Szczecin, Łódź and Wrocław. These cities were chosen because they represented the main centres of the movement's activity. How could we avoid situating our study in the two great Baltic ports and in the two regions of Silesia, Poland's industrial heartland? Łódź, the capital of the textile industry, saw a big hunger march in the summer of 1981; we also wanted to know the views of its women workers. Warsaw seemed essential, firstly because one of the starting points of the movement had been the Ursus factory in the suburbs of the capital, and also because the Masovia branch of the union saw itself as the spearhead of Solidarity's most radical wing.

---

1 A more detailed discussion of the method of sociological intervention may be found in Alain Touraine's *La Voix et le regard*, Paris, Le Seuil, 1978; trans. as *The Voice and the Eye*, Cambridge University Press, 1981; especially Part Two, pp. 139–222. (Tr.)

Introduction

The groups first met interlocutors from the Party, industry, the Church, the press and the political opposition, as well as the leaders of Solidarity; they then went back over these meetings and, with the help of the researchers, formulated a first analysis of their action. Then the researchers submitted to them their own hypotheses and examined the way in which these were received – accepted, rejected or modified – in the course of long joint working sessions. The first three groups were later able to meet in pairs in Warsaw, and we saw them again in the autumn before beginning work with the new groups.

In each group, the research was led by a Franco-Polish team, composed as follows:

Gdańsk	*Katowice*
Grażyna Gęsicka	Tadeusz Chabiera
Paweł Kuczyński	François Dubet
Krzysztof Nowak	Malgorzata Melchior
Michel Wieviorka	Jan Strzelecki

Warsaw	*Szczecin*
Anna Kruczkowska	Tadeusz Chabiera
Ireneusz Krzemiński	François Dubet
Włodzimierz Pańkow	Włodzimierz Pańkow
Alain Touraine	Jan Strzelecki

Wroclaw	*Lódź*
Paweł Kuczyński	Grażyna Gęsicka
Malgorzata Melchior	Anna Kruczkowska
Krzysztof Nowak	Ireneusz Krzemiński
Alain Touraine	Anna Matuchniak
	Michel Wieviorka

This primary source of material was supplemented with shorter talks with Solidarity members and officials in Kraków, Nowa-Huta, Bielsko-Biała and Lublin. Michel Wieviorka and Jan Strzelecki attended Solidarity's Congress in Gdańsk in September 1981. We also had many interviews with Solidarity leaders and advisers, and with various sociologists. The research began in April 1981 and was completed at the end of November the same year.

PART ONE
THE MOVEMENT

1

1956 – 1968 – 1980:
Resistance to Communist rule
in Central Europe

TWO EXPLANATIONS

After the invasion of Czechoslovakia, the future seemed bleak for popular opposition movements in Communist Central Europe. In Poland in 1968 the intellectuals, fighting in isolation, had been brutally silenced, and in December 1970 the Baltic strikes had been crushed with heavy loss of life. So in 1976 the workers' uprisings which began at the Ursus tractor plant in Warsaw and in the town of Radom showed the scale of popular discontent, but seemed incapable of leading quickly to any social or political counter-offensive.

And yet August 1980 saw the outbreak, on the Baltic coast, of the most widespread and the longest-lived popular uprising yet to challenge Communist rule, its autocracy, its economic failure and its subservience to foreign domination. The repression taking place today must not obscure the force of the message: a working-class rising against those who claim to speak in its name; a mass movement inventing its own democracy in the face of arbitrary government and bureaucracy; a nation turning to its history and its religion, not to impose fanaticism and persecution, but as a ground upon which to give fresh life to democratic freedoms.

Whatever the future holds for Poland, Solidarity has already obtained what hardly anyone outside Poland itself thought possible: it has forced the acceptance, at least for a time, of the unacceptable, and for all this ground to be lost would require repression much more brutal and much more sustained than that which followed the revolution of Budapest and the Prague Spring. Any analysis of Solidarity must therefore situate it within the history of social and political struggles in the Eastern bloc or, to be more precise, in the group of Central European countries which have been part of the Soviet sphere of influence since the Second World War: Czechoslovakia, Hungary, the GDR and Poland. Such an overview must show the historical similarities between these countries over the last thirty-five years; but it must also bring out the originality of the movement which began in Poland

13

with the strikes of August 1980, and make this originality more clearly understood.

Over the last few years, the notion of totalitarianism has often been used to define Communist societies, particularly in France, where intellectuals had for long enough rejected this idea, refusing to read Hannah Arendt so as to avoid having to class Hitler's Germany and Stalin's Soviet Union together. For a long time there was practically no analysis of these 'people's democracies', apart from a few ambiguous remarks about the distance still separating the reality from the ideal and socialism as actually constituted from true socialism. Even this highly abstract perspective, which was cultivated for a long time by the review *Les Temps modernes*, was more respectable than the laziness which sought to explain present crises by reference to the weight of the past, or the actions of Stalin, not to mention underdevelopment or the continuing influence of pre-war inequalities.

The notion of totalitarianism represents a considerable advance on such superficial explanations, in that it recognises the existence of a certain type of regime, in its diachronic coherence. Instead of taking refuge in a search for particular and occasional causes, it asserts, with the same force as Montesquieu, the general nature of the totalitarian regime: not despotism in the traditional sense of the term, but the hegemonic grip of a despotic government on society as a whole, the rule of the arbitrary through bureaucracy, the subordination of all social relations, and in particular of class relations, to the great All – which is at the same time the One, in the form of the Party, and more often than not the First Secretary, as Prince. The notion of totalitarianism seemed a useful tool for the description of Eastern bloc societies at a time when more and more credence was being given to a vision which saw the discourse of the ruling class and the transmission of privilege as the central mechanisms of Western societies. In both cases, intellectuals disillusioned by the failure or corruption of socialist or revolutionary movements were taking refuge in the assertion that society was an order resting on the twin foundations of self-interest and violence, an order so absolute that there was no place for the social agent, for innovation and opposition, for debate and negotiated change. When Marcuse spoke of one-dimensional societies, he was thinking just as much of the United States as the Soviet Union.

These analyses, whether they present themselves as Marxist, post-Marxist or non-Marxist, have sometimes exalted the idea of rebellion, but they have never believed in conflict nor, especially, in the ability of the oppressed successfully to challenge the domination which is imposed on them. Such pessimism is easy to understand at a time when the economic and political managers of the growth economy seemed to have a free hand, when fine social-democratic feelings were easily reconciled with capitalist domination, and when those who spoke for the liberating revolution politely doffed their hats to the masters of the Soviet empire who were assassinating, deporting and imprisoning militant workers, intellectuals and millions of ordinary people.

And yet the notion of totalitarianism is of only limited use in understanding present events in Poland. The very fact that Solidarity can exist forces us to reject excessive use of the term. Hannah Arendt was more cautious, restricting her analysis to Hitler and Stalin and not considering at all the Soviet Union after 1953. As far as Poland is concerned, how can we understand the extraordinary events which have taken place there recently if we do not first recognise that Poland has never, except for the last few years of Stalin's rule from 1949 to 1953, been a totalitarian society? That the country has been ruled by an all-powerful Party, imposing its political monopoly and demanding the right to dominate the whole spectrum of social life, and therefore totalitarian in inspiration, is self-evident. But Polish society has almost never submitted to this domination, and the primary reason is that the Polish sense of nationality, formed by more than a century's experience of being denied the status of nation-state, has its roots in consciousness and culture rather than in institutions and government, and that Poland since Stalinisation has continued, as at the time of partition, to live through its national consciousness. To a great extent this is due to the resistance of the Church, which has for a long time been identified with the sense of nationality, and to the intellectuals, often the heirs of the gentry, who felt that the responsibility for the cultural survival of the nation lay with them. After 1956 and the return of Gomułka the Church was recognised, even if new pressures came to bear on it fairly soon; at the same time the majority of the peasants were freed from forced collectivisation, and the intellectuals were able to participate almost without restriction in international scientific and cultural life.

Such relative autonomy of society in relation to the dominant regime goes against the image of a totalitarian society. Poland has always had two faces: the real country has never been entirely obscured by the official one, intellectual life has never been reduced to the dominant ideology, and the subjection to socialist realism, however brutal were the pressures which sought to impose it, was only a brief, black episode. Above all, the working class has never identified with the institutions, particularly the official trade unions incorporated into the state apparatus, which claimed to speak in its name. It is this resistance on the part of society to absolute rule which explains the fact that we feel directly concerned by events in Poland. Those events demonstrate in that part of the world, as the movements which began in Western universities from Berkeley to Nanterre between 1964 and 1968 did in ours, that it is high time to give up resigned, bitter pessimism and the anti-humanist rationalisations which flow from it. It is not History which makes men and women; they, constantly, through their conflicts, their cultural orientations, their imagination, create a history which is always open-ended, even if what they build is often destroyed by force.

If we are to prevent excessive recourse to the notion of totalitarianism, we must look in greater depth at another interpretation, of similar inspiration but closer to the observed facts. This view sees the history of Eastern Europe as a series of cycles which always return to the same starting point. At more or less regular intervals, the contradictions between the life of the nation, including the economy, and the dominant forces which in more than one sense of the word are foreign to it, can no longer be held together, and explode. At first the regime, incapable of negotiating, is outflanked, and it seems that it might be swept away by popular discontent and above all by the opposition of the working class whose representative it claims to be. But fairly soon it seeks to negotiate, to halt its retreat, and gradually it regains control of lost ground and re-establishes its hegemony. If the Party has lost its powers of recovery, the Red Army intervenes, but, once the opposition is crushed, the Party has, like Kadar in Hungary after 1956, to carry out reforms at the same time as it re-establishes its domination.

At the heart of this interpretation lies the definition which it gives of the central contradiction upon which the cyclic conflict between society and the regime is based. Ferenc Fejtö, the best-informed and most lucid proponent of this view, has defined it as the contradiction between the dominant Soviet model and different national roads leading to socialism or, more simply, to economic and social change.

Hence the importance which Fejtö accords in his analysis to the great trials at the end of the Stalin era, particularly that of Slansky in Czechoslovakia, which he sees as the trial of Gottwald himself and, in short, of the Czech road to socialism.[1] That independent road was very real in a country where the Communist Party had been strong at the end of the war – as was not the case in Hungary or Poland – and where it had come to power in 1948, not unaided by the most direct forms of pressure but nonetheless using the democratic institutions. To the extent that the national–foreign dimension is fundamental, Fejtö is quite right never to forget that the Communist regimes of Eastern Europe were installed under the shadow of the Red Army, inside what was considered *de facto* as the zone of Soviet domination.

And yet analysis of Solidarity must distance itself from this thesis of the cyclic repetition of uprising, concession and final recovery of power. In the Polish case, but also in that of Hungary, the destruction of the hopes of 1956 did not mean that the country returned to the previous type of domination. Kadar was an old victim of Rakosi, and he did not take over where the latter had left off, while the last years of Gomułka did not bring Poland back to the

---

1 Rudolf Slansky: Secretary General of the Czechoslovak Communist Party, executed in 1952; Klement Gottwald, President of Czechoslovakia from 1948 until his death in 1953. (Tr.)

forced collectivisation of the countryside, the persecution of the Church or even the close control of intellectual life. The totalitarian intention of the regime was still present, giving a certain unity to the general historical picture, but the forms of resistance to it were transformed at the same time as the regime tried, with varying degrees of success, to reinforce its position by achieving positive economic results rather than by toughening its ideological principles. The political police still intervened at all levels, but internal problems, particularly in the field of the economy, took on growing importance, which in turn had a profound effect on the nature of social opposition movements. It became more and more difficult to separate the struggle for national survival from internal social and economic conflicts. The social history of Poland from 1953 to 1980 is dominated by a progressive merging of social and national claims, and therefore by the increasing importance of internal social problems. Solidarity is first and foremost a workers' movement, even if its social objectives are inseparable from the struggle against national domination and for democracy.

The two versions of the view which sees a society crushed by totalitarian domination from outside should, then, be treated with a good deal of caution, which should in turn encourage us to examine a very different thesis which has been put forward by some very perceptive commentators, concerning the modernisation of Polish society. In this view, Poland (and certain other countries like Hungary and perhaps even the Soviet Union itself) is affected in its own particular way by the great movement of secularisation which is a mark of modern industrial societies. Just as in the West the industrial revolution brought about a far-reaching modernisation of society, by the most violent of means, so Communist industrialisation, at first resting on economic, military and ideological violence and having no room for economic rationality and the autonomy of science and art, is gradually forced by successive crises to come to terms with pragmatic considerations. Technicians begin to replace the ideologists, a growing number of social activities are granted a certain functional autonomy, and the consequence is the gradual establishment of *de facto*, if not *de jure*, political pluralism.

This analysis, which was practically the official ideology of the Gierek era after 1970, can be seen in its most comprehensive form in the work of the sociologist Jan Szczepański, but it was also taken up by Alexander Matejko, even though he was living in exile in Canada; and it can even be found in certain works by Leszek Kołakowski, the principal intellectual influence on the present opposition movement. Szczepański speaks of a 'weakening of the doctrinaire and ideological approach' and even of a 'gradual democratisation of the Soviet bloc'. This idea is all the more important in that it reflects the expectations of part of the 1956 opposition movement, including the workers' councils. Then, criticism of economic policy dominated by ideology and arbitrary rule often rested on a call to realism, in turn supposing that the hold of the Party on society should be limited, not in favour of competing political forces but rather in the name of internal criteria of rationality in economic and scientific life. Economists like Lipiński or Bobrowski, whose careers were to be very different to Szczepański's, made proposals in 1956 which foreshadow the general theory which Szczepański was to outline later. And in 1980 and 1981 a marginal Party figure like Bratkowski, President of the Journalists' Association, and a central figure like Rakowski, the Deputy Prime Minister, could both put forward the idea that the crisis provoked by Solidarity should lead to economic reform along Hungarian lines, in other words greater autonomy in economic management combined with the maintenance of the political primacy of the Party.

These reformers hoped for a gradual evolution towards a less divided society, and perhaps towards a time when ideologies would hold less sway, and confrontation between East and West might therefore cease. But they must now recognise that history has not followed their predictions. Almost constantly – in 1956, 1968, 1970, 1980 – Poland has been shaken by political passions going far beyond a call to place economic rationality over arbitrary political rule. In this sense the proponents of the cyclic theory are closer to the truth: these movements, even when they manage to impose limits on their ambitions, are propelled by a desire for complete rupture, for total rejection, and belong to the diverse, contradictory family of popular and community movements directed against authoritarian industrialisation and the new forms of exploitation and repression which it creates. Supposedly enlightened despotism is rejected by a vast popular movement appealing to its cultural and national identity as well as to its own material interests. In Poland this community movement is democratic in character, whereas in other, especially Islamic countries, it is often traditionalist or fundamentalist. But these two forms have more in common with each other than with the more sober ambitions of a rationalist, moderate liberal elite. The contribution of the theory of modernisation is that it stresses that the social conflicts in Poland are those of an industrial society, with the workers, particularly in the main industries, taking a leading role. The stakes are no longer the same as they were before, during and in the dramatic period immediately following the war. The workers have no desire for a return to capitalism, and if they feel that the responsibility for the interests of the nation lies with them, it is precisely because Communist Poland has given the workers a central place in society.

THE COMMUNIST COUNTRIES OF CENTRAL EUROPE:
A HISTORICAL VIEW

The two interpretations which we have looked at so far – the theory of a national struggle and the idea of social modernisation – both shed light on important elements in the life of the Communist countries of Central Europe, but neither of them is a sufficient account of the great protest movements which have arisen in these countries nor, especially, of their historical evolution. The context for the working-class protest which gave birth to Solidarity is much more an industrialised society subjected to brutal and inefficient methods of economic development than a country living under foreign domination. On the other hand, the theory of modernisation reflects more closely the hopes of certain members of the ruling elite, and probably those of some technicians and managers trained after 1956, than it does the objectives of militant workers.

We should therefore look more closely at the nature and the dynamics of the social movements which have repeatedly shaken these societies. What they have in common is that they are all, simultaneously, a democratic movement, a national protest against subjection to a foreign will, and a working-class struggle. What differentiates them is the changing relationship between these component elements. If it is possible to speak of a history of the Communist countries of Central Europe, and not simply of the cyclic repetition of the same contradictions and forms of constraint, then the reason is that for the last twenty-five years, slowly, intermittently but unmistakably, these elements have been coming together and merging. The present situation in Poland can be seen as a result of this process: the main confrontation is between a mass organisation on the one hand and the hegemony of the Party on the other, while in the middle, but leaning towards Solidarity, the Church, and more precisely the Episcopate, tries to remind the nation of the conditions for the survival of the nation-state and for the strengthening of the national identity itself.

From 1956 in Hungary and Poland to the Prague Spring and finally to Poland in 1980, the gap between revisionist criticism coming from the top, above all from intellectuals, and mass national resistance to an artificially imposed regime, is eroded and gradually replaced by a united movement centred on economic demands but broadening out into a struggle against the Party's pervasive domination of society. The culmination of this important shift is Solidarity, a movement which is both more radical than the others, the bearer of a more far-reaching challenge, and less violent, more capable of self-limitation and self-control than the revolutionary rebellion and the intellectual radicalism of previous uprisings, a movement which constantly seeks to stay on the right side of the invisible boundary of what is acceptable to the Soviet leadership. Over these twenty-five years the roots of protest, at first ideological, have gone deeper, reaching down to the level of economic policy and now making contact with working-class consciousness itself as it is determined by the material conditions in which the working class works and lives. But these demands are not purely economic, they will not be satisfied with partial adjustments to the ideological line or economic policy; their concern is to defend society against the regime, and they rest upon the awareness of a fundamental conflict between the people and its rulers. When economic demands and the national consciousness meet, they produce a democratic movement the aim of which is to free social life, sector by sector, from the grip of the Party, and which is carried by its own momentum to demand the whole range of political freedoms. Solidarity went much further than any previous movement in its attempt to force the Party to recognise the independence of certain key areas in society: it created free trade unions, it tried to establish freedom of the press, and it fought for a principle of self-management, the main thrust of which must be to reject the Party's privileged role in the management of the economy.

Starting with the complete domination of society by a Party backed by a powerful foreign ally, protest began, then, at the top, often among the very people who had been most enthusiastic in their acceptance of the regime; after the failure of 1956, it was taken up and extended by managers who wanted to free the economy from the hold of bureaucrats and ideologists; but only in Poland from 1970 onwards was the struggle led by the working class, and only after 1976 did the intellectuals turn away from the revisionism so brutally crushed in 1968 and join the workers in the preparation of the victorious uprising of the summer of 1980.

REVISIONISM

Protest in Hungary and Poland in 1956 began at the top, even if working-class uprisings broke out before the great political crises, in Berlin, Plzen and Poznań. Intellectuals and students played a major role in both the Polish and the Hungarian October. *Po Prostu* in Warsaw and the Petöfi Circle in Budapest were the nerve centres of opposition. The contrast with the central role which the working class played in Solidarity, which is first and foremost a trade union, is so marked that we must begin with a brief review of the problems facing Eastern bloc societies, and particularly Poland, at the end of the Stalin era.

In 1949, when the Stalinist system became firmly established in Poland, the country had just experienced ten years of slow death. From 1939 onwards Poland was split between Hitler's Reich and the Soviet Union, and was systematically dismembered. More than one Pole in five died in the war, twice as many as in Yugoslavia, the other great sacrificial victim of the war, and five times as many as the Soviet Union, whose losses were nevertheless extremely heavy. Hitler's self-avowed policy in the administration of Poland was the destruction of the Polish nation. While Polish Jews were exterminated with consistent fury, other Poles were to lose their identity, their national territory and their language: they were to be dispersed. The destruction of the intelligentsia was all the more brutal for the fact that, as the heir of the petty aristocracy, it identified with the nation and the national sense of honour. On the Soviet side, a similar policy of destruction was directed against the intelligentsia and the life forces of the nation: army officers were executed *en masse* and militants of the Jewish Bund deported and assassinated. As Hitler's empire crumbled, Soviet troops watched from the other side of the Vistula as the young soldiers of the Home Army (AK) were massacred amidst the ruins of Warsaw.

Somewhat earlier, the Polish Communist Party, which had never been strong, had been the first victim of a similar policy of destruction on the part of the Soviet Union. Stalin had had it dissolved in 1938 by the Comintern, and had lured its leaders to the Soviet Union, where they had been assassinated. At the end of the war the People's Army (AL) and the Lublin Committee, inspired by Communists in exile in Moscow, became the centre of gravity of the new regime. The AK, although bigger, was banned, and the socialist and peasant parties were broken, divided and integrated into the dominant party which, as in the other 'people's democracies', became the only party. The ruling group which took complete control of the country, especially after the removal of Gomułka and the rejection of the 'Polish road to socialism', represented only a small section of the population. The country, torn apart by massive population shifts, sank into silence, people jealously guarding their private existence and seeing to their immediate economic needs.

Accurate as this picture of the circumstances in which a Communist regime was installed in Poland is, it is nonetheless incomplete. Those who lived through those traumatic years and could no longer look back with any nostalgia to a previous society and political regime which had been unjust and odious, were often carried along by the new regime, not because of what it was, but because it was the only reality; because, at least during its first few years, it did not impose, either directly or completely, its dictatorship, and above all because it was the only possible instrument for the rebuilding of the nation.

No one has better analysed the motives of post-war intellectuals than Czesław Miłosz. He does not simply bewail the cynicism, vanity and weakness of those who renounced their integrity to become the propagand-ists of the Stalinist regime. As someone who shared their hope of a national revival but later chose exile, he understands the collapse of an intellectual class which was separated from social reality, which lacked commitment and whose cohesion had been broken by events. He shares still more strongly their devotion to the nation, still present even under foreign domination. The writer wanted to go on living in Poland for it was there that his audience lay; the engineer wanted to rebuild Polish factories; the researcher wanted to re-establish his country's position in international scientific and cultural life. When intellectuals and young workers joined the

21

Party, they were not simply bending to necessity and the desire to build a career, it was not simple hypocrisy. It was a willing, even an enthusiastic act, as well as being dictated by the fate of the nation. It was when the dictatorship of the Stalinist faction was at its strongest, from 1949 to 1953 and even through to 1956, that consciences began to show signs of strain, and intellectuals began to resort to what Miłosz calls 'ketman', a term borrowed from Gobineau's writings on Persia, by which he means the separation of tough, conformist appearances from a hidden private world where beliefs and feelings were kept. Behind the sham conformity fear and hatred grew. Despite important reforms and the destruction of the old ruling classes, 'the entire country was gripped by a single emotion: hatred. Peasants, receiving land, hated; workers and office employees, joining the Party, hated; socialists, participating in the government, hated; writers, endeavouring to get their manuscripts published, hated. This was not their own government; it owed its existence to an alien army.' (Miłosz 1980: 164)

Intellectuals threw themselves into the building of a future which was to see the nation reconciled with itself, a future in which the intelligentsia[2] would no longer be separated by an enormous void from peasants and workers seen through the twin distortions of disdain and idealisation, and in which the lords of the land and of the factories would no longer hold arrogant sway. Many, at least up to 1968, did not lose their faith in the eventual results of the upheaval through which they were living, however painful it may have been. But the greater their expectations, the greater became their anger at political rulers who were brutal and incompetent, who abolished freedoms, exploited the workers, wasted resources and openly lied to the population. These recently recruited Communists, intellectuals and workers, were the main protagonists of October 1956 in Poland and Hungary.

But they were themselves powerless to displace Stalinist rule in Poland or Hungary. Change in a society so close to the totalitarian model can only come from the centre. 'It was divisions within the Communist political elite which created a situation in which intellectuals, the intelligentsia and finally society as a whole could express its desire for emancipation from the ruling bureaucracy.' (Fejtö in Kende & Pomian 1978: 38) Not until the death of Stalin in 1953 and the succession struggles which followed was the power of the ruling elite in the satellite countries weakened. It was Khrushchev's

2 In Eastern Europe, the intelligentsia is a huge group, comprising those who have received secondary and higher education and who feel, and display, their cultural superiority over workers and peasants, who are perceived as uneducated. This cultural class relationship is a consequence of the relatively small size of the industrial sector and of the business and middle classes. The intelligentsia generally identifies itself with the nation, its past and its present. The intellectuals only represent a small part of the intelligentsia, which also includes civil servants and the majority of office workers.

secret report to the 20th Congress of the Soviet Communist Party, in February 1956, which sparked off the revolutionary movements of that year.

In Hungary, the new Soviet leadership had, as early as June 1953, pushed Rakosi from power and given its support to Nagy. Admittedly, they had abandoned him in April 1955, but they had prevented Rakosi from resorting to the violent police repression which he had used before, and had forced him to clear the reputation of Rajk, executed in October 1949. The Party's principal tool, the political police, was everywhere weakened by these political changes. In Hungary, Gerö was unable to rebuild an effective political police: in Poland, Bierut and then Ochab were themselves responsible for preparing the return of Gomułka.

1956

It is true that the workers' uprising in Poznań, and the repression with which it was met, precede and prepare the ground for the Polish October. But any analysis must begin with the revisionist intellectuals, for they represent the first and most direct challenge to the regime. The intellectuals' motives were above all moral: they wanted an end to the lies and the fear.

The Hungarian writer Gyula Hày wrote on 22 September 1956: 'The most essential problem in my opinion . . . is that of truth. The best Communist writers – after many difficulties, many serious mistakes and violent spiritual struggles – have decided that never again, in any circumstances, will they write untruths.' (Quoted in Broué, Marie & Nagy 1966: 167) The reaction of what Molnar calls 'the sentimental elite' broke out when the prisoners who had survived the trials were released. In Warsaw Krzysztof Pomian, then the leader of the Communist students at the university, used the same words as Hày: the intellectuals wanted to live truthfully and honestly. Their action was directed not against the Party, now the only source of power, but against the centre, already shaken by events in Moscow.

The action of the intellectuals had two senses. The first and most obvious was their revisionism, the criticism of Stalinist rule, of political arbitrari-ness, of economic mistakes and the constraints which socialist realism imposed on intellectual and artistic life. But beyond these relatively circumscribed ideas emanating from within the Party, the voice of the intellectuals could be heard more and more distinctly speaking in the name of a nation and a people reduced to silence. Hence the confusion and ambiguity of these protests, sometimes so hesitant to break with the past. Kazimierz Brandys, who had been a Stalinist, wrote *The Defence of Granada*, the story of an avant-garde theatre company which accepts the orders of Doctor Faul and agrees to put on mediocre plays conforming to the canons

23

of socialist realism. When finally the wind turns and the company can present Mayakovsky's *The Bath*, previously banned, Brandys concludes: 'They know that when great things have been lost one thing remains, never lost and constantly reborn, and that it is more important than any one of us.' At the time, many considered this to be an absolution of Stalinism. Sometimes the intellectuals' protests seem very elitist: the special issue of *Les Temps modernes* (February–March 1957) devoted to Polish socialism is a case in point. Not only does the author of the Introduction, the Frenchman Marcel Péju, give rather hasty acceptance to the idea that the pieces which follow show us 'what Communism freed from Stalinism should be, could be today and will be tomorrow', a judgement which history quickly and cruelly refuted; the reader is also embarrassed to see intellectuals talking so much about themselves and so little about their society, with its exploited workers, dispossessed peasants, political prisoners and persecuted Church.

But beyond this court revisionism there was a revisionism taking as its object the society and the nation as a whole. The Hungarian students and writers who took part in the huge demonstration on 6 October 1956 to commemorate the anniversary of the execution of Rajk and who, the same month, were responsible for the Petöfi Circle's calls to action and the fourteen demands of the Polytechnic on the evening of 22 October, the eve of the revolution, went far beyond simple revisionism. They sought to re-establish a link between the political regime and the society and the nation: not only did they demand the removal and prosecution of Rakosi and Farkas, they went on to call for workers' management of the factories, in other words the scrapping of the *nomenklatura*,[3] and even the withdrawal of Soviet troops and free elections.

From the very beginning of the revolution, revisionism was totally overtaken by more radical movements. Throughout the revolutionary period, during and after his first government, Nagy, the best theoretician of revisionism, was unable to regain control of the movement which had called him to power but which now wanted to free the whole society from the grip of the Party. Nagy still wanted to create a people's democracy, a kind of regime which was defined for him by its difference from the Soviet model of socialist society and which he conceived as a more broadly based kind of Popular Front. In his memoirs he speaks with obvious sincerity of his faith in a regime freed from degenerate forms of Bonapartism, led by the workers themselves. His aim was political neutrality, and his appeal was to humanist values.

But he was squeezed between the political and ideological crisis at the top

---

3 *Nomenklatura:* the principle by which the Party appoints its nominees to important posts throughout the country's institutions. The term may also refer collectively to the posts which are filled in this way. In the case of Poland, a list of such posts is appended to Macshane 1981. (Tr.)

and the sudden explosion of the long silent forces of the society and the nation; how empty these fine words now seem, how incapable of channelling the irresistible torrent which was now bursting forth. Nagy was quickly swept away; he did not go far enough for the revolutionaries, and at the same time he allowed himself to be drawn into breaking with Moscow, announcing, at the height of the revolution in Budapest, that Hungary was withdrawing from the Warsaw Pact. It was this which cost him his life. The example of the intellectuals, and the Communist militants and officials from both civilian and military spheres, who started off as revisionists but gradually committed themselves to the revolution and as a result sometimes lost their lives, also points to the unbridgeable gap between criticism coming from within the regime and a national rebellion against the regime and the international alignment of the country.

What was a revolution in Hungary was never more than a revolutionary climate in Poland. There, the Communist leadership had been able to prepare the gradual return to power of Gomułka, the Party had been weakened by the bloody repression of the workers' uprising in Poznań on 28 June 1956, and on the dramatic night of 19 October 1956 the regime had been strong enough to resist Soviet pressure and the coup which the Stalinist 'Natolin' group was preparing.[4] But in both countries the general nature of the regime meant that the same gap existed between the tensions at the top of the political hierarchy and the social and national demands of the mass of the population.

In Hungary the national dimension of the struggle became central with the first Soviet invasion of 24 October and especially after the second military intervention on 4 November. Even the workers' councils saw it as crucial. In Poland the regime was able to resist Soviet pressure precisely because of the strength of national feeling. In both cases, the national movement represented more than nationalism: it was primarily a desire to free society, politically but also economically and culturally, from foreign control brutally and incompetently managed by the country's leaders. On 18 October the text of the Polytechnic's demands could still include a statement like this: 'We believe that the alliances with the Soviet Union, China and the other people's democracies are and must remain the basis of our country's foreign and economic policy. Such alliances can in no circumstances restrict the sovereignty of each of the allied countries and their right to choose independently their respective roads to socialism.' The revolutionary situation was soon to radicalise such positions, but old forms of nationalism, so strong in Hungary and Poland before the war, played only a marginal part in the national movement of 1956. As for the theory that foreign subversion was the force behind the revolution, it is too poor

4 'Natolin' group: named after the chateau in which they met. (Tr.)

and too arbitrary to be seen as anything other than a justification of the repression which followed the restoration of order, and a pretext for the elimination of those who had challenged the supremacy of the Party and the over-riding interests of the Soviet Union.

Does the working-class element in 1956 foreshadow Solidarity? The differences between these movements are more striking than the similarities. It is certainly true that such working-class rebellions have economic causes which are quickly transformed into political problems: in a state-owned economy, economic decisions such as sudden price increases, planning errors, or the imposition of unpaid overtime, are inevitably also political decisions. But here the similarity between the various working-class rebellions, and the respective demands which they made, ends: and between the beginning and the end of the period there is one essential difference. Earlier workers' movements are torn between two opposing tendencies: either they constitute a total rejection of the regime, or they are revisionist in the sense that they are led by those who call for more rational management of industry and a return to true socialism. There is no such gap in Solidarity, which is simultaneously a working-class movement, a central agent articulating the whole society's rejection of social and political domination by the Party, and a defender of the right of individual factories to make their own economic decisions.

Pure trade unionism cannot exist in a Communist country, since the worker's boss is also the master of the whole social fabric. But this intermingling of social, political and national demands may or may not have as its focal point problems arising in the workplace. In 1956 and 1968, in Hungary, Poland and Czechoslovakia, the working class did not perform this crystallising role; from the start, the workers rejected the regime, its leaders, and its submissiveness to a foreign power. In Plzen in 1953 the workers invaded the town hall and set fire to portraits of Stalin and Gottwald. In Berlin on 16 June of the same year, the workers demonstrated for the removal of Ulbricht, free elections and the reunification of Germany. In both cases it is impossible to separate the rebellion of the workers from the general social and political crisis sparked off by the death of Stalin. The immediate cause of the uprising in Poznań was price increases, but it is no coincidence that this took place just after the Twentieth Congress, at a time when Ochab was preparing the return of Gomułka. The workers' councils in Poland and even in Hungary were never the expression of a pure class struggle: in Hungary their short life, from 23 October to 9 December 1956, was overshadowed from beginning to end by Soviet military intervention. In Miskolc and in Györ they became a kind of regional people's government; in Budapest itself, the leaders of the central workers' council for Greater Budapest were mainly concerned with negotiating with Kadar and the occupying forces in order to limit the consequences of the military intervention. Ideas about workers' self-management were certainly present, often in the form in which they were to reappear in Poland in 1981: a way of freeing the factories from the domination of the Party and the *nomenklatura*, but with a constant concern to distinguish very clearly between the trade union, whose job was to protect workers' pay and conditions, and the workers' council, concerned with management and management supervision. But it was impossible, at a time when the revolution was fighting and losing, to prevent the councils becoming first and foremost centres of political and national resistance.

In Poland, on the other hand, the opposite tendency was predominant: revisionist economists seeking to improve economic management tried to use workers' movements as a basis for creating a free space where the Party had no hold and in which new state enterprises could operate. Babeau states categorically that, under the terms of the Act of 19 November 1956 and the supplementary statutes of 29 July 1957, the planning of production strategy is the joint responsibility of the State and individual enterprises. Even the most important of the workers' leaders, such as Godździk, placed themselves firmly in the revisionist camp: 'The movement at Żerań [a large factory in Warsaw] was first formed by isolated Communists fighting for control of the Party from inside.' One could and one should fight for the control of the apparatus. In 1956, both in terms of rank-and-file rebellion and of strategies at the top, workers' movements were essentially political in their objectives; they were not yet able to form a truly social movement extending out into a political dimension, as they would in Poland twenty-five years later. Their action was directly political, and the important role played by the workers from the large factories can be seen as a consequence of the privileged position of these key workers under industrialising regimes which consider themselves to be the representatives of the proletariat.

1968: THE PRAGUE SPRING

At the end of 1956 Hungary and Poland seemed to be going in opposite directions. Hungary had been invaded, its political leaders had been imposed by the Soviet Union, and the principal figures of the revolution executed, imprisoned or forced into exile. In Poland, on the other hand, hopes were running high: the peasants had been freed from forced collectivisation, the Primate had been released from prison and the Church was no longer persecuted. The intellectuals were now free to express themselves and to maintain their contacts with the West; workers' councils were active and the population in general placed great hopes in Gomułka, whose return had meant a break with Stalinism.

Soon, however, the paths of the two countries started to converge. Kadar, a victim of the Stalinist trials, had not been put in power by Khrushchev to return to the policies pursued by Rakosi. He undertook a double policy: the political pacification of the country – 'those who are not against us are with us' – and far-reaching changes in the management of the economy. In Poland, the period of freedom did not last long. Already in 1957 the workers' councils were once more placed under the supervision of the trade unions, which to all intents and purposes meant that they were abolished. The highly critical periodical *Po Prostu* was banned. Throughout the 1960s this toughening of the political and ideological line increased, culminating in the spring of 1968 in the brutal repression of student protest and a violent nationalist and anti-Semitic campaign which forced the great majority of Jewish intellectuals into exile.

If the two countries seemed to be in a roughly comparable situation in the middle of the 1960s, it was because, more than ten years after the death of Stalin, it was no longer possible to define the Communist regimes of Eastern Europe as Stalinist. Soviet domination was still of course enforced, but these regimes were no longer under the direct control of a despot and his henchmen. Their status was an intermediate one, half-way between satellite states and genuinely Communist societies. The regimes would probably not have withstood the test of free elections; but it was becoming more and more false to see a complete opposition between the regime and the society because, once the desire for political and national autonomy had been crushed and, on the other hand, the chaos of forced industrialisation in the Stalin era recognised, the regimes had no choice but to become the managers of their respective societies. Marc Rakovski is right to insist that the countries of Eastern Europe must be analysed as a particular type of society.

The increasing importance of economic problems in the Eastern bloc was the clearest sign of the growing autonomy of internal social reality. This appeared most clearly in Czechoslovakia, which at least as far as Bohemia and Moravia were concerned was an industrially advanced country. Before the others, Czechoslovakia was faced with the exhaustion of its rural workforce, the effects of excessive and badly planned investment and a balance of payments deficit. The response was an increasing concern for economic reform within the Party and its ruling circles. The proposals of the leading Communist economist Ota Sik were accepted and became, under Novotny himself, the official policy of the Party and the government. The priority which was given to reforming the management of industry meant that technical managers had a greater say, and that the direct hold of the Party on the economic life of the country was reduced. The unions and workers' organisations acquired new responsibilities within the enterprise.

This new direction corresponded to Soviet policy under Khrushchev, which was to give economic decision-makers greater autonomy from Party bureaucrats and ideologists. In Hungary, economic reform was adopted in

1968. Once it had removed the threat of political opposition, the Party was able to reconstitute a civilian agent in the life of society: enterprise managers became a ruling class which was at the same time autonomous and subordinate. But in Poland the organised resistance of social groups like the peasantry, the Church and the intellectuals soon caused Gomułka to re-establish former priorities: the Party had to maintain its hold on society, and Poland returned to economic policies which took no account of economic rationality and which could only be explained as a reflection of power relations within the ruling circle of the Party. In Czechoslovakia economic reform led to a political leadership crisis which had been avoided in 1956, and which in turn led, as had been the case twelve years previously in Poland and Hungary, to a social liberation movement. Events in Czechoslovakia therefore belong simultaneously to the end of the Stalin era and to the post-Stalin period with its central problems of industrialisation and social change. On the one hand the Prague Spring is a great movement of social and cultural liberation directed against an imposed regime; on the other, it is the expression of the various forces of economic and social change at work within the new type of society.

The absence of a great opposition movement in Czechoslovakia in 1956 is largely due to a lack of collaboration between intellectuals and workers. This was only overcome in the revolutionary atmosphere of 1968, above all after the invasion. In 1967 and 1968, the intellectuals led the assault. At the Fourth Congress of the Writers' Union Ludvik Vaculik pronounced the first great indictment of Party policy and called for democratic reforms. Karel Kosik took the argument beyond questions of political management: 'Reason unaccompanied by conscience becomes utilitarian, technical, self-interested and calculating, and the civilisation which is based on such reason is a meaningless civilisation in which man is subordinated to things and to their technical logic.' Milan Kundera expressed his anxiety that Czech and Slovak literature was losing its European character.

This agitation precipitated a crisis which was already latent in a political leadership which satisfied neither the expectations of the population nor the wishes of the Soviet leaders. Ota Sik led the attack on Novotny; on 5 January the latter was replaced as First Secretary by Dubcek, although he remained head of state. This break was in no way provoked by popular pressure. And yet these political changes quickly brought about a liberation of the press and hence of public opinion, bringing to the surface the demand for real political freedoms in the form of free elections between different parties. Democracy, in the great tradition of T. G. Masaryk, was alive again in Czechoslovakia. Młynar concludes: 'Radical changes in the structure of power, leading to a few changes in key jobs, were enough to paralyse for a time the rest of the totalitarian machine.' (Młynar 1968: 157) This relatively restricted change created the conditions for the explosion of 'a vast popular democratic movement in which the moral element plays a preponderant, not to say essential role', he adds.

The large but quickly bridged gap between revisionism at the top and a popular movement at the base – simultaneously cultural, political, national and moral in character – situates the Prague Spring in the direct line of the Hungarian October. In each case a challenge to the Party's domination of society – and not just of the state – leads to military intervention by the Soviet Union, because the power of the Party is the keystone of the whole system, and the Soviet leadership cannot tolerate the Party being reduced to impotence and swept away by the society which it is there to rule.

On the other hand, what distinguishes Czechoslovakia in 1968 from Hungary in 1956 is the part played by economic problems and workers' movements in the national uprising. It is true that, as in Hungary and Poland, workers' councils were slow to develop in Czechoslovakia: the first ones only appeared in May, and the movement did not gather momentum until after the Soviet invasion of 21 August, reaching its height in the winter of 1968–9. It is also true that these councils played a political role, sheltering the Left after the secret congress in August. But economic concerns were much more clearly present than in the workers' councils in Hungary or even in Poland in 1956. The trade unions and a majority of factory managers supported this orientation. Two-thirds of the members of these councils were technicians and engineers. So that while they certainly fulfilled an important political role, the workers' councils were following the Programme of Action adopted by the Party on 5 April 1968, the third chapter of which was entitled: 'Socialism cannot do without the spirit of enterprise'. The emergency Congress of 22 August had itself adopted this orientation. Speaking of the workers' councils, it had declared: 'To ensure local participation in this general socialist spirit of enterprise, various organs for self-management within the enterprise may be used: workers' councils, as long as they ally the direct interests of the workers to the wider interests of the enterprise and society as a whole, provide a firm and dynamic framework for production management which is qualified and competent in technical and operational terms.' Some councils, for instance at the W. Pieck CKD factory in Prague, certainly had more radical ideas about what self-management meant. But the idea that, in the words of the chairman of the workers' councils at Skoda in Plzen, 'we must ensure that the socialist enterprise is a successful business concern', was constantly present.

We should not be too hasty in seeing technocratic tendencies here; what was being sought was rather an alliance between the interests of the workers and the defence of economic rationality against political decision-making. At the time of the national uprising and in the immediate wake of the Soviet invasion the idea of self-management was inseparable from the political role of the workers' councils; but the call for rational economic decision-making shows a desire on the part of the workers not only to defend their rights but also to reconstruct the economy and the whole society. Hungarian economic reform at this time had the same aims, but it went about the rebuilding of the economic system from the top, under the control of the Party and firmly opposed to any political democratisation. The Czech workers' councils (there were few of them in Slovakia), on the other hand, took as their starting point the demands of the workers, and strove to rebuild the economy, according to the wishes of Ota Sik, by freeing it from political control. Such a notion was of little importance in Budapest in 1956, and remained marginal in Poland at that time; but it was to become crucial in Poland in 1981.

THE POLISH SITUATION

This review of the main popular political uprisings between 1956 and 1968 should make it easier to place the action of Solidarity in Poland in 1980–1. The differences between Solidarity and Hungary in 1956 or the Prague Spring are obvious. Solidarity conducted its struggle in the factories and avoided violent confrontations with the state. It did not question Poland's international alliances. In 1956, on the other hand, a limited drive for the revision of the political and ideological line sparked off a huge popular movement challenging the very basis of the regime and, in the case of Hungary, bringing about the intervention of the Red Army. In 1968 in Czechoslovakia the distance between initiatives at the top and the thrust of demands from the base was smaller: criticism at the top was directed mainly at the economic policies of the Party and the government, while the country as a whole was inspired by a climate of freedom but did not know a truly national movement. Working-class demands, democratic convictions and national consciousness had come closer together. But, as in 1956 in Hungary, the country's political leaders lost control. Like Nagy in Budapest in 1956, Dubček was impelled far beyond the moderate programme adopted by the Party in the spring and, a faithful supporter of Soviet policy, he fell victim to the Warsaw Pact armies. The tragic outcome of the Prague Spring should not, however, obscure the differences between the events in Hungary and those in Czechoslovakia. The gap between criticism at the top and popular demands was less great in Czechoslovakia, the climate never became truly revolutionary, and there was no insurrection.

The situation in Poland in 1980 seems to be the opposite of 1956 and 1968. The initiative came not from the intellectuals or a section of the political leadership, but from the workers. The intellectuals were essentially present as advisers to the union. Similarly, Solidarity was in no sense a revolutionary movement, and its political action was an extension of its trade-union role. How can we explain this reversal, the construction of a workers' social movement which was the bearer of the most fundamental democratic and national demands but which kept firm control over its own momentum, seeking not to destroy the Party but to free society, sector by sector, from its grip?

The first explanation has to do with Poland's economic situation. Nowhere else in Communist Central Europe is the failure of the government's industrial and agricultural policies so strikingly obvious. There were constant shortages. Serious imbalances paralysed the production system, especially since the regime's isolation within society meant that political criteria weighed even more heavily in economic decisions. Incompetence and corruption increased the anger which the population felt at the repeated failure of industrialisation programmes. The working class, especially sensitive to economic realities because it perceives them most directly, was in a constant state of discontent; even the best paid groups of workers, the miners in particular, complained that they were exploited, pointed to poor working conditions and standards of hygiene and safety, and denounced the spuriousness of official figures and mistakes in investment and production planning.

The large Polish working class has changed over the years. On the one hand, young workers no longer have the prospects for social advancement which skilled workers enjoyed just after the war, when some of them rose to organisational and management positions within the factories, central administration and the apparatus of the Party itself. On the other hand, industry has seen an influx of workers from the country, in close touch with rural traditions, particularly religious ones. The presence of cultural traditions within an industrial world is reinforced in certain regions, among them Silesia and the Baltic coast, by large numbers of people originally from the Eastern areas of the country annexed by the Soviet Union. The working class is therefore at the heart of the national problem, and at the same time it faces the reality of political power in its everyday life, because the Party, the supreme authority in the land, decides national economic policy and working conditions in the factories. The unions are integrated into the state apparatus and the management of the enterprise, and cannot therefore be a free expression of the workers' demands.

Public reaction to the bloody repression of workers' demonstrations deepened popular discontent and mistrust of the authorities. The Poznań demonstration of 28 June 1956 had ended in nearly eighty deaths, and many more were killed during the Baltic strikes of December 1970, at the Lenin shipyard in Gdańsk and in particular at Gdynia railway station and in Szczecin. One of the first acts of the clandestine trade union at the Lenin shipyard was to commemorate the dead of 1970. The working class became more inflexible in its economic, cultural, political and national opposition to the regime.

The revisionist intellectuals, for their part, were losing their influence and their convictions. Most of them soon lost their faith in Gomułka. Some became more radical: Kuroń and Modzelewski were imprisoned for the *Open Letter to the Party* which they wrote in 1964, in which they condemned the domination of the workers by the 'new class', to use the expression of Djilas. The philosopher Leszek Kołakowski openly questioned the meaning of socialism: in a text which was widely read, he began by saying that he was going to define socialism, and went on to a long catalogue of all the things which socialism was not, but which was an accurate description of the Polish situation. He concluded in a tone of derision, simply saying that socialism was . . . a good thing.

The authoritarian reaction, nationalist and anti-Semitic, orchestrated by the Partisan faction led by General Moczar, silenced many revisionist, reforming and liberal intellectuals, not to mention those of Jewish origin. The students and intellectuals received no support from the workers in the spring of 1968, and the intellectuals likewise failed to support the workers on the Baltic and in Łódź in 1970 and 1971. The disappearance of the traditional role of the intellectuals and students was to be a lasting one: in 1980 the universities were not at the centre of the movement. Adam Michnik was one of the first to show that the time of revisionism had passed, but he maintained as well that the 'neopositivism' of the *Znak* group which, like the revisionists, sought to initiate action from the top, was on the decline. He called on intellectuals to refuse to conform, and to defend human rights by encouraging political consciousness among the working class. He was to be heard.

Finally, apart from the factors which put the working class in a central position in Poland, and those creating a gap between the working class and the intellectuals, we must mention a more general characteristic of Polish society, which has been best described by the sociologist Stefan Nowak. Poles feel very close to their relatives and friends, and very attached to Poland; but social and political institutions are perceived as foreign to their values and needs. Between private life and the national consciousness lies a social and political vacuum. Institutions have no legitimacy. The population habitually thinks and acts with realism within the given state of affairs, but the idea that those who hold power represent the people, or that official norms should be accepted and internalised, is totally alien to them. Poles think of official speeches as being delivered in a language which is not their own. Nearly everyone listens to them as a source of information, but, apart from Party officials, very few people see them as expressing ideas which they should discuss, accept or reject. Officials are only really listened to when they appeal to the national interest and wish to speak 'as one Pole to another'.

CONCLUSION

Up until 1956, and in Czechoslovakia until 1968, political life in Communist Central Europe was dominated by the contradiction between a totalitarian regime imposed at the time of the partition of Europe and the creation of a Soviet sphere of influence and, on the other hand, the national society. Totalitarian domination by definition excluded all recognised internal conflict. Resistance under such a regime led not to the formulation of demands, but to exile at home or abroad. After the death of Stalin and the Twentieth Congress, the only voices which were heard within the regime itself were those of a few revisionist intellectuals; but as soon as the political leadership of the Party was shaken, silent popular opposition would begin to swell, beating at the gates of power.

A quarter of a century later the situation had changed totally in Poland. The totalitarian hold of the Party had been loosened by successive crises, and the leaders no longer sought their legitimacy in ideology, but in the management of the economy. The revisionist intellectuals had disappeared, persecuted, coopted, and recuperated as professional intellectuals or, alternatively, having joined forces with the people. It was at that moment that a working-class movement, strengthened by the economic failure of the authorities, undertook to win back the social space from the hegemony of the Party. The latter had already been expelled from several important areas, but Solidarity sought to liberate the central social activities: trade-union organisation, industrial management, the media and, perhaps, political representation. The regime was on the defensive; on occasion, it seemed totally powerless. For twenty-five years popular movements had simply rejected what was imposed on them; here at last was a rank-and-file movement for the rebuilding of the life of a society, taking as its starting point the condemnation of economic failure seen as the sign of the failure of the political system itself. This movement appealed neither to the past, nor to foreign models; on the contrary, it was firmly rooted in contemporary Polish society, its political and economic structures. But this realism in no sense made the movement less radical. In 1956 in Hungary, society had tried to shake off Stalinist rule; in 1968 Czechoslovakia had lived for one brief spring under the illusion of freedom; in Poland in 1980 all the forces of society, clustered round the workers' movement, set about winning back the social space from a regime weakened by the failure of its economic policies.

2

vwvwvwvwvwvwvwvwvwvwvwvwvwvwvwvwvwvwvwvwvwvwvwvwvwvwvwvwvwvwvwvwvw

Class, nation, democracy

THE BIRTH OF THE MOVEMENT

At the beginning of the 1970s opposition forces were weak and divided; in August 1980 they merged with Solidarity or came out in support of the new trade union, and in the space of a few weeks the great mass of wage-earners had been won over.

Workers, intellectuals and the Pope

How is this reversal to be explained? Listening to members of Solidarity, we shall be able to define the component elements of their action and the way in which these elements are bound together, but a preliminary study of the Baltic strikes and the movements which preceded it will allow us to formulate working hypotheses, to identify the elements which will interlock at the height of the strike. The history of Poland between 1970 and 1980 is marked by three fundamental changes.

The first is a reversal of economic fortunes. After 1970 Poland was carried along by the wave of euphoria associated with a huge programme of industrial investments which won the support of Western banks and seemed set to increase living standards and put an end to shortages. These economic aims went hand in hand with increased pragmatism and tolerance, and a reduction of the Party's political and ideological hold on society. But after 1975 it started to become clear that the investment programme had been badly planned and managed, that the foreign debt was taking on overwhelming proportions, and that the price structure and production planning were as irrational as before. Once again the economic survival of the country was at stake, and in this context the working-class movement, with its denunciation of bad management and corruption, spoke for the interests of the whole nation.

Secondly, the intellectuals, who had been brutally silenced in 1968, now abandoned revisionist attitudes, and no longer thought to criticise the Party in the name of a more accurate interpretation of socialism: instead of

35

attacking the top of the social hierarchy, they aimed at the bottom, first by supporting the workers imprisoned or otherwise sanctioned for their part in the rebellions at the Ursus factory and in Radom in June 1976, and later through the creation of workers' newspapers and the organisation of free trade unions on the Baltic coast and in Silesia.

Here, the KOR (Workers' Defence Committee) played the major role. Its very existence shows the coming together of various tendencies: the 'red' tendency of Kuroń, Michnik, Lityński, Wujec and others, and the more nationalist group, revolving around the review *Głos*, and including Naimski and Macierewicz. In the KOR, socialists of various shades like Lipiński, Cohn, Lipski and Zawadzki rubbed shoulders with men whose political education had been in the internal resistance, such as Rybicki or Father Zieja. Its meetings brought together the former Stalinist writer Andrzejewski and the famous actress Mikołajska, and workers and intellectuals, who had for many years lived in different worlds, met and united through the KOR and other groups. As a result the workers were able to organise a campaign going far beyond the riots of 1976, and the intellectuals were at last able to escape their isolation.

Finally, the role of the Church and Catholic circles became much more important over this period. Not only was there a broadening of the public reached by the Clubs of Catholic Intellectuals (KIK), the periodical *Więź* (comparable to *Esprit* in France[1]) and the Kraków monthly *Tygodnik Powszechny*; above all, on 16 October 1978 the Catholic Church chose a Polish Pope, Cardinal Wojtyła, well known for his democratic stand and his links with the workers' movement. When John Paul II visited Poland in 1979, the whole nation felt that it could now take its destiny into its own hands. The dominant factor in Polish life was the gap between the society and the centres of power, the almost total divorce between the citizens and the regime, which they saw simply as an unavoidable reality held in place by the international balance of power. The peasants felt tolerated but excluded, held back by archaic methods of production; the workers were crushed by the weight of a pyramid of bosses all acting according to a logic which had nothing to do with producing goods; and the intellectuals were above all indifferent towards an official ideology in which even the representatives of the Party hardly believed any more. The forces of society had withdrawn from the regime; they wanted to shake off its hold and to build a social and national life aside from it, if possible without entering into conflict with it, but rather using it as their most powerful ally.

To forget conventions, pretence and absurdity, to return to things which were real, to use words which had meaning, to tell the true history of the

---

1 *Esprit:* a review associated historically with an intellectual tendency known as the 'chrétiens de gauche' or left-wing Catholics. (Tr.)

nation, to run the factories in a rational way: these were the real aspirations of a people which was reduced to feeling a foreigner in its own country, absent from its own life. A big gap separated the campaigns of a few isolated groups and these widespread feelings of alienation from the regime. But this gap could be more easily bridged by a great popular movement occupying the void left by the institutions than gradually reduced by the slow advance of pragmatism. In August 1980 this social vacuum was suddenly filled, and Poland was once again itself.

August 1980

Solidarity was born in the strikes of August 1980, not simply in the sense that it was through them that the union gained the right to exist, but also because every aspect of the movement was present then. In the course of that summer, the workers' struggle took on democratic and national meanings, culminating in the Gdańsk, Szczecin and Jastrzębie Agreements which also defined the limits of Solidarity's action. The idea of free trade unions was in the air but only with the Gdańsk strike did it become the main objective of the movement.

Even on 15 August the only thing at stake was a wage claim, and the management of the Lenin shipyard agreed to an increase of 2000 zloties. Wałęsa announced that the strike was over. Then came the turning point: a large number of workers demanded that the strike continue out of *solidarity* with the other enterprises in the area which had not obtained the same advantages. At that point some hesitated and withdrew, but many remained, and Wałęsa declared: 'We must continue the strike out of solidarity, until everybody has won.' The same day, the tram drivers had refused a rise of 2100 zloties, almost half their wage, out of solidarity with the general movement. The MKS (Inter-Factory Strike Committee) was formed on 16 August, with nineteen delegates representing 388 enterprises. On Saturday 16 and Sunday 17 August, the delegates drew up their list of demands. The first was for a free trade union. The first version of these demands seemed more radical than the programme agreed later with Jagielski, including as it did the demand for free elections and the abolition of censorship. At this point the more politicised militants, Bogdan Borusewicz and Andrzej Gwiazda, tried to exert a moderating influence.

The dominant tone of the August events was one of working-class and trade-union action. But the intellectuals were soon to make their voice heard, and their arrival on the scene was crucial in defining the composition of Solidarity over the months to come. Already, militants linked to the KOR and the ROPCiO (Movement for the Defence of Civil and Citizens' Rights) were involved. On 20 August, sixty-two Warsaw intellectuals, many internationally known and some of them members of the Party, came out publicly in support of a free trade union, demanding the recognition of the MKS and warning the government against a trial of strength. 'History will not forgive anyone who attempts a different solution.' On 22 August, Bronisław Geremek and Tadeusz Mazowiecki delivered a letter of support to the Gdańsk MKS. The delegates asked them to go further in their support and to help in the negotiations which were about to start with the government. A 'committee of experts' was formed on 24 August to assist the MKS; its members, apart from Geremek and Mazowiecki, were: Bogdan Cywiński from the Catholic periodical *Znak*, the economists Tadeusz Kowalik and Waldemar Kuczyński, the sociologist Jadwiga Staniszkis, and Andrzej Wiełowiejski of the KIK. Starting from this nucleus, other intellectuals became involved, many of them members or sympathisers of the KOR, others known as being more moderate, like Jan Strzelecki. These experts did not take a direct part in the negotiations: they were rather political advisers, preparing files and meeting government advisers. Everyone involved is unanimous in saying that the experts, whatever their individual tendencies, were astonished by the radical nature of the MKS's first proposals and that they tried to exert a moderating influence. This was the beginning of collaboration between trade unionists and intellectuals which was to continue and evolve over the next few months in all the MKZ (regional organisations of Solidarity). In Szczecin, meanwhile, the movement was going in a more or less similar direction, and received the support of a number of intellectuals who assisted during the negotiations at the Warski shipyard. These intellectuals, often radical or moderate militants in the democratic cause, constitute the essential link between trade unionism and democratic themes in Solidarity.

While the first strikes were beginning on the Baltic coast, a demonstration took place in Warsaw in memory of the dead at Katyń. Five thousand people were present. But in Gdańsk the link between the workers' movement and national consciousness was less clearly focussed. Working-class and national elements were intertwined in the symbolism of the movement. The *Internationale*, played over the shipyard loudspeakers during official speeches being broadcast to the workers would be met by a rendering of *God save Poland*. The national flag, red and white, replaced the red flag, and everyone has seen images of workers kneeling during the masses which were held in the factory and outside the yard. When the Gdańsk group met Father Jankowski, the priest from a neighbouring parish, the militants stressed how important the religious affirmation was in giving the movement a national legitimacy at a time of great fear. Wałęsa himself spoke as a Pole, a Catholic and a worker. But if the strikers immediately affirmed their national and religious identity, the position of the Church hierarchy and the Episcopate in the last week of August brought only cautious approval from the strikers. A letter from Cardinal Wyszyński on 22 August gave support to the movement, but many found its advocacy of caution rather excessive. The television broadcast of the Primate's address to the pilgrims at Częstochowa provoked even more criticism, and the Episcopate had to intervene to point out that the passages expressing support for the strike had been censored. On 24 August, the Bishop of Gdańsk, Monsignor Kaczmarek, called on the workers to return to work. Not until the following week did the Church hierarchy express unqualified support, and even then there was a call for moderation. But just as the role which the experts were later to play became clear during this period of August, so the Church's position was beginning to emerge: one of the voices of the national consciousness, but also an agent of moderation ever conscious of the international threat hanging over Poland.

Between 17 and 23 August the Lenin shipyard and the whole country continued to mobilise. On the day when negotiations began, 1000 delegates representing 600 enterprises were present. The first issue of the newspaper *Solidarność* ran to 40 000 copies. Fourteen issues came out in eleven days. The workers refused to back down and forced Jagielski, the Deputy Prime Minister, to come in person to the yard. Hard bargaining continued until 30 August. Those negotiations are now part of the public memory. Everyone remembers the arrival of the government delegation between silent ranks of workers. In the main hall of the shipyard the government negotiators sat beneath a statue of Lenin while the Solidarity delegation sat beneath a cross; between them stood the Polish eagle. All the proceedings were relayed by loudspeaker to the workers outside, who applauded, or protested by their silence. Wałęsa and his colleagues showed themselves to be formidable tacticians and gave their opponents little respite; Jagielski was forced to back down, and several times returned to Warsaw to consult the government. The agreement on the twenty-one points was signed on 31 August. 'I'm signing, I'm signing', Jagielski told the cameras before leaving the yard, accompanied by Wałęsa. Then came the explosion of joy, the tears of happiness. Wałęsa was carried aloft in triumph and declared that the fight would have to continue if the agreement was to be implemented. The previous day, an agreement similar to the Gdańsk one had been signed at Szczecin between Jurczyk and Barcikowski. On 1 September 30 000 workers went on strike in Silesia; on 4 September they signed the Jastrzębie Agreement with the government. On 30 August the political militants arrested during the events of the previous week were released, but the Party press continued to denounce them as criminals and anti-socialist agitators.

In the middle of August the strikers had feared repression as bloody as that of December 1970, but two weeks later the nation, in the person of the workers from the key industries in the economy, had made its economic, political and national demands, the Party and the government had stepped down and the agreements were signed, without the threat of Soviet military intervention. The movement was born.

In the countries of the Communist bloc, the Party-state is both the master of all political life and the employer of practically every wage-earner; but it is itself subject to the authority of the imperial power. This general situation determines the three facets of all social movements which set about challenging its totalitarian rule. In the central capitalist countries of Western Europe and North America, truly social problems, those involving socio-professional and economic groups and, in the last analysis, social classes, occupy a central position, and are increasingly independent of national problems, whose importance has diminished, at least in Europe where the traditional nation-states are now subordinate to a confrontation between empires taking place over their heads. In countries recently freed from colonialism or from the older forms of economic dependence, the creation of a truly sovereign national state is the principal stake in political struggles. In those countries which are ruled by a Communist Party which is the master of the state but which has its own imperial master, how could economic demands, democratic action and the national struggle possibly be distinct and separate? Social problems characteristic of industrial society are intertwined with those concerning the independence of the nation. In such a climate, the aim of a democratic movement must be to liberate a social space in which class and national action can meet and unite in the fight for self-determination. If we are to understand Solidarity, we must first look carefully at the nature of this union between social, political and national claims.

Class action and trade-union activity

Solidarity is a trade union, and as such it is one of the representatives of Polish workers at the International Labour Organisation. The movement which was born in the explosion of August 1980 was not directed against autocratic rule or foreign domination. These themes were certainly present among the strikers, but the principal aim of their action and the first of their demands accepted in the Gdańsk Agreement was the recognition of free trade unions. From the beginning Solidarity operated chiefly in the enterprises. This is the most obvious difference between the Polish movement and its counterparts in Hungary in 1956 and Czechoslovakia in 1968.

But is this trade-union activity really class action, or is it simply the form which the struggle against the political and social dominance of the Party takes at factory level? In all our research groups, but especially at Katowice and Gdańsk, the activity of the trade union was constantly defined in terms of class struggle, even when these were not the words used by the militants. For the miners, the union's main job was to be 'against the bosses'; at Gdańsk, Marian, who had become Solidarity's standard-bearer, explained why he took part in the August strikes in the following way: 'I took part in the events of 1970; I was on the quayside when Kociołek appealed to us to go back to work. I was at the demonstration outside Party headquarters. I'd been through all that, and this time I was afraid that it would end the same way, with my mates being killed. I wanted to win the things we'd been fighting for in 1970 – better working conditions, an end to this monotonous work from morning till night followed by the pub. We wanted work to be more than just drudgery which you forget by spending everything you earn on drink. Often we were at work, not just for eight hours, but for sixteen, on Saturday and Sunday. I wanted work to be better organised, because they so often gave us deadlines we couldn't meet. We had to work non-stop, day and night, for forty or fifty hours at a stretch, before we could go home. And this work was badly paid. Sometimes we worked really hard and we got nothing for it. That's what we were fighting for, to get a better deal for every worker in Poland.' In Silesia, the word 'exploitation' recurred frequently.

The first task of free trade unions had to be to protect the interests of the workers against the employer and to obtain better pay and conditions, as well as freeing the workers from the arbitrary decisions, incompetence and corruption of their bosses. The miners are acutely conscious of being the productive base of the country: without coal, the economy would crumble; and indeed they are better paid than other groups of workers. But they felt crushed by brutal working methods and conditions, in which their health and their lives were disregarded and put at risk.

Such language is identical to that of workers subject to the laws of productivity and profit in the industry of the West. Should this come as a surprise? Socialist and capitalist countries are radically, indeed sometimes diametrically opposed in their methods of managing social change and industrialisation, but, to the extent that both belong to industrial society, they are both based on the same central class relation between a workforce, with its strength, its skill, its experience and its group solidarity, and, on the other hand, the organisers, the managers, who impose on the workers production rates, working conditions, and a pay structure: who, in short, exploit them. Polish workers, for example, complain as do most others that they do not understand their wage-slip, and they see this as proof that they are being robbed, that they are not being paid for the work they have done. They do not criticise the managers of the economy for the same things as workers in a capitalist economy, accusing them of incompetence and

41

corruption rather than blindness to anything other than the profit motive; but as far as their direct masters are concerned, their complaints are the same, bearing on working conditions, pay, and the exercise of authority.

In Poland, as elsewhere, the workers' movement clearly goes beyond the particular problems of the individual factory to recognise the common interests of the working class as a whole. We have already seen how in Gdańsk in 1980 the shipyard workers, having already won considerable material gains, were prepared to put these at risk when workers from other enterprises in the city asked them to support them in their demands. But such class action is not the only possible form which the protection of workers' interests can take. It is the most positive, offensive aspect of such class action, but there is a more defensive side to this. The workers are also consumers, suffering shortages, the victims of a system of distribution in which favouritism, blackmail and misappropriation are rife. Political leaders have a free hand in the allocation of housing and promotion at work. The workers, in many ways, therefore need to seek protection against the omnipotence of those who claim to represent them and whose prime concern is to reinforce their own power and privileges.

In this case, the rise of Solidarity reflects not class mobilisation but a search for protection against arbitrary decision-making, bureaucracy and dishonesty. One miner told us how one evening he came home to the block of workers' flats where he lived to find his neighbours shocked and surprised. The town-planning department had started to rip up the workers' allotment gardens to lay some pipes. When they found out that he was a union official, even people who did not know him pleaded with him to go to the council offices to have the work stopped. He saw the architect at the town hall, who panicked in the face of this new authority and managed to have the line of the pipes altered and the gardens saved. As shortages became worse, it was to Solidarity officials that people turned to get food, clothing and cigarettes for workers in the factory. A member of one of the groups told us about an incident in which there had been a fight at a hotel; the militia refused to intervene unless a Solidarity official went with them. Incidents involving theft and rape were brought to the union, which would reluctantly take them up, knowing that it enjoyed the confidence of the population, mistrustful of any initiative coming from the authorities and above all from any Party official. Here, another dimension is added to the workers' struggle against their employers: the defence of 'ordinary people' and 'good citizens' against the 'plotters', the 'monopolists' and the incompetent. The situation only needed to get worse and one would hear 'honest folk' calling for the guilty to be strung up, which has precious little to do with the creation of free trade unions and the improvement of working conditions. On the one hand, then, the workers were fighting a ruling class which was also, and above all, the master of the state; on the other, the whole population was set against an economic order perceived as unjust and designed to preserve the monopoly of those who held power and information.

As long as the movement was carried forward by enthusiasm and hope, class action and the desire to free the workers were stronger than popular discontent and mistrust, and succeeded in keeping them in control. But in the most difficult periods there was a danger that the authorities might quite simply be rejected in the name of the people, leading to more and more irrational behaviour which could one day backfire on Solidarity, obliged as it was to take over certain roles which had previously been the responsibility of the Party.

This popular discontent sometimes became an appeal to the base against the leaders and intellectuals, tinged with aggressive nationalism. The force uniting this popular mistrust with class consciousness was an increasingly strong perception of inequalities which were widening under socialism. Here, the surveys conducted by S. Nowak are particularly revealing. In 1961 and again in 1975 he asked a representative sample of the population which social distinctions were a cause of social division. Economic and social distinctions were a greater source of conflict in 1975 than in 1961.

	1961	1975
Differences in earnings or wealth	82%	91%
Differences in education	71%	76%
Differences between managerial and non-managerial positions	69%	77%
Division into manual and non-manual workers	57%	66%

Differences of political or religious conviction, on the other hand, were of diminishing importance as factors leading to social conflict, and social origin was of minor importance on both occasions (Nowak 1981).

This accentuation of class consciousness is partly due to the increasing difficulty of social advancement. Workers can no longer rise to managerial positions through the Party; Party and state officials constantly reinforce their privileged position and workers find their path to promotion blocked, as Matejko observes (1974: 110–12). Within Solidarity, this popular and working-class consciousness was just as strong as outside it: it was expressed as a constant mistrust of the leaders and particularly of experts from outside the working class. Even the militants of the KOR, whose role prior to 1980 is recognised as decisive, were the object of a certain amount of suspicion, and could not have been certain of the support of worker members of the union if they had been threatened. Not that there was any difference of opinion between the rank and file and these individuals: the majority simply thought of belonging to the working class and having direct experience of social relations within the factory as being the firmest and most fundamental guarantee for an effective defence of their interests. It should be remembered that non-wage-earners were not allowed to join Solidarity, which immediately excluded the majority of the student population.

At the most critical and dangerous moments in the union's history, particularly in the wake of the Bydgoszcz incidents in March 1981, in the tense period leading up to the signing of the Warsaw Agreement, anxious militants turned first of all to the workers in the large enterprises, seeing these as the best place to prepare resistance. In the same way, the clandestine Congress of the Czechoslovak Communist Party in August 1968 had taken place in one of the capital's large enterprises. This was our reason for choosing to work with militants in the factories.

Solidarity is a trade union, but it is also, more broadly, a workers' movement, animated by class consciousness as well as by a need to defend the people against profiteers and bureaucrats. But this economic action and class struggle are themselves inseparable from a third dimension: the fight for national liberation.

In the name of the nation

Multinational Central Europe in the period of industrialisation before the First World War provided the arena for the first meeting between working-class and national consciousness. This coming together was sometimes a source of conflict and sometimes produced fruitful combinations. In Poland, Róża Luxemburg was the theoretician and organiser of an international working-class struggle which was enormously suspicious of Polish national-ism. But the very year in which the Polish–Lithuanian Social Democratic Party was formed, 1892, also saw the creation of the Polish Socialist Party of Józef Piłsudski. After the resurrection of the Polish state, Piłsudski's campaign against the Russian armies and his coup of 1926, the distance separating nationalism from class action, from now on the preserve of the Communist Party, grew progressively greater. The Second World War created new divisions amongst those who fought Nazism, some of them joining ranks with the Red Army and others fighting in the Home Army (AK), close to the London government in exile, in which Christians and socialists were united above all by their common hatred of the national enemy. Since 1945 Poland has been independent but its sovereignty has been of a limited nature. The nation as a whole has never forgotten that it was living under a political regime imposed by the partition of Europe and Poland's *de facto* dependence on the Soviet empire. The new institutions and above all the new management of the economy were not rejected by everyone – nothing indeed could be further from the truth – but even among those who threw themselves enthusiastically into the rebuilding of the country by Communism there remained a persistent awareness of the rigid limits which the country's geopolitical situation imposed on the ambition of national sovereignty.

The events of 1956 were a clear demonstration of the fact that the interests of the working class and national feeling represented a united force against the regime, which was held responsible for economic failure, the attacks upon democracy and the domination of the country by foreign rule.

Since that time, working-class militants have undoubtedly held the view expressed by Lech Wałęsa: 'The interests of the Polish nation will always override our own particular interests.' The priority which is given to national problems stems from Poles' unanimous view that the driving force behind Polish society, in terms of economic organisation and political regime, is Poland's membership of the socialist camp and, more specifically, of the Warsaw Pact. This represents neither adherence to an ideology nor participation in an economic system, since membership of Comecon has not prevented the country from being much more deeply in debt to the West than to the Soviet bloc. The fundamental tie is political and military.

National consciousness in Poland takes two distinct forms. Poland's lack of sovereignty maintains a dissociation between the nation and its state brought about by many years' experience of being deprived of a nation-state. The national consciousness is the consciousness of a collective cultural existence of which the main components are the language, religion and national history. The language has not been threatened by the Communist regime, but it has been impoverished by the regime's refusal to allow access to the writings of exiled authors. The militants of Solidarity invited Czesław Miłosz to come and address them, and gave him a triumphant reception, showing their respect for a strong, free literature written by Poles who had refused to accept Stalinism. The national history has been kept from the Polish people; school history courses usually ignored the period between the wars, and official sources seriously distorted the history of the Polish resistance, the nature of Soviet occupation and, especially, the Soviet massacre of thousands of Polish officers at Katyń and the real circumstances in which the Communist Party came to power. One of Solidarity's first concerns was the setting up of a working group to revise school history textbooks, and the teachers whom we met in Kraków told us that they no longer had any respect for official history courses and wanted to restore Polish history and literature in their entirety to the country's children.

But the essential component in the Polish national consciousness and in the action of Solidarity is the Church and Catholicism. It is in this area that the misunderstanding between the Poles and Western opinion is most obvious. At the demonstration in support of Solidarity which took place in Paris the day after the introduction of martial law, some groups of demonstrators could still be heard attacking 'the priests' and the Pope as well as Jaruzelski and Brezhnev. But it is false to assume that 'Catholic' and 'Polish' are inseparable terms. Three attitudes to the Church can be discerned in Solidarity. The first is the assimilation of religious belief to a sense of national identity. For the miners of Silesia, who for so long had to work under Prussian and Protestant employers and foremen, the affirmation of their Catholic faith was a means of resisting this domination. Later, when the Communist regime encouraged them to greet each other with a comradely 'Cześć pracy' (literally: 'honour to work'), they continued to use the traditional greeting 'May God give you happiness'. Religion here is inseparable from private life, which in turn cannot be seen in isolation from national consciousness, whereas public life is dominated by a Party which is perceived as foreign to the nation and to the interests of the people. The priests are seen as the natural leaders of a community which they have never let down since the imposition of foreign rule.

The second attitude has been best expressed by Adam Michnik. Michnik, a historian, an adviser to Solidarity and an eminent member of the KOR, himself recalls that, like Leszek Kołakowski, he for many years adopted atheist and anti-clerical positions. If he had been a Frenchman at the beginning of the twentieth century, he told us, he would have taken part in the fight against clericalism and would have been in favour of the separation of Church and state. But, he added, it is impossible to compare a democratic situation with a totalitarian one. In the latter, the Church is a force resisting absolute power; it protects civil society against the state, and therefore plays a fundamentally democratic role, even when it continues to adopt culturally conservative positions which reinforce its hold over the population. That the Church performed this role was made obvious to everyone during the sustained confrontation between Cardinal Wyszyński and the regime which led to him being put under house arrest from 1953 to 1956. The personality of John Paul II strengthens this image of the democratic role of the Church. Cardinal Wojtyła was seen as a democrat, and his election as Pope and subsequent visit to Poland were experienced by the Poles as a decisive reinforcement of the nation's capacity for action in the face of state power. One of Solidarity's main advisers, Bogdan Cywiński, has called the Polish Church Julian, to contrast it with the Constantine Church. From Constantine onwards, the Church triumphant became identified with state power; under Julian the Apostate, on the other hand, it suffered the attacks of a state which wished to destroy it, and had therefore to seek closer links with the people, the social base.

Finally, the Church is also the Episcopate: a political force which is distinct from the regime, but also from Solidarity. It seeks above all to safeguard what it considers to be the first interest of the nation, in other words the survival of the national state, while at the same time it tries to extend its own influence in society. Great trust is placed in the Episcopate, but Solidarity militants often found it hard to accept what they saw as its political role of moderating or, some would say, discouraging popular mobilisation. In some of our groups, particularly at Katowice and Gdańsk, clearly anti-clerical views were expressed: as long as the people are poor and oppressed the Church is strong, because it is the only force protecting them; but if they were free and happy, they would soon shake off its restricting patronage. It was even said that the priests were perfectly aware of this and deliberately encouraged the traditional dependence of the people in order to maintain their own influence as a political counterbalance.

Father Jankowski came as an interlocutor to the Gdańsk group. At first the group was welcoming and deferential towards him, and they all clearly saw the Church as an expression of national community and of an ideal of justice. Then, after he had left, the tone changed. First came a phase in which the group voiced various criticisms of the Church. Janusz wondered whether it was not in fact an independent force which had 'gained more than us' in the struggle. Mirosław was the most critical: having first said that he was a believer, he went on to describe how a priest in his parish was selling washing powder which he was receiving free from an international charity, and asking three times the marked price for religious books. Jan quoted similar examples, and added: 'Let's be frank, society in the past has often suffered from the way the Church has behaved.'

Bogusław thought that the Church was a kind of lever operating against political action as this gained momentum and became more radical; it pointed to the reality of the limits beyond which the movement must not go. Therefore, its position was not somewhere on the axis between social and political action: it acted in a purely political perspective. It had its own interests, distinct from Solidarity's: the proof was that it had managed to have new churches built and was allowed to give religious instruction in schools. Paweł put it very succinctly: 'It sees things from a different point of view to us, and that's why it exerts a stabilising influence.' It was clear that the movement was quite independent of the Church, especially when the application of the Gdańsk Agreement was at stake.

The desire to maintain this independence with respect to the Church, and the refusal, shared by the Episcopate, to accept any political intervention on its part, came out very clearly in our work with the groups. Wałęsa was the first to reject any notion that the union was a Christian-democrat movement and to reaffirm its independence, even though, of all the leaders of Solidarity, he was the one who most frequently insisted on his religious commitment. Religion cannot therefore simply be seen as part of a traditional sense of community, and it certainly cannot be seen as fulfilling a conservative role as a refuge for the people. A militant in Warsaw summarised everyone's feelings: 'The cross symbolises a set of spiritual values which define us as a nation. We have always wanted to be the subjects, the creators of our national life, and not just a labouring mass. The feeling of being treated like objects was crucial in bringing about what is happening now, and it was the Church which made us conscious of that.' On its side the Church defined the part it had to play very well in a communiqué issued by the Episcopal Conference which emphasised that the regime must respect a certain number of rights: the right to God, in other words religious freedom, the right to a decent existence, the right to truth, the right to know the complete history of the country, the right to the past, the right to work, the right to fair pay, the right of assembly, the right to independent representation and therefore to free trade unions. The alliance between Solidarity and the Church was forged through the movement, in a common struggle to free society from the totalitarian grip of the Party. But whereas Solidarity was a social movement built on a working-class base, the Church acted first and foremost as the guardian of the interests and the survival of the national state.

The national consciousness, with its double foundation of cultural identity and the desire for democratisation, and which led Solidarity to choose 3 May, the anniversary of the liberal Constitution of 1791, as the national holiday, never ceased to dominate the movement. But as danger became more immediate and difficulties increased, a more aggressive nationalist reaction developed, defined more as the rejection of the enemy than as the affirmation of an identity. Hostility towards Russia and the Soviet Union, although always present, was much stronger in the autumn of 1981 than during the first phase of our research. An opposition between the Western model of society, in which civil society and the state remain separate, and the 'Asiatic' model where the state's power over the society is total, was not the only basis of this: it was also, quite simply, the rejection of the overlord. This hatred which, we should stress, never makes the Poles forget what the Germans inflicted on them, leads some people, not to seek confrontation with such a powerful enemy, but to consider it inevitable and to be determined to run the risks which it involves. The Poles are convinced that a Soviet invasion would provoke violent clashes with the population, which would not be prepared to accept events with the same sad despair as in Czechoslovakia in 1968.

This nationalism even caused radicals to criticise with increasing violence Wałęsa's policy of caution, and to reject his moderation, perceived as premature submission to the permanent blackmail directed at the Polish nation by the Soviet state and its army. It also found expression in an appeal to 'true' Poles and a growing hostility to opposition intellectuals and political programmes, an intransigent and intolerant form of populism. And such nationalism was exacerbated by the exasperation of the people at growing economic difficulties, causing them to look more and more often for scapegoats. Here, at national level, as at the level of the trade union, the attitudes of Solidarity militants had a positive and a negative side. National consciousness was closely linked to their desire for democratisation, but a form of nationalism hostile to anything foreign or redolent of minorities quickly came to the surface in a population which felt let down and exhausted.

Overall, national feeling was of fundamental importance for everyone and was responsible for some of the most emphatic expressions of unanimity which occurred in the research groups; but it could rarely be separated from the desire to protect the interests of the workers and the urge for greater democracy. The groups thought that the social and democratic struggles constituted the fundamental movement upon which the national demand, the last to be made because of the almost insurmountable international obstacles in its way, must be carried forward. Solidarity is a national liberation movement, but its strength is built on its desire to create free trade unions and its struggle to extend democracy into all areas, but first of all into the factory.

Democracy everywhere

In many countries, class action and the movement for national liberation have coalesced around an armed struggle led by a centralised party or by a military staff subordinating a popular movement to the demands of a war of liberation. In Poland, a country ruled by the type of regime which was produced by the Russian Revolution, this fusion has taken place at the furthest possible remove from this model, in the name of democracy: the right of citizens and workers to choose their representatives freely and to decide as directly as possible on things affecting their lives. Trade-union action is not pursued through a militarised class struggle: on the contrary, it proceeds by demanding the recognition of workers' rights. Solidarity was born in Gdańsk during the strike which was to lead to the Gdańsk, Szczecin and Jastrzębie Agreements, the first article of which is the recognition of free trade unions. From another point of view, rather than being a glorification of the nation, the national movement represents the desire to separate society from the state, to restore their freedom to the citizens, to allow them to choose, and to have control over, their representatives, and to inform and organise themselves as they wish.

Two opposing notions coexist in the term 'democracy'. One has to do with the sovereignty of the people, in which case the emphasis is on the unity of society; the second stresses the idea of individual freedoms which allow minorities to express their point of view and organise themselves. The first emphasis, one which came to dominate the French Revolution and led to the Terror, was rarely present in Solidarity. The second, on the other hand, was constantly in evidence: for the militants of Solidarity, democracy

49

and liberty were inseparable from individual freedoms, and in particular from the separation of powers, which in the Polish context takes on a new sense, referring above all to the autonomy of those sectors of society hitherto under the omnipotent rule of the Party. The judges must be independent, but the managers of enterprises too must be chosen for their competence and their respect for the workers, and not because they belong to the *nomenklatura*. The freedom of Solidarity's newspapers was considered fundamental, as was Solidarity's right of access to television. At no point was the defence of the interests of the workers separated from the restoration of civil liberties. How could the rights of workers be protected without free trade unions, and how could the unions be free if they were unable to make their voice heard?

'Rights', 'institutions', 'laws': we found these words constantly associated with the notion of democracy. And at factory, regional or national meetings of Solidarity, rules and procedures were followed with such scrupulousness that the actual business of the meeting was slowed down. Solidarity has given Poles the basis of all democracy: the right to vote for the candidate of their choice. Members' trust in their representatives was always accompanied by a desire to restore democracy to the rank and file, which explains a certain mistrust of the union's advisers, even when the importance of the part they had to play was recognised: the fact that they had not been elected, and that they were not themselves workers, was held against them.

When Poles speak of democracy, they clearly associate it with the West. Poland's kinship with all those countries which respect the basic freedoms, hold free elections, can change their government and accept the independence of the judicial system and the freedom of the press, is constantly affirmed. The people of Poland do not want to become part of the capitalist world, and debates about the ownership of the means of production do not interest them. But they do very clearly wish to be allowed to return to their normal place among the nations which limit the powers of the state and protect the rights of the individual. The militants of Solidarity repudiate the term 'Communism', and the same fate is reserved for the word 'socialism' if by that is meant socialism as actually constituted today in Poland or the Soviet Union; on the other hand it is accepted by some militants if it refers to civil liberties and the workers' right to manage their enterprises themselves. In the later analysis of Solidarity's evolution and the rise of the theme of self-management during the spring of 1981, we shall see the meaning of the latter term, but it should be said straightaway that it refers primarily to the desire to eradicate the Party from the enterprise and to revert to free social relations between, on the one hand, competent, independent enterprise managers whose completely normal concern is to act first and foremost in the interests of production, and, on the other, trade unions whose job it is to defend the workers and to protect both the national interest and the freedom of collective bargaining.

Is there within Solidarity a less open conception of what democracy should be, associated with aggressive, intolerant forms of nationalism or conceived as a means of protecting workers' interests against a hated group of rich and powerful? The answer must be no. In the groups in which we worked there was no trace of this egalitarian notion of democracy of the austere, Committee of Public Safety variety, refusing to acknowledge the freedom of the enemies of freedom. Conversely, a less institutional and more moral idea of democracy was always present. One member of the Warsaw group said: 'Economic changes will have to bring about political changes, because corruption is caused by the political system. The one-party system creates corruption.' The condemnation of the Communist regime rests not simply on principles, but also on the scandalous privileges, fraud and cynicism of the ruling class within it. Hence the urge to bring together groups of honest people motivated by convictions and principles, respectful of the rights of others and courageous enough to stand up and be counted in the defence of the workers and the nation. Solidarity's discourse is never purely political, and it speaks even less in pseudo-scientific terms of the laws of history and the demands of reason. It is a moral movement, setting honesty against corruption, the openness of its own debates against the secretiveness of Party decision-making, and the frankness of its militants against the dissembling of the bureaucrats. Solidarity knows that its strength lies not only in its numbers but also in the conviction of every one of its members. In every group each person felt a personal responsibility for the whole of the movement.

THE UNITY OF SOLIDARITY

Solidarity was born when three forces came together in Gdańsk and Szczecin: the demands of the workers, the affirmation of national identity and a call for democracy and free political expression. How did the fusion of these elements take place? The militants with whom we worked can give us the answer.

Trade-union and national action

The miners of Silesia are underpaid, badly housed and their diet is poor; they are obliged to do badly paid overtime, and their working conditions are exhausting, particularly when the four-shift system is in operation. They consider themselves doubly exploited: their economic exploitation is aggravated by a colonial dimension. The Silesian miner is a Pole who produces wealth for a foreign master, and if he is exploited as a worker, then it is because Poland itself is exploited too: is it not true that the coal he mines is sold to Poland's allies, especially to the Soviet Union, at a price which does not even cover the cost of mining it? Such a feeling of being exploited is perhaps based on an ignorance of economic processes, and several interlocutors pointed out to the Katowice group that things were not as simple as that, and that the general balance of trade within Comecon had to be taken into account. But that does not alter the fact that a working-class awareness of exploitation and national consciousness are closely allied in the mind of the Silesian miner. Moreover, the miners are often described as having been Gierek's favourites, a privileged section of Polish society, and in our group this clearly caused the miners to insist even more strongly on this alliance between working-class and national feeling.

This was why, when the group met one of Solidarity's national leaders, they finally, after long discussion, accepted the argument which he was putting forward. He maintained that if Solidarity restricted itself to a purely trade-unionist attitude there was a danger of slipping into a kind of corporatism, organised on a trade basis and not, like Solidarity at present, regionally. Problems connected with individual trades had their import-ance, but they must not become the mainspring of action. Jan put it in the following way: 'Problems concerning Poland come first, and individual branches must be subordinate to the regions.'

Working-class and national consciousness were also manifestly in-separable for the Gdańsk group. The dock workers, well informed about the movement of goods, and above all the shipyard workers of Gdańsk and Gdynia, several times attacked the unequal trade balance with the Soviet Union and its catastrophic effects on the life of Polish industry. Working-class consciousness in this group was different to that of the exploited, exhausted miners of Silesia: it had more to do with the professional pride of highly skilled workers who, because of an economic system which to them is colonial in nature, could not use their skills to the full and, moreover, saw their wages diminishing in real terms.

In Silesia and in Gdańsk, working-class and national action fused spontaneously in the call for the freeing of the workplace and of the nation's productive forces. But the combination can also take another form, in which the positive side of national consciousness goes hand in hand with the political awareness of the workers. For thirty years the miners of Silesia have been fighting against the forces which seek to deny their religious faith and, through that, their national identity. They condemn the inhumanity of a system which imposes the four-shift system and compulsory overtime on them, and one of the reasons is that they see in this a form of exploitation which prevents them from going to Mass.

Similarly, when the Gdańsk group was visited by Father Jankowski, the priest of the Chapel of St Brigitte close to the Lenin shipyard, the idea of a close interrelation between workers' action on the one hand and, on the other, religious activity explicitly Polish in character, was self-evident to the whole group. Zenon recalled how, on the fourth day of the strike, he telephoned Father Jankowski to ask him to come and give a sermon to the workers. He found this sermon 'politically very mature', he said. Father Jankowski, having explained how he divided his time equally between his parish and the union, recalled how, after some reflection, he had organised his sermon around the theme of 'work as a blessing and work as a curse'. With Father Jankowski the group relived this crucial period in the struggle, and the dominant image of this particular session was of the indissoluble union between the problems of the workplace and the affirmation of a specifically Polish Catholicism. Working-class consciousness, then, whether it takes the form of professional pride or perception of exploitation, is bound up with national feeling expressed either as a rejection of foreign domination or as an affirmation of religious identity.

Trade-union and democratic action

In a situation in which a Party-state entertains totalitarian ambitions, anything which wrests any activity from its control immediately takes on a directly political character. The demand for a free trade union is therefore in everyone's eyes an eminently political act.

In Gdańsk, Warsaw and Katowice, even if the relation between trade-union and political action was seen from very different and sometimes diametrically opposed points of view, it was nonetheless unanimously accepted as more than self-evident: it could not be otherwise. In the words of Janusz, a member of the Gdańsk group, this interrelation was one of the terms of 'a struggle for survival'. For all the workers, Solidarity was first of all a trade union, but in order to perform that role it must constantly defend the political conditions of its very existence, as defined by the Gdańsk, Szczecin and Jastrzębie Agreements. The groups constantly insisted that Solidarity was not a political party, but that in order to remain a trade union it had always to ensure that the agreements were respected; some maintained that their scope should even be extended.

As we shall see later, there was much highly charged debate as to whether the movement should become more political, exerting constant pressure against censorship and all political detentions, or indeed try to facilitate the formation of new political groupings. But no one was prepared to relinquish a minimum definition of the interrelation between trade unionism and democracy: Solidarity was a trade union, but as long as it did not have absolute institutional guarantees for its freedom of action it must also be a political actor fighting for those guarantees. In the words of Tadeusz, a member of the Warsaw group, 'If we are going to be a union, we must strengthen present democratic institutions and create new ones.'

Democratic and national action

The political and national dimensions of Solidarity's action are equally interdependent. This emerged very clearly when the groups met members of the PUWP. The Party against which Solidarity is fighting has no legitimacy and draws its power from abroad. The session during which the Gdańsk group met a delegate to the forthcoming Party Congress was a good illustration of the way in which political action directed towards the democratisation of society is also a struggle for national independence and an opportunity to proclaim a national identity which the Party cannot represent. The interlocutor was not a hard-liner wishing to have done with Solidarity quickly and if necessary by violent means; he was a moderate, a supporter of some kind of renewal, who would probably back Kania at the Congress which was to open in a few days' time. A level-headed university teacher, he was an advocate of political realism.

The meeting began slowly, with no concessions on either side. The Solidarity militants criticised the Party for its paralysing totalitarian grip on society and, after long tirades from the Party delegate, finally exploded. The Party, said Zenon, had never been an authentic representative of the will of the people, and very few members were workers. It was time to establish a political system recognising the existence of several political parties, continued Janusz, knowing full well that this would mean an immediate break with Moscow. The whole group affirmed that Polish society must be freed of the Party-state, and that democracy also meant putting an end to an 'enforced friendship'. The session ended in complete disorder with everyone on their feet, the interlocutor beside himself with anger, his appeals for moderation no longer even heard. The final word came from Mirosław: 'Which is better: to die on your feet or live on your knees?' Weak and decayed, it was the Party which was the obstacle to democracy; the instigator of censorship and political imprisonment and the force which silenced all political expression. And it did all those things because it was the agent of a foreign power ruling Poland.

Democratic and national action, then, are brought together in the desire to live in a free society not dominated by an omnipotent Party-state, and in a national consciousness defined in opposition to foreign domination. But the two also come together in the assertion of a religious identity articulating a set of values specific to Catholic Poland. In the Warsaw group, for instance, Staszek said that by identifying itself as Catholic and Polish the movement revived the great ideals of a humanist, democratic nation. Similarly at Gdańsk, during discussion with Father Jankowski, both sides saw the Church as one which, in Jan's words, 'sides with justice', and Zbigniew summarised this particular part of the discussion when he said: 'As a union we have taken over from the Church in the fight for human rights. The Church has given us the strength to fight against men being made into machines.'

In the spring of 1981, the trade-union, national and democratic dimensions of Solidarity's action were not only linked: they were fused to such an extent that no one would risk putting himself on the fringe of the movement by adopting one dimension, or even a combination of two of them, to the exclusion of the others. An exclusive concern with the protection of workers' interests was never accepted by any of our groups. In the same way purely political action, although certain people did not reject it out of hand, extended outside the movement's boundaries and was seen as a threat to its strength. Finally, although it represented the movement's ultimate horizon, the national struggle was never presented in isolation from its democratic and popular dimensions.

Leszek Moczulski, the founder of the KPN and a political figure who can justifiably be termed a nationalist, and another leading figure from his organisation agreed, shortly after his release from prison, to come and spend a morning with the Warsaw group. Moczulski laid out his position very clearly: the long-term objective was national independence. He did not win any converts, but he was listened to sympathetically, because his very presence was symbolic of the resistance to political oppression and above all because, in the exposition of his ideas, he had succeeded in appealing simultaneously to the political and working-class dimensions of the movement. Friendly debate was possible to the extent that Moczulski's nationalism accepted the usefulness of democratic action and considered trade unionism an indispensable first step along the road to national liberation.[2]

THE SOCIAL MOVEMENT AND THE LIBERATION OF SOCIETY

Solidarity did not mobilise the workers simply by offering to defend their interests at work: it demanded action of a much wider kind, and led the workers to make far-reaching changes in their lives. That is why when Lech Wałęsa was asked what Solidarity was, he replied that it was more than a trade union, and not the same thing as a political party, but rather a social movement. Every one of the members expected Solidarity to speak for the

---

2 The leaders of the nationalist KPN, released from prison in the spring of 1981, were arrested again and put on trial in July. The trial crystallised nationalist aspirations, and there were plans for a march in support of the defendants, which Solidarity opposed. Some miners testified at the trial. The organisation only had a few dozen militants, and it would not appear that the trial widened its militant base to any significant extent; but it did become a symbol of nationalism, and received some support from popular opinion.

workers, but also for the nation and for political freedoms. Hence the irresistible force with which it mobilised the country: Solidarity's success was experienced as the revival of popular action which up to then had been banned, manipulated or repressed by force. Unlike the Prague Spring, the movement which gripped Poland in 1980 and 1981 never ceased to be primarily a workers' movement, even when it extended to affect practically every group in the country. Solidarity's struggle took place in the factories; at the same time, it was the meeting point of the whole country's hopes and demands.

What then was the main aim of this social movement? The seizure of power followed by the imposition of the dictatorship of the proletariat or the rule of workers' councils? Not for a moment. Firstly because the Gdańsk Agreement, which throughout remained Solidarity's code of conduct, explicitly recognises the Party's leading role in the state; and secondly because the militants themselves wanted to be free from the grip of the regime, and not to take over its powers from it. The constantly reaffirmed aim of Solidarity was to free society from the totalitarian domination of the Party. In the factories, rank-and-file militants were just as clear about this as their national leaders. They did not speak of a workers' state, rarely of 'true socialism', and even less of the total independence of Poland. They wanted to drive the Party from their lives, and to limit it to its proper functions within the state, so that a free society might once more exist. They thought that the rebirth of Poland requires not only a strong, independent workers' movement, but also enterprise managers who are competent and unhindered by any administrative or political control, and media open to all. They wanted free elections, first at local, then at *województwo* (district), and finally at national level. It is an astonishing programme. When was the last time that we saw trade unionists defining one of the principal tasks of the movement for self-management which they are in the process of building as the appointment of managers with whom they know that they will enter into conflict? Freeing society from the Party-state means recognising the existence of social relations and conflicts, and this entails repudiating claims made by anyone, and first of all oneself, to be able to speak for all. These are not the abstract formulations of ideologists or observers: they were constantly made in our research groups, recurring throughout debates on self-management, the media or elections.

The social movement and the programme for the liberation of society are complementary, but they nevertheless represent two distinct sides of Solidarity's action, each with its respective supporters within the movement. The first group is above all concerned with developing the movement's momentum, its capacity for mobilisation, the strength of its conviction and its internal democracy; those who situate themselves on the social liberation side are more committed to thinking about the institutions which must be rebuilt and the political solutions to be conceived. Some of those who see Solidarity first and foremost as a social movement are mistrustful of political action and would like to see the union return as quickly as possible to its proper function as a defender of workers' rights at factory level. On the other hand, some of those who are above all concerned that Solidarity should bring about a revival of freedoms would like to move quickly on to strictly political action. These are both very strong tendencies. The first was to be seen more often in Katowice, the second in Warsaw and Gdańsk. But what defines Solidarity is the association of both these tendencies. The central role of Wałęsa is in part to be explained by the fact that he himself is the best representative of all of the power of the social movement, while his principal advisers, Tadeusz Mazowiecki and Broni-sław Geremek, want more than anything else to rebuild free institutions and to create, in the words of Geremek, 'intermediary institutions with a capacity for negotiation and mediation going far beyond the present head-on confrontation of society and state'. Mazowiecki, for his part, insists on the need for 'supervisory trade unionism' which neither becomes locked in purely defensive action nor takes a direct responsibility in the running of the economy. The complementarity of these two conceptions of Solidarity's role serves to underline how different it is both from a form of trade union whose main function is in the area of wage bargaining, and from a political movement seeking to gain power. Solidarity does not even have to trouble to dismiss the first of these ideas: from the very first, its action went far beyond such a limited role. Conversely, the second meets with constant and categorical rejection: Solidarity is not and does not want to be a political party.

The life of Solidarity and the internal discussions within it are dominated by the relations between these complementary and partly opposed tendencies. But the two sides of the movement are in turn each subdivided by the opposition which has already been noted in the areas of trade-union, democratic and national action, between, on the one hand, a defensive, community-based orientation and, on the other, one which is more reforming and institutional, and which might also be called counter-offensive. It is therefore possible to distinguish four main tendencies within Solidarity:

1. The defensive, community-based tendency within the social movement pushes Solidarity towards a form of trade unionism centred round the enterprise, sometimes moderate in character and sometimes closer to revolutionary trade unionism. The latter is above all the case in Silesia, where there is widespread acceptance of the idea that the miners are the most productive group in the nation, and that their economic importance and cohesion as a group give them sufficient weight effectively to set themselves against the regime. The miners of Katowice often think of self-

management as a regime of workers' councils, concerned with economic management but at the same time revolutionary in character. This first group sometimes adopts a radical, and occasionally violent, tone; sometimes, on the other hand, it falls back on a concern with problems connected with the workplace and immediate economic needs. In both cases there is a strong mistrust of specifically political action.

2. This is not the case for the workers of Gdańsk and Szczecin, who still identify with the spirit of the agreements which they forced on the authorities in the strikes of August 1980. They do no separate the creation of free trade unions from the recognition of the rights of all working people and a modification of relations within the workplace and of the decision-making process. This tendency, then, represents the reforming, institutional side of the social movement.

3. The community-based, defensive tendency, when combined with the desire to free society of the Party's domination, most frequently takes on very radical and even aggressive forms. The populist appeal to the base, containing elements of nationalism and of the ideology of workers' power, is heavily laden with images of combat, open conflict between the Polish people and its overlords.

4. On the other hand, the reforming vision of the liberation of society envisages the gradual creation of free institutions leading ultimately to the establishment of true internal independence limited only by relatively minor constraints, comparable to those which apply to Finland. The main representatives of this tendency, which is both political and moderate, are the opposition intellectuals, especially from the KOR. Rulewski, on the other hand, can be seen as representing the radical, defensive, nationalist tendency to which those who are referred to as the 'true Poles' also belong. We should however be wary of the labels 'radical' and 'moderate', superficial in that their content is constantly changing.[3]

Differences of position can be better understood if they are defined in terms which correspond to what Solidarity is as a movement. Solidarity is a workers' movement, and it is also a movement for the liberation of society. It is the affirmation of a social and national community rebelling against an imposed regime, and it is also an attempt to restore democracy to the economy, to politics and to culture.

But Solidarity's unity remains the essential fact. Certainly, defensive community-based tendencies became increasingly important as the crisis deepened, but the will to reform and negotiate never left the movement, as Wałesa's continued presence at its head showed. In the same way, the theme of the liberation of society and its corollary, political objectives, took

3 The four tendencies are set out in the table on p. 176. (Tr.)

on increasing importance as the original movement of August 1980 receded into history, but Solidarity never ceased to be a movement of the workers, a social movement resting on strongly held convictions and a highly developed sense of responsibility.

THE NATURE OF POPULAR MOVEMENTS IN COMMUNIST CENTRAL EUROPE

Like any social movement, Solidarity can be defined in terms of the identity of the people in whose name it speaks, the adversary which it is fighting, and the stakes of this conflict. The preceding analysis may be summarised as follows: Solidarity's base is the working class; its action is directed against the obstacles in the way of democracy, the autocratic power of the Party and of the state which it dominates; and the stakes of this struggle are the form which the life of the nation is to take. The Party sees itself as having been responsible for the creation of an industrially strong and socially egalitarian society, and this claim is not without justification. Compared with pre-war Poland, Communist Poland is indeed a more socially and culturally integrated country, and the French observer is struck by the relatively small social distance between the major professional groups. But Solidarity shows the unity of the nation in a very different light: the movement represents the consciousness of the Polish people in their opposition to the hierarchy which runs the Party and the state. Ordinary members of the Party are closer to members of Solidarity than they are to their own leaders, and indeed many members of Solidarity also belong to the Party. It would be wrong to consider the political leaders of Poland as pure agents of Soviet rule. They are aware that they have helped to bring about a strengthening of the Polish nation, and have little difficulty in reconciling this with their obedience to their Soviet masters. The militants of Solidarity recognise this: for them, the country's political leaders are also the masters of Polish society and of the economy. Solidarity is as much a social movement as a national one. If we call the definition which the actor gives of himself the principle of identity (I), the definition of his adversary the principle of opposition (O), and the stakes over which the two adversaries are fighting the principle of totality (T), we can represent Solidarity, in as much as it is a social movement, as in Figure 2.

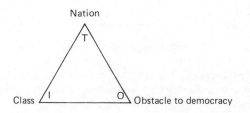

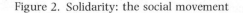

Figure 2. Solidarity: the social movement

The movement

The other side of Solidarity's action, as a movement for the liberation of society, defines the stakes in exactly the same way: what is being fought over is still the Polish nation, or society, as the Poles call it, controlled at present by the regime. But in this case (Figure 3), the principle of identity is different: here, Solidarity is fighting against the power and privileges of a ruling class and its monopoly of information and economic life, and speaks in the name of democracy and citizens' rights. The similarity of the stakes represents a close link between the two sides of Solidarity, since in each case the popular movement is opposed to the Party's hegemonic control of society: but one tendency represents a class struggle, whereas the other situates itself on more directly political ground.

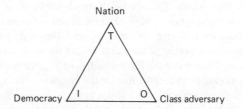

Figure 3. Solidarity: the social liberation movement

The differences between Solidarity and the other main popular movements in Communist Central Europe since the end of the Stalin era will be more clearly shown if we represent their component elements in the same diagrammatic form.

Democracy represented the principal stakes of the movement in Czechoslovakia in 1968. Changes in the leadership of the Party opened up a breach for public opinion to express itself. Students, writers, intellectuals and the press played a central role in the Prague Spring, which was a social liberation movement rather than a social movement in the strict sense of the word. The Czechoslovak nation took on the ruling class, defined as the groups holding power in all its forms, in an attempt to establish democracy (Figure 4).

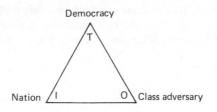

Figure 4. Prague Spring

After the Soviet invasion, the nature of the resistance changed, becoming concentrated in the large factories where workers' councils sprang up. The basis of opposition was defined in class terms, and the adversary in national terms, since the country was occupied by a foreign army dictating the course which the government was to follow (Figure 5).

Class, nation, democracy

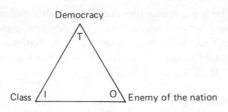

Figure 5. Czech workers' councils

A common thread links the popular movements of 1968 and 1980–1: in each case the struggle takes place in the political field. There is however a difference of emphasis. In Prague in 1968 the social liberation movement preceded the workers' movement, whereas in Gdańsk, Szczecin and Silesia it was the workers' movement which developed before the institutional and political action for the liberation of society. Going further back, we come to the so-called revisionist movements, led by counter-elites seeking to replace regimes inherited from Stalinism with 'true' socialism or a specifically national form of socialism. These revisionist campaigns were, certainly, often overtaken by truly national movements repudiating the Stalinist terror which the trials of the 'Titoists' came to symbolise. But the ruptures of 1956, and the Yugoslav schism of 1948, took place within the Communist hierarchy. Stalinist forms of socialism were rejected in the name of the principles of socialism: the field remained defined in class terms, in the sense that one type of class power confronted another, rather than one class actually entering into conflict with another.

In the case of Titoism, the basis of action was defined in national terms: Tito was the leader of the internal resistance and as such he represented the nation as well as the Party. The adversary, on the other hand, was defined in social as well as national terms, as the idea of self-management, launched by the Yugoslav regime in the aftermath of the break with Moscow, shows (Figure 6).

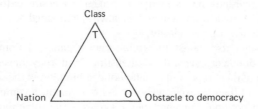

Figure 6. The Titoist schism

Turning to events in Budapest and Warsaw in 1956, it is clear that for the Petőfi Circle or in the pages of *Po Prostu*, the stakes of the struggle were defined in terms of a revisionist criticism of Communist rule, appealing to the principles of Communism or Marxism. Unlike the Titoist schism, the basis of the struggle was defined in democratic and not in national terms. The people spoke up, rejecting the totalitarian system and therefore being drawn into conflict with the foreign domination which was the final guarantee of autocratic rule. In this first period of opposition to Communist rule in Central Europe, we see the same combination of two distinct kinds of action, both defining the stakes in the same way but each mobilising social forces differently (Figure 7).

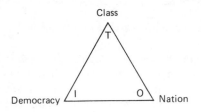

Figure 7. Budapest–Warsaw 1956

In short, as we move from 1956 to 1968 and then to 1980, we see the stakes of the conflict becoming wider and wider. At first it was a question of reforming the regime according to the very principles upon which it rested. Then a call for democracy was heard as a reaction to autocratic rule which had brought about deep economic crisis and had resorted to Stalinist methods for controlling public opinion. Finally, culminating in the events in Poland in 1980, we see the formation of a social movement powerful and complete enough to have as its objective the liberation of the whole society.

It may appear surprising that the more restricted of these movements led to the most open conflict, while Solidarity, far more powerful than the others, managed to control and limit itself and, as a result, to last longer. But the paradox is only apparent: the more a movement broadens and deepens its base, the more it is the expression of a whole society rather than a dispute at the top. Furthermore, as a movement broadens it takes in more and more opposition elements, whereas, sooner or later, revisionism was always overtaken by a desire for total rupture with the regime, by a radicalism which has always remained a small and highly controlled element within Solidarity.

Popular movements against the totalitarian regimes of Communist Central Europe are undoubtedly separate and distinct, but they nevertheless form a paradigm: each of them represents a different combination of the same component elements. None of them is exclusively a class movement, a campaign for greater democracy or a national uprising: they all possess the three dimensions. Those which lack this plurality of meaning are weak.

Nowhere else in the world have such powerful social movements developed. In the West, the workers' movement is losing its momentum, either absorbed into the political system or devoting itself to the management of the field of which it has gained control. In the Third World, nationalist movements are more often than not the work of ruling groups. It is in Communist countries that mass working-class strikes take place, for it is there that the brutal effects of accelerated industrialisation are most directly felt. At the same time, it is there that the workers' movement finds itself associated with agitation for democratic reform, for these countries had previously known democratic freedoms, sometimes very restricted and sometimes extremely wide, but in no case so completely destroyed as under Stalinism. Finally, domination by the Soviet Union is a constant source of resentment: in these countries, the Soviet neighbour is not seen as a powerful, rich and brilliant Rome, but as a backward, autocratic and militarised country. For all these reasons, it is here that the most wide-reaching movements appear.

Solidarity is the fullest and most highly integrated of these *total social movements*.

vw

A self-limiting movement

Observers who have followed the history of Solidarity since August 1980, and the militants in our groups who were the actors in that history, all stress the extraordinary degree of control which the movement exerted on itself. How can one fail to be struck by the self-control of a movement which seems to have a whole people behind it and which is in conflict with an increasingly paralysed and disintegrating Party? The movement's self-control must be seen as a function of the paradox which determines its aims and its strategy. On the one hand, Solidarity is a movement which, by virtue of its aspirations, its strength, and the importance of the stakes, is not to be satisfied by partial reform of the system. But, on the other hand, the militants know that this global rejection of the system has its limits, which are mainly determined by the international situation of Poland. Solidarity is therefore obliged to have constant regard to this gap between its aspirations and the action which it can realistically undertake.

Jacek Kuroń was the first to describe Solidarity as a 'self-limiting' movement, articulating radical criticism of the regime and of the state of Polish society but admitting at the same time that the international situation makes it impossible for it to overthrow Communist rule, since this would be intolerable to the Soviet Union. The movement is self-limiting in the sense that, against a background of radical aspirations, it is prepared to adopt strategies involving compromise with the authorities. The self-limiting nature of the movement was shown for the first time during the negotiation of the Gdańsk Agreement, when the workers recognised the Party's leading role in the state. But even before 1980 the theme of self-limitation was present among opposition intellectuals: Kołakowski, for instance, in his theses on 'Hope and hopelessness', put forward the idea that a self-limiting popular movement would have a chance of surviving in Poland.

The aim of this chapter is not to analyse these limits, in particular the workings of the Soviet regime. It is rather to show how the movement adopts and modifies the limits which are imposed on it, always acting within its capacities. The tensions which flow from the need for self-limitation affect every aspect of Solidarity's life: how can it push back the limits without the risk of confrontation? How, conversely, can the movement avoid being stifled by them? Debate on these questions, in which the intellectuals who are the movement's advisers took an important part, changed in character over the months, as the economic crisis deepened and the Party became increasingly weak.

It should be understood that the image of Solidarity as a movement split down the middle between those who accept and those who reject the limits to its action is false. The truth is rather that each and every militant lives with the internal contradiction between the movement's momentum and the recognition of limits.

THE LIMITS

The external threat

Krzysztof Pomian writes that the existence and development of Solidarity over a period of more than a year seemed at the time to be a miracle (Pomian: 1981). Such a miracle is to be explained largely by factors which have nothing to do with the nature of Solidarity itself: the choices made by Soviet and Polish leaders, the international situation, etc. But Solidarity too contributed to the definition of an area of action which would be 'tolerable' to its adversaries, and the militants were always conscious of an external threat. From the first few hours of the strike of August 1980, the workers were apprehensive.

The militants in our groups never spoke as though anything were possible, as though Solidarity were not, as it were, on probation. 'As a nation we realise that we are caught between a political system and certain geographical facts, and that we have to exist within that framework. The problem is to recognise those limits and to know how far we can go', said Andrzej, from the Warsaw group. All the militants had a clear awareness of the limits and were keen to make it publicly known that there could be no question of going beyond them. The majority were explicit in saying that Poland's alliances must not be tampered with, and the Gdańsk group thought that 'it would be madness to leave the Warsaw Pact'. When Solidarity militants publicly restored monuments to the Soviet Army which had been defaced by persons unknown or by provocateurs, they were unambiguously showing that they were conscious of certain limits. As late as May 1981, when Warsaw Pact troops were carrying out manoeuvres, and the Party received a threatening letter from its Soviet counterpart, many militants were less than enthusiastic about the 'anti-socialist' emblems which some students were sporting. The Soviet threat is not seen as a danger just for Solidarity: it concerns the whole of Poland.

The limits which Solidarity must observe were defined principally in terms of external threat and domination, and yet in the course of our research we found that the militants rejected direct appeals for a struggle of national liberation. The Polish national consciousness was not transformed into a pure form of political nationalism. In the spring of 1981, strictly nationalist discourse laying the emphasis on the struggle against the Soviet Union remained extremely weak, and acts hostile to the Soviet Union, such as satirical drawings and caricatures, though rare, were often seen as acts of provocation or the work of minority groups. Nothing could show more clearly the weakness of political nationalism, carrying with it the risk of going beyond the prescribed limits, than the meeting between the Warsaw group and Leszek Moczulski, the leader of the nationalist KPN who had recently been released from prison as a result of Solidarity's campaign for freedom of opinion.

Moczulski's courage was applauded, but no one was ready to accept his proposition that they must fight for 'the creation of the Third Polish Republic'; as we have already seen, debate with this interlocutor was possible, but a gulf separated him from the group, which sought to take account of the balance of power and to observe a set of limits which the KPN would blithely ignore. A meeting between the Katowice group and Andrzej Czuma, who defends a certain kind of national radicalism, followed the same pattern: the Silesian miners' nationalist feelings and their hostility, to say the least, towards the Soviet Union, did not obscure their consciousness of the limits within which Solidarity must act.

The Party

The leading role of the Party is considered to be the keystone of the Soviet domination of Poland, and therefore represents a limit. This was clear for everyone, including Party militants. When they talked to Solidarity members about the danger of foreign intervention, this was not meant as a form of blackmail. The delegate to the Party Congress who met the Gdańsk group reminded the militants that, apart from the Party, the real danger was an international one and that Solidarity must beware of weakening a political force which, despite all its failings, nevertheless protected Poland from the excesses of 'Soviet friendship'. A Communist militant who was invited to meet the Katowice group took a similar line: he was not contradicted when he said that 'we are on the edge of a precipice, and we cannot bring down the Party because we know who we would have on our backs then'. In the same way, Bogdan Lis, a member of Solidarity's Presidium, urged militants in September 1980 not to leave the Party so as not to weaken it too much. Despite profound hostility to the PUWP, the majority of militants seemed to agree with this argument, accustomed as they were to moderating their desire to settle the score with the regime in a proper confrontation.

This refusal to attack the Party directly is the clearest manifestation of Solidarity's voluntary self-limitation: the primary demand is for free trade unions, and it is an explicitly non-political demand. Certainly, militants would not deny that free trade unions are unavoidably a political fact in a system in which politics seeks to involve itself in every sphere of social life. But at the same time, in August 1980, Solidarity recognised the 'leading role' of the Party, and in doing so it committed itself to respecting the boundaries which it had set itself, and which the base of the movement, often more radical than the leadership, had to be reminded of. This self-control, which was a relatively conscious attitude among the militants in our groups, can be seen as a direct contrast to the explosions of working-class anger which caused the strikes of December 1970 in Gdańsk, Gdynia and Szczecin, when the workers left the factories to attack local Party offices.

An effort should be made to understand this apparently paradoxical attitude on the part of the workers: on the one hand, they say that they can make their peace with the Party, and at the same time they see it as their main enemy. This mixture of hostility and acceptance was a constant feature of meetings between our groups and Communist officials. Many militants spoke of the history of a Party brought to Poland in the lorries of the Red Army after it had crushed the internal resistance to Nazism. Many also recalled the disappointments of the Gomułka period which ended in the bloodshed of 1970, the instigators of which are in many cases still in power. Such memories were not passed over in the discussions with Communist militants, and as a result these were extremely violent. The journalist from the Party newspaper *Trybuna Ludu* who met the Gdańsk group denounced the strikers as economic saboteurs and hooligans, defended the 'success propaganda' of the Gierek period, and declared his absolute opposition to a free trade union. The militants, however, did not turn their interlocutor out: despite their anger, they explained to him that they were demanding neither the elimination of the Party, nor the abolition of *Trybuna Ludu*, that they simply wanted an honest Party and honest journalism. Some of them even reminded him that Solidarity itself sometimes had to censor its own newspapers, that it could not go beyond all the limits and say whatever it wanted. These are astonishingly moderate reactions. The reasons are to be sought in the fact that the militants, without entertaining unrealistically optimistic hopes, knew that Solidarity and the Party were 'condemned to get on together'. The limits were clearly perceived by everyone, and the movement's action had to try to internalise them. Janusz, from the Gdańsk group, put it like this: 'The term "freedom" means setting the limits which you will respect yourself, not just respecting those which someone else imposes on you.' Many saw such self-limitation as a kind of self-mutilation, but everyone agreed that everything had to be done to avoid reaching the point of rupture.

'You have to know the right tone to adopt', said a militant from Gdańsk. Liberation could only be brought about gradually, by avoiding open conflict. In a society which only seems to progress from one conflict to another, that is a difficult axiom to apply. The need to have a clear image of the limits, and not to go beyond them, was seen as the price of survival which the movement would have to pay if it was to avoid the fate of the Budapest revolution of 1956. One of the reasons why these limits were accepted by the militants was their feeling that history was on their side: they believed that the wave of liberation would eventually reach the Soviet Union. The militants who took part in our research were moderate people, but they were in no sense half-hearted: they felt that the general struggle in which they were involved was so powerful and so legitimate that compromise was no retreat. The power of the Party was simultaneously an obstacle to be overcome and a boundary which must not be crossed, and that explains why, for more than a year, Solidarity consistently agreed to last-minute compromises with this increasingly fragile adversary.

The history of Solidarity could therefore be described as a succession of advances towards the limits of its action, each time resulting in a last-minute compromise. In this series of crises and compromises, Solidarity can be defined as simultaneously a force leading towards rupture and a moderate, limited movement. Wałęsa and most of the union's other leaders are perfect representatives of this double nature, appealing at the same time for total struggle against the social, political and national order, and for reasonable compromise. Such a strategy requires calmness and skill, the very qualities which astonished the world for over a year.

The Church

One of the moments of greatest tension in the history of Solidarity was the Bydgoszcz crisis at the end of March 1981. On 19 March, a delegation led by Jan Rulewski, the president of the Bydgoszcz MKZ, came to present a motion from a group of individual farmers to a meeting of the official regional council. The group of thirty militants was met by a squad of militia who charged them, seriously injuring three of the delegation, including Rulewski. The incident was filmed by the police and shown on television in May. Everyone, including the Communist members of the *Sejm* for the region, understood that this was a deliberate provocation planned by the hard-liners in the Party. Photographs of the victims were made public, posters were printed, and in an atmosphere of great tension a general strike was planned for 27 March. This was a great success, not least because of the participation of large numbers of Communists. When the authorities failed to name those responsible for the provocation, the union announced another general strike for 31 March; everyone agreed that this would mean a total rejection of the regime. From 28 to 30 March, a Solidarity delegation negotiated in an atmosphere of enormous tension. The only card which the Party had left was the threat of Soviet intervention. On the evening of 30 March, Wałęsa and a few advisers took the decision to call off the strike without having been able to consult the KKP. This courageous retreat in the face of inevitable confrontation provoked a serious crisis within the union. At a moment when it had reached its greatest strength, it was for the first time confronted with its own limits and experienced its first serious internal conflicts.

Wałęsa's retreat from confrontation cannot be understood without reference to the moderating influence of the Church, which sees itself as the guardian of national survival, and therefore sought to avoid disastrous foreign intervention. Since 1956, the Church has known what the ruling Party judges to be the limits of tolerability, and has been an expression of an irreducible national identity while at the same time making quite clear how far resistance could go.

The meeting between the Warsaw group and Professor Kukołowicz, the Episcopate's adviser to Solidarity, brought out very clearly the Church's moderating influence on the movement. The Church's identification with the national consciousness makes it back away from any nationalist confrontation with the authorities. The Polish identity has survived four partitions and thirty-six years under the Soviet model, and the sense of attachment to Poland is so strong that it is seen as far more important to avoid the catastrophe of the destruction of the Polish state than it is to embark on a struggle for political power. Kukołowicz explained that the Episcopate supported Solidarity to the extent that it was an expression of the national identity, but that it was equally aware of the danger of foreign intervention. The Episcopate's decisions, he said, were dictated far more by a desire for the survival of the nation than by a preference for one social model as against another. Kukołowicz, whose influence remained great well into 1981, did not seek to promote a clerical or Christian-democratic tendency in Solidarity: his role was to warn the movement of the dangers to which it might expose the very life of the nation.

In the weeks following the Bydgoszcz affair, many militants criticised the Church for being too moderate and for having too great an influence on Wałęsa and his advisers. The same period saw the death of Cardinal Wyszyński, who had symbolised a double attitude of firmness and moderation towards the regime. The combined result of this was a change in relations between the union and the Church, Solidarity advisers with close connections with the Church being increasingly criticised by militants. The influence of Kukołowicz and Cywiński was weakened, and the moderating influence of the Church on Solidarity became less direct. The new Primate, Archbishop Glemp, seemed to be leading the Church towards a more pastoral and more autonomous role, and Father Tischner was the representative of this new direction, in which the Church intervened less directly in the life of the union. The Episcopate began to affirm its own independent policy of moderation, acting as mediator at the request of both parties when negotiations became too difficult, as for instance during the discussions in June over legal action to be taken on the Bydgoszcz affair. Mistrust between Solidarity and the authorities was such that only the Church could offer both parties and public opinion in general some guarantee that the agreements which had been reached would be respected. In this way, the Church helped to keep the union's action within the limits of tolerability.

The economic crisis

The limits of possible action, then, were defined by the Soviet threat and by the role of the Communist Party, and the Episcopate constantly reminded the nation of these limits. But the worsening economic crisis also imposed limits on Solidarity's action and on the demands which it could make. The responsibility for the crisis was obviously seen to lie with the Party's disastrous management, its incompetence and its dishonesty. Many people, particularly at Gdańsk and Katowice, also thought that Poland was being more or less pillaged by the Soviet Union. As a result, discussions on the economy always led to the most violent criticism of the regime.

But militants also felt that not everything was possible on the economic front, that the situation was so serious that it would not be enough simply to replace a few leading figures, and that everyone's cooperation would be needed. The calls for responsibility and cooperation from district officials in the Gdańsk and Katowice *województwa* were generally accepted by the members of the groups in these towns. The militants saw themselves as the only force capable of mobilising the nation in the rebuilding of the economy. When the Warsaw group met Mr Gluck, an economist, their criticism of the domination of the economy by bureaucracy, but also of certain forms of protection enjoyed by the workers under the present regime, was made in the name of 'economic laws'. They admitted, although in some cases reluctantly, that they would have to accept unemployment and some price increases. Rank-and-file members rather than the union leaders were the ones who spoke of the 'laws' of economics. Jerzy, from the Warsaw group, expressed the idea in the following terms: 'We, Solidarity, are in an exceptional situation, because for the first time in the history of the trade-union movement a trade union is going to have to accept unemployment and be a party to making workers redundant.' This is a clear case of trade-union activity taking on other meanings, in the sense that, beyond the class confrontation between workers and bosses, there is a more general call for the reconstruction of the ruined economy.

At first, the economic crisis appeared to constitute a force limiting the range of the demands which the union could make. But from the summer of 1981 onwards, the crisis took on such proportions and the economy was in such urgent need of reform that the field of confrontation shifted more and more towards the economy. The question of political power, which could not be posed in directly political terms, was then posed in the field of the economy, in which the Party seemed too weak to be able to carry out reform unaided. And it was here that the conflict which had always been avoided by last-minute compromise was going to take place.

PUSHING TO THE LIMITS

The boundaries which Solidarity must not overstep are defined by the Soviet threat, the hegemony of the Party and the economic crisis. But what was the actual mechanism of the movement's capacity for self-limitation? How far did one have to go before awareness of these limits weakened or paralysed the ability to act?

The ideal and the possible

The notion of self-limitation does not imply a stable and harmonious state. As the months went by, the effect on the movement of the gap between its aspirations and a set of voluntarily accepted constraints was sharper and more painful. The members of our research groups had within them a project for far-reaching change in society, but were also conscious of the need for self-restraint. The same was true of advisers, leaders, and rank-and-file militants alike: one could quote back at them declarations of war juxtaposed with appeals for caution. The internalisation of the notion of limits never damped the urgency of their aspirations: the militants lived at two levels, the desirable and the possible, and had to struggle to manage the tension between them. Solidarity was born of a struggle against a state of totalitarian inspiration, and within it there can still be seen traces of the internal split described by Bulgakov, Kundera, Miłosz or Zinoviev. A case in point was Zenon, from the Gdańsk group, a member of the Young Poland movement. To a certain extent he had overstepped the limit in joining a political party, but at the same time, as a trade unionist, he urged the workers in his factory to remain calm and to respect the Gdańsk Agreement to the letter, and even thought that the union's newspapers should practise some limited form of censorship. This should not be seen as inconsistent or

71

contradictory: it is a concrete expression of the double nature of Solidarity.

The work of all six of our research groups is an illustration of this life on two levels. Often the absence of an interlocutor was a signal for deep aspirations to be expressed: attacks on the Party were frequently violent, and the whole system created under Communist rule would be rejected as foreign, totalitarian and incompetent. A sense of deep antagonism between Solidarity and the authorities was constantly present, especially as the period in which the research took place was one in which the Party was at best delaying and at worst sabotaging the implementation of the Gdańsk, Szczecin and Jastrzębie Agreements. Militants increasingly believed that the internal crisis within the Party made it incapable of any action not backed by the threat of Soviet intervention. This was the language of aspirations, the inner language, but even then the militants were not prepared to transform such statements into political strategy. On the occasions when the groups had before them a Party member hostile to Solidarity, they would attack this figure for his political affiliations, for belonging to the propaganda or administrative apparatus, but sooner or later the theme of limits would appear on both sides, and all these meetings involved a return to a more moderate tone. With local government officers, the groups entered into detailed discussion of measures to be taken to improve the economic situation and, on a more urgent level, food supplies. When Party delegates were present, the groups would come round to accepting the idea of some kind of coexistence with the Party. Here, the shift to the level of the possible was expressed as an alliance of the 'moderates' against the 'hard-liners'. On both sides, the moderates were those who accepted the existence of limits. The militants of the Warsaw group, for example, imagined an alliance with the base of the Party against the Party apparatus, the former being seen as part of society while the latter was considered to be under the control of Moscow. Certainly such meetings were not notable for their effusions of comradely sentiments, and war was never far away, but everything pointed to the fact that these were people who frankly hated each other but were forced to live together. The meetings nevertheless ended in mutual recognition of conflict.

The two levels are also clearly reflected in militants' ambivalent reactions to events like the Bydgoszcz crisis. The reader will recall that, after a first protest strike, the movement saw its leaders call off a second stoppage in order to remain within tolerable limits. The Katowice militants described their feelings at that moment: disappointment at the fact that the movement had not gone all the way, and because the desire to confront the regime with a general strike had not been satisfied; but disappointment tinged with relief that the catastrophe which everyone could feel hanging over them had been avoided. The militants' feelings were contradictory, moderate and radical at the same time. Andrzej Gwiazda's position as he explained it to the Gdańsk group is significant here. He explained how he had taken an important part in some of Solidarity's famous last-minute compromises, especially in December 1980 during the crisis over the union's registration. He believed that the union had to take account of what was defined as acceptable to the government by ideological and external constraints. The compromise reached in the wake of the Bydgoszcz affair seemed a good one, since the government had promised to find the provocateurs and had recognised Rural Solidarity. But he was violently opposed to Wałęsa and his advisers over the secrecy of the negotiations which led to the agreements. For him, Solidarity had acted contrary to the basis of its own legitimacy, behaving in a 'Bolshevik' manner. Moreover, no reference should have been made to a general strike if the leaders knew that that was setting the bar too high and that they would have to back down. Gwiazda therefore thought that the union should have gone ahead with the strike, even if only for an hour, to prevent the Party from taking the offensive and to show that Solidarity did not go back on its commitments. Gwiazda's position can be described neither as moderate nor as hard-line: it simply tries not to widen the gap between the movement's aspirations and the limits which are given. It seeks, in other words, to reconcile the two levels of the action.

The advisers

The union's advisers (often referred to as 'experts') played an important part in the brinkmanship which this simultaneously radical and moderate strategy involved. But who were these intellectuals, presented to the world first as dangerous extremists and then as timid advisers paralysing the revolutionary energy of the workers? We should make a distinction, although it is perhaps a little arbitrary, between the specialists who gave the union the benefit of their knowledge of the law or of economics, and, on the other hand, better known and more influential advisers whose role was more political. The latter group is important: these intellectuals were involved in defining limits which could never be totally objective, and which had to be established by the actors themselves.

When Bronisław Geremek and Tadeusz Mazowiecki arrived in Gdańsk on 22 August 1980 with a message of support signed by sixty-two Warsaw intellectuals, the strike leaders asked them to join in the preparation of the negotiations. Relatively quickly, it appeared that these advisers had coalesced into three distinct groups, and these groups were to be consulted independently by the union. The first was the Episcopate group with Professor Kukołowicz at the centre; the second was the moderates, with Geremek, Mazowiecki and Wiełowiejski, close to the KIK; and finally there was the group made up of members of the KOR, with Kuroń, Michnik and

Lipiński. Among the advisers attached to each MKZ these distinct tendencies are often reproduced.

The way in which opposition political thought developed after the massacres of 1970 is in itself a sign that intellectuals and other groups hostile to the system did not think that the time had come to embark on a struggle with the direct aim of overthrowing the political order. Many people admitted that the political system had not fulfilled its totalitarian ambitions, and had been forced to leave a certain margin of autonomy in which the intellectuals, and the national consciousness through the Church, could operate. This led to the conclusion that limited action was still possible. For Leszek Kołakowski, this path represented a rejection of the false alternative between silence and total revolution. Of course it did not mean that opposition intellectuals believed that Communism or its leaders could be made to be good.

With the movements of protest against the revision of the Constitution in 1975 and against the repression of the Radom riots in 1976, and the creation of the KOR and the ROPCiO, a strategy of self-limiting struggle began to emerge. The intellectuals' concern was to defend freedoms on the basis of the law and the Helsinki Final Act, and to give concrete help to the workers, rather than to aim directly for a change in the nature of the regime. The road ahead seemed to be one of resistance on the part of society, and not political struggle. The writings of the major personalities behind these opposition groups, notably Michnik and Kuroń, define very powerfully this cautious, limited strategy. The regime's totalitarian logic leads it immediately to treat the slightest act of resistance as a fundamental attack on its own national and international legitimacy, but the opposition refuses this almost automatic escalation towards the political level. This strategy is obviously more marked in the case of opposition intellectuals close to the Church, the members of the KIK, and also those who have chosen to remain in the Party, like certain members of the DiP group. By different routes and from sometimes diametrically opposed starting points, these intellectuals seemed to converge during this period: their common aim was to promote a self-limiting struggle which would avoid the catastrophes which had befallen Hungary and Czechoslovakia, and bypassing the Leninist model of revolution, used by the Party as a justification for its own dominance. 'True socialism' was no longer set against socialism as actually constituted.

In direct opposition to the usual pattern, in which it is the intellectuals who provide the radical consciousness in social struggles, what the intellectuals brought to Gdańsk in August 1980 was moderation and an awareness of the limits of possible action. Most of the advisers were much more moderate than a radical rank and file which was, generally speaking, very young. Kuroń defined the strategy of self-limitation which refuses to threaten the power of the Party or to commit acts which the Soviet Union would find intolerable in this text written in September 1980: 'Is it possible to set limits to the movement's dynamic? Not only is it possible, it is necessary; but the only way of achieving this would be to define a programme of action which would allow the movement to develop without losing sight of the limits' (KOR news-sheet, September 1980). Such statements are not an attempt to allay suspicion: they were soon acted upon. During the registration crisis at the end of October 1980, Kuroń and the majority of the union's advisers opposed the decision to base the Gdańsk MKZ at the Lenin shipyard, fearing that this would be seen as a gesture of provocation. In November, at the time of the Narożniak affair[1], Kuroń and his friends went to the Huta–Warszawa steelworks to ask the workers to call off their strike. Such acts on the part of advisers considered to be the most radical were repeated throughout 1981. They show that the advisers defined themselves by their awareness of the limits of possible action and their desire to prevent the movement becoming caught in an uncontrollable logic which would inevitably lead to rupture.

Radicals and moderates

On 19 March 1981 a group of Solidarity militants were beaten up when they tried to read a statement to the regional council at Bydgoszcz. The decision to call off the second strike, called for 31 March, which led to the signing of the 'Warsaw Agreement', was strongly criticised within the union. It was after the Bydgoszcz affair that a split began to emerge inside the union, and above all within the leadership and the different groups of advisers, between radicals and moderates.

This split is less simple than it appears: no one believed that there were no limits to the action which Solidarity could undertake, but, conversely, no one imagined that the union could advance without bringing heavy pressure to bear on the regime. Far removed from Kuroń, whose appeals for caution we have just seen, Mazowiecki, generally considered to be a moderate, thought that constant pressure had to be put on the government, since it took advantage of the slightest slackening of pressure to win back lost ground, and only carried on with the implementation of the Gdańsk Agreement when strike action was threatened. Moreover, both men were in agreement in September 1981 that a compromise on self-management should be accepted.

A divergence between radical and moderate tendencies also became apparent in our groups. As at the top, the distinction was relatively imprecise, since the militants, at Katowice for instance, saw themselves

---

1 Narożniak was a militant arrested for passing on secret official directives concerning the repression of Solidarity.

primarily as trade unionists and admitted that the boundary between trade unionism and political action was itself not clearly defined. Furthermore, the internal life of Solidarity was not polarised in any concrete way around organised factions. But the idea of a split did exist: in Silesia for instance, the miners saw the Katowice MKZ as 'radical' and the Jastrzębie MKZ as 'moderate'.

Political radicalism was not necessarily reflected in radical attitudes at the level of trade-union action. At Katowice, Jan was politically radical but more moderate as a trade unionist, whereas Henryk supported radical demands at union level but was more cautious on the political front. Other militants, such as Mirosław, considered themselves relatively moderate at both levels. The opposite was true, for example, of Józef.

It appeared that the main touchstone for this distinction was a militant's attitude to the adversary, the PUWP. This came out particularly clearly in discussions of the Bydgoszcz affair. At Katowice the radicals, such as Krystian, thought that Wałęsa had been wrong to call off the strike and saw this as the union's first retreat. Since then, they maintained, the Party had returned to the offensive over the media and the Agreements, and the judicial investigation of the Bydgoszcz affair had led to the withdrawal of the case: it had therefore been a mistake to give in to the threat of foreign intervention. The same militants criticised the secrecy of the negotiations and said that 90% of the workers were in favour of a general strike which everyone knew might have become insurrectional in character. The moderates, on the other hand, thought that the agreements of 31 March were right and that the first strike had been a sufficient show of force. Henryk said that if Wałęsa had lost two million radicals, he had gained five million Poles. Stanisław took up the Episcopate's argument that the most important thing was not to endanger the Polish state. The moderates were not simply those who thought about the limits laid down by Poland's geopolitical situation; more often than not they believed that there was some room for compromise with the Party, and they saw the Bydgoszcz incident as a provocation by Party hard-liners directed at more moderate elements within the Party. The less radical Solidarity members were no less disgusted than the others: they simply thought, unlike the radicals, that compromise with the regime was possible.

After September 1981, the internal split seemed to be between the 'pragmatists' and the 'fundamentalists'. The first group, of which Wiełowiejski is a representative, thought that the leading role of the Party must not be directly challenged and that all the possibilities of the Constitution must be exploited. There was talk of 'rebuilding public life' in Poland, and the Gdańsk Agreement was seen as a basis for continued progress, as long as Solidarity and the authorities both acted realistically. The texts which the pragmatists published after the Congress spoke of the

Party as one of the *partners* in the Gdańsk Agreement. The pragmatists reminded the movement of the existence of the external threat, and said that the creation of political parties might have the effect of dividing the union. But more hard-line positions could be found in association with these moderate ones, like the call for free local elections which would inevitably unmask the illegitimacy and weakness of the Party.

The fundamentalists, for their part, maintained that the political system was illegitimate, and that the Party could not meaningfully be a partner to the union or society as a whole. They made direct demands for political pluralism and the 'realisation of the ideals for which the workers have been fighting for more than a century'. But, these principles being stated, they also said that 'in the present situation there can be no question of destroying the Party' and that 'Solidarity is not fighting for power and has no ambition to become a political party'. In other words, the actual positions were more moderate than they would appear from the way they were expressed.

'Radical' and 'moderate', followed by 'fundamentalist' and 'pragmatist', are words which refer to a problematical area within which militants must find their way, rather than to a clearly defined split. For instance in September 1981, delegates to the Congress criticised the leadership for signing an agreement on self-management which they saw as backing down. But, simultaneously, the Congress passed a vote of confidence in the leadership by 567 votes to 60. Wałęsa's power was confirmed, but Gil, the union leader at Huta-Lenin, was criticised for having supported Wałęsa's positions. The effect of the paralysing constraints on the union's action was to create among the rank and file a strong mistrust of the leaders and their advisers. But is it therefore possible to say that the base is radical or fundamentalist and the advisers moderate or pragmatist, and to conclude that the principal rift is between the base and the top, the workers and the intellectuals? Certainly not. Conversely, it is even less justifiable to imagine that the opposition is between a spontaneously moderate rank and file and a set of radical intellectuals. Adam Michnik was one of the radical intellectuals who were violently attacked by the Party and the Soviet press. And some members of the Gdańsk group were very mistrustful of this politico, on the grounds that he might tend to push Solidarity beyond the bounds of the possible, and because they saw him as the representative of those intellectuals who were said to have too much influence on the movement's working-class leaders.

And yet, when Michnik met the group, he set about defining the system of constraints within which the whole movement had to act, the intellectuals' job being, he said, simply to present a clear image of these constraints. He refused to define Poland simply as a subject nation: the situation was not comparable with that of the Ukraine or Lithuania, since Poland possessed a state, not a sovereign one, certainly, but a state all the same, and its very existence meant that it was not true to say that the movement had 'nothing to lose'. Solidarity could only act within limits which for the moment had not to be touched: no one was overestimating the danger of Soviet intervention, but until there was a change the partition of Europe which had stood since Yalta had to be respected, 'unless the Pacific overflows . . .' 'We must build our own house within these limits.' Intractable problems were caused by the coming together of a desire for general liberation and a set of limits whose existence was recognised but whose exact location was unknown; the role of the advisers was to help the movement to square that circle. This, said Michnik, was the psychological problem which the Poles had to face, 'at the risk of going mad'. Michnik's vocabulary, and indeed that of the militants in general, was peppered with ambiguous phrases and jokes playing on these contradictions. He thought that, at least in the short term, it would be a mistake to form opposition parties because 'for the Russians, that means war'. He also said that he had proposed the disbandment of the KOR (which was to take effect in September) not only because it had been superseded by Solidarity, but also as a way of denying the enemy an excuse for attacking the movement. The union's aims had necessarily to be limited ones: 'Let's win what we can, and not bother if some people call us defeatists.' The man who was saying this can nevertheless be considered as one of the 'radical advisers' to the extent that he thought that the conflict with the regime was by its very nature a total one, even if circumstances dictated extreme caution. Michnik was concerned to define the limits of possible action, and within them to put up a strong defence of what had been won. But he did not want to go beyond them.

As the time went by, it became increasingly difficult for Solidarity to be simultaneously a total social movement and a self-limiting one. The balance which, in the first few months, had seemed easy to attain, now grew weaker each time Solidarity reached the limit and retreated. The Party and the economy were in such a state of crisis that they no longer presented a sufficiently solid definition of the limits to be observed, thus opening up dizzying prospects to the movement. With the limits becoming more and more hazily defined, appeals to nationalist sentiment and uncontrolled hunger marches began to appear. In general, militants felt that the movement was becoming progressively paralysed as the radical and moderate tendencies, instead of meeting head on, went their separate ways or became superimposed one on the other.

The militants with whom we worked and the union leaders whom we met are driven by convictions of enormous strength, which can be heard in the way the movement speaks and seen in its actions. Many knew that the situation was extremely dangerous, and yet we rarely heard excessive or bellicose statements. People spoke the language of values, principles, responsibility, honesty and morality. This tone is usually attributed to the influence of the Catholic Church; but in our opinion the conviction of Solidarity militants is a direct result of the imbalance between the movement's aims and aspirations on the one hand, and on the other, its awareness of the limits which it must not overstep. This transformation of ideas through the internalisation of limits is most clearly illustrated in the case of the national consciousness.

Political nationalism is not possible in Poland in the present climate. Under the pressure of this constraint, it is transformed into an affirmation of national identity, a search for a sense of community which never dissociates the idea of society from that of the nation. The national theme often takes on popular and democratic meanings, and in the case of Wałęsa, with his appeals to Polish culture and values, a populist dimension is added. Many observers have stressed the calm and steadfast way in which the Poles are bearing the difficulties of the economic crisis, and one of the reasons why incidents are as rare as they are in the food queues is the strong sense of collective responsibility. Even during the strikes, there were very few clashes which could be attributed to Solidarity. The militants cannot undertake here and now the building of a democratic political system, so they establish an exemplary form of democracy amongst themselves. Principles fill the vacuum between the movement's inner desires and the restrictions which it has to impose on itself.

Nevertheless, militants rarely identified the movement completely with its underlying values: there was a general refusal to separate principles from the actual means by which action was to be pursued. We found that the individuals who stood for the movement's convictions felt that they had been relegated to the wings during negotiations and compromises. This was true of Anna Walentynowicz and to some extent of Andrzej Gwiazda. Conversely, a purely instrumentalist, tactical attitude was absent or well hidden. Wałęsa, the very image of political skill and negotiating ability, constantly reminded the movement of the principles which guided its action, however short of the principles that action might fall. The movement is condemned to the difficult task of reconciling its aspirations with the possibilities actually open to it.

PART TWO

THE LIBERATION OF SOCIETY

4

The movement evolves

A YEAR OF STRUGGLES

The Gdańsk Agreement defines Solidarity as a trade union 'having no role to play as a political party', but also as a force of social liberation which must 'enjoy genuine opportunities for publicly evaluating the new decisions that determine working people's conditions'. Solidarity also made it clear that it intended to see that freedom of opinion and expression were respected. The union did not seek to challenge the Warsaw Pact and Poland's links with the Soviet Union, but its aim was to fight the power of the Party and its domination of society. How was this action for the liberation of society integrated into the social movement in the first year of Solidarity's life?

For the first few months, the two elements were highly integrated. The strikes which took place all over Poland were directed not only at enterprise managers but also at the political and administrative authorities who were attempting to slow down the establishment of the union. The movement's general goals meant that all professional groups became involved in the action: teachers, workers in the health service and the judicial system . . . The regime's opposition to the independent farmers' union weakened, and Rural Solidarity was registered in May 1981. The movement advanced more and more quickly, partly through its own success within the factories but also because the Party retreated, releasing the majority of political prisoners and seeing its control over society questioned and more and more effectively undermined. Political leaders from the Gierek period were denounced and the new First Secretary of the Party, Kania, went to meditate publicly at the memorial to the dead of 1970 in Gdańsk. This liberation of society, and the retreat by the Party, were all the more spectacular for the fact that the regime's attempts to impede the union failed before the threat of a general strike. This was the case in November 1980 when the Warsaw District Court was obliged to accept Solidarity's statutes without any of the changes which it had tried to introduce. It was also the case in many conflicts at local level. At this stage Solidarity was a highly integrated movement, more and more clearly identified with the whole of Polish society by virtue of the size of its membership and its capacity for uniting the democratic and national aspirations of the population around the theme of free trade unions. But it remained conscious of the limits to its action which were dictated by economic problems and the danger of Soviet intervention.

Faced with this liberating drive, the Party was incapable of setting out a consistent political line, blowing alternately hot and cold. The leadership changed hands constantly, reinforcing the impression of inconsistency at the top: Kania replaced Gierek as First Secretary in September 1980; Jagielski, seen as the strong-arm man, was removed; in February 1981 Jaruzelski took over from Pieńkowski as Prime Minister. At rank-and-file level, the Party was in a state of decay: many members were leaving it and joining Solidarity, expressing their mistrust of the leadership. Members of the Politburo had great difficulty getting themselves re-elected at the Congress, which replaced 80% of the membership of the Central Committee. Party militants in favour of renewal within the Party and agreement with Solidarity met in 'horizontal structures',[1] while hard-liners instituted Forums like the one at Katowice in order to recall the faithful to Marxist–Leninist orthodoxy and 'friendship' with the Soviet Union. The Bydgoszcz crisis of March 1981 represented the high point of Solidarity's power; the crisis also showed clearly how the movement's progress could be halted by a set of limits which it would be suicidal to overstep. From this point onwards, although trade-union activity continued, increasing importance was attached to the theme of self-management, seen as the means of freeing industry from Party domination. As early as April 1981, a 'network' for self-management (*sieć*) was formed after meetings between union representatives from the shipyards of Gdańsk and Szczecin. It brought together militants from seventeen large enterprises, and put forward proposals for methods of self-management. Later another network, more radical and oriented more towards workers' control, was established at the initiative of workers from Łódź and Lublin. Solidarity's Centre for Socio-Professional Research also made a series of proposals, paying more attention to general economic problems than to specific questions of

1 The 'horizontal structures' movement is an indication of the crisis within the Party. It first met at Toruń in April 1981 at the initiative of Iwanów. Its sympathisers, numbered in tens of thousands, proposed the creation of several organised tendencies within the Party: only democratic reform of the PUWP could, they believed, stave off the otherwise inevitable confrontation with society. Similar preoccupations can be seen in calls for pluralism within the Party made by Bratkowski, the president of the Journalists' Association, and Lamentowicz, the head of the School for Party Officials. These democratic forces did not present any organised front at the Party Congress in July 1981: it would appear that many of them chose to support the moderate position of Kania as a way of keeping out the hard-liners.

organisation within the enterprise: according to Jakubowicz, the idea was to 'socialise the plan'. Generally speaking, it would appear that the category most involved in questions of self-management were technicians and engineers from the larger enterprises. Outside Solidarity, self-management councils were set up with the aim of electing new managers for the enterprise and seeking solutions to the most urgent problems posed by the crisis. The impression of moderation was accentuated at this time by the distress caused by the death of Cardinal Wyszyński, and by preparations for the Party Congress to be held in July.

The central phase of our sociological intervention took place during this period of relative calm, at Gdańsk, Warsaw and Katowice. The situation seemed to have stabilised itself, self-management councils were establishing themselves, and the Party, getting ready for its Congress, seemed to be consolidating its position, thus considerably reducing pressure from the Soviet Union.

But from July onwards the trade-union struggle began to look more like a rebellion. The population, used to food shortages, was beginning to feel the effects of something starting to resemble famine: people could no longer be sure of finding staple foods even after long hours of queueing, and the food supply became a dominant element in trade-union activity. In July, hunger marches were organised at Kutno, Łódź and in other towns. On 3 and 4 August Warsaw was occupied by demonstrators protesting about the deterioration in living conditions.

At its Congress the Party seemed to consolidate. Kania's position seemed safer since he had shown that he was capable of resisting Soviet pressure by refusing to yield to the threatening letter which the Soviet Party had sent to its Polish counterpart in June. He was elected directly by the delegates to the Congress, and he set out a centrist policy equally removed from the 'hard-liners' and the 'liberals'. Having regained its stability, the Party then launched an offensive against Solidarity, reaffirming its monopoly of the media, arresting the nationalists of the KPN, and refusing to hand over control of the large enterprises to the self-management councils. The Party adopted, for instance, a very firm position over self-management in the national airline LOT, where the first confrontation on the principle of self-management took place in July. The election of Kimajze by the council was rejected, and a general appointed as manager instead. Solidarity responded by hardening its attitudes. On the one hand the liberation of society came to be more and more identified with demands for free local elections, for access to the media, and for participation in the planning of economic reforms which were under discussion in Parliament. On the other hand, the climate of nationalism became more acute, with support being given to the KPN militants on trial, and several incidents between police and nationalists were reported in various towns.

The liberation of society

The history of Solidarity is determined by three factors: its own internal dynamics, the evolution of its adversary, and the changing situation. On the other hand, the very nature of Solidarity incites it progressively to raise the level of its demands, as long as its general priorities are not changed. The struggle for the liberation of society, at first undertaken in order to obtain free trade unions, is then extended to include the management of the enterprise and economic life in general, and finally reaches out into the political field, in the strict sense of the term. It is as if the defence of free trade unions had to take place on ever widening ground. A constantly accelerating movement towards political action can be seen in the debates of Solidarity's National Coordinating Committee. This process culminated, in the summer of 1981, in a demand for free elections which represented a direct challenge to the Party's control of the state. On the other hand, Solidarity moves on from the affirmation of its principles and its independence to more pragmatic action, increasingly limited by the economic situation and the danger of Soviet intervention. At first the movement behaves as though it could carry all before it, but it gradually reverts to the defensive. The strikers who at the end of August 1980 followed the great public negotiation between Jagielski and Wałęsa were, fifteen months later, overwhelmed by their awareness of the generalised crisis affecting society and the economy.

It is therefore just as false to speak only of the rapid development of a revolutionary movement for the seizure of power as it is to reduce Solidarity's history to a movement away from principles and towards pragmatism. The movement's double evolution leads rather to a dissociation of the component elements of its action. While the leaders fought increasingly on political ground, the rank and file retreated more and more to defensive positions. The optimism of those who believed that the movement would go on to greater victories was matched by the pessimism of those who saw the widening gap between the leadership and the base.

At the beginning of its life, Solidarity had a clear vision both of the extent of its ambitions and of the limits which it had to respect. One year later a double change can be seen to have taken place: the movement seemed no longer to be clear about the limits to its action, but at the same time it had become less triumphant and increasingly presented itself simply as a response to the economic and political crisis. The movement's successes encouraged it to broaden the scope of its action, but at the same time they revealed the accelerating disintegration of the Party. In August 1980 the latter was prepared to engage in open negotiations, hoping to overcome this first crisis. In the spring of 1981 it organised a serious act of provocation (Bydgoszcz) and then took shelter behind the threat of Soviet intervention;

at the same time it sought to avoid or slow down reform in the enterprise and in the economy generally. Finally, in the autumn, just after Solidarity's Congress, it began to hide behind the army: generals began to enter the government, and groups of military started to replace the powerless local authorities.

We found that when militants, both rank-and-file and at the top, looked to the future course of their action, they increasingly emphasised their expanding aims, but at the same time their concrete actions were designed to defend more and more directly their own immediate interests. As a result, conflict with the authorities became more and more open, not because they were directly attacking the centres of power but because they increasingly resorted to wildcat action. In our groups, the image of a stable movement with a solid base of principles and strategy was at first dominant. This gradually gave way to the notion of action rising by stages towards an increasingly general liberation of society. In the autumn this image in its turn began to be replaced by a representation of Solidarity as a movement whose very nature set it on a course of radical opposition to the Communist regime, but which was at the same time confined to defensive behaviour by a set of external constraints. As was the case in the groups, we shall refer to these three theories by the names of those who formulated them.

(a) *The Jerzy theory* (Figure 8), after an engineer in the Warsaw group. This view reduces evolution in Solidarity to a minimum. The movement is defined primarily by its trade-union activity, and is seen as intervening in political problems and in the national question only inasmuch as these dimensions are bound up with the defence of workers' interests. In this sense, it is close to the spirit of the Gdańsk Agreement. Solidarity is bound progressively to extend its trade-union action onto the political and national fronts, but this must only take place where the three levels are inseparable. Jerzy produced a diagram representing his theory which was often discussed with the other research groups.

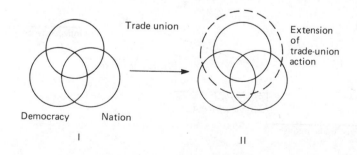

Figure 8. The Jerzy theory

In this view, trade-union action takes precedence over other types of action, and the social movement is seen as having the priority over the wider movement for social liberation. Purely political action is regarded with a certain mistrust. Jerzy insisted that the rank and file expected the union to defend them in the factory and in society as a whole, as producers and as consumers. The theory was at first widely supported in the Warsaw group itself and in the others, perhaps because it seemed to confirm the straightforward idea of Solidarity being made up of three component elements. Even the more politicised militants were convinced that theirs was first and foremost a workers' movement with its base in the factories. The idea that action should develop from this professional and economic base was unanimously seen as being in accordance with the spirit of the Gdańsk Agreement and with the origins of the movement. At a time when the movement was carried forward by a great momentum, everyone accepted that it had to limit itself and avoid becoming involved in certain types of political and national problems.

(b) Nevertheless, at about the same time a different theory was put forward: the *Grzegorz theory* (Figure 9), after a technician in the Warsaw group. He rejected the image of a movement centred on trade-union action, and proposed instead the model of a movement rising by stages towards increasingly political and national action. The Gdańsk Agreement, he said, had freed the trade unions, and since then, and especially since the spring of 1981, the union's central preoccupation had been self-management, in other words the liberation of the enterprise. But the nature of the Polish economy meant that any action at factory level inevitably entailed action at the general economic level, since the autonomy of the individual enterprise presupposed general economic reform, an end to the centrally administered economy and its replacement by a rational price structure and a free market system. Finally, once it had rebuilt the political system, Solidarity must attempt to restore the true independence of the country.

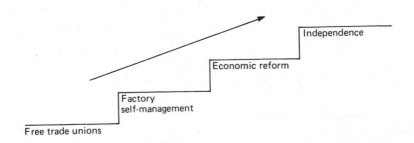

Figure 9. The Grzegorz theory

Despite the differences, this theory is not diametrically opposed to the previous one, in the sense that it still sees trade-union action as the most important concrete element of the movement. In Western countries, too, trade-union action goes beyond a simple defence of workers' interests, seeking to establish various forms of industrial democracy: this represents an involvement in the political system as a whole, and trade unions which undertake action of this kind are not accused of being politicised. But a difference remains: where Jerzy sees a social movement, Grzegorz sees an evolution culminating in the liberation of the whole society. Solidarity must rebuild relations between management and workforce in the enterprise, and attempt to lay the foundations of economic reform by demanding the creation of a second, economic chamber in the *Sejm*, in which it would have considerable influence.

The Grzegorz theory, then, although it remains essentially moderate, nevertheless begins to tip the balance in favour of the idea of the liberation of society rather than that of a social movement. We shall see later how the Warsaw group discussed these two theories put forward by two of its members, and how the positions of each individual and of the group as a whole were modified in the course of these discussions. At Gdańsk the two theories were also present, in the form of a strictly trade-unionist tendency and a political tendency which were clearly identifiable within the group. At Katowice the Jerzy theory was readily accepted, but was given a rather more radical meaning than in Warsaw. The miners' action was indeed based on the defence of workers' interests, but their highly developed class consciousness meant that they constantly saw a very clear opposition between the interests of the working class, particularly the miners, and methods of economic management which exploited them for the profit of a privileged Party apparatus and ruling class, against the fundamental interests of the nation.

By the autumn, however, the Jerzy theory no longer reflected the militants' predominant view, and the theme of self-management had also lost some of its importance. From now on, the main question was this: should Solidarity confine its action to the economic sphere, or should it be extended to encompass the whole of society?

(c) It was at this point that the *Józef theory* (Figure 10) made its appearance in the Wrocław group, with similar views being put forward at the same time at Łódź by Andrzej and by several members of the Szczecin group. The Wrocław group had the diagrams in front of them and were discussing the two previous theories when Józef, a young technician from a research department, suddenly turned the reasoning on its head. Solidarity must not be defined by the aims from which it started but by its ultimate objective, which was nothing less than Polish independence. The only guarantee of free trade unions was political democracy, which in turn could not survive until the Poles were in control of their own affairs, and could establish the democratic institutions of their choice. Only Solidarity had been able to initiate this process. Whereas Grzegorz saw Solidarity building up its action stage by stage, Józef and others thought that the movement's action could not be anything less than total, even if they admitted that the movement had to take account of external constraints and impose limits on itself which meant, at a practical level, that it proceeded step by step. Józef, like Leszek Moczulski who seemed to have been an influence on him, was no extremist: he was relatively silent in the group, and when he did speak it was to ask questions rather than to make statements, but he was followed by most of the group when he said that the movement's evolution had to be seen from above and not from below, which inevitably meant that the centre of gravity shifted. Whereas the other theories placed it respectively at union level and within the enterprise as a whole, it was now clearly situated in the political field. The social movement and nationalism were coterminous. And if the ultimate aim was independence, then the decisive moment would be free elections, at which point, another member of the group said, Solidarity would split into a number of political forces, at the same time retaining the classic functions of a trade union. This transition from a single social movement to a pluralist political system would mark the ultimate victory of Solidarity.

Here, the progression from social movement to the liberation of society is pushed to its logical conclusion. The movement's victory will signal its own abolition, as a united movement representing everyone is replaced by a diversity of political choices which is the condition of democracy. The necessary consequence will be the fall of the PUWP, which was variously predicted as receiving 30%, 10% and 1% of the vote in free elections.

Between the first and third of these theories, Solidarity's image of itself has shifted decisively: the social movement has become a force for the liberation of society in its entirety. There is no complete discontinuity between these three views: Józef did not for a moment think that the

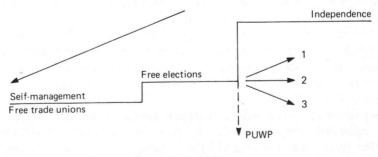

Figure 10. The Józef theory

90

movement towards independence was possible without the mobilisation of the working class which Solidarity was capable of bringing about.

At Wrocław, Łódź and Szczecin it was never questioned that Solidarity had begun life as a trade union, and that its action was and must remain rooted in the factory. But the workers and technicians in our research groups were increasingly convinced that the problems they faced at work were ultimately determined by the political and national subordination of Poland to a Party whose only support came from abroad. There is no reason to believe that trade-union problems were less important to them than others, or that they saw the national question as more central than social ones. What can be stated with certainty is that as the crisis worsened and, above all, as the disintegration of the Party became more glaringly obvious, the more Solidarity realised that its own attempts to limit its action could not prevent the question of political power from being confronted, that indeed that question had been on the agenda since the very first day, and that the conflict could not be confined to one particular area. And the reason was quite simply that the adversary's domination is not confined to one sector of society, but is a totalitarian force which by its very nature subjects the press, industrial management, the workers and the interests of the nation to its own power.

Must we conclude from this series of views that the militants of Solidarity, at first united in the limited aim of creating a free trade union, were progressively drawn into political action, that they ceased to perform the self-limiting role which had allowed them to pursue their action without coming into direct conflict with the regime, and that they were therefore themselves to blame for their downfall? Such a conclusion is unacceptable, and is contradicted by the minutes of our groups' meetings. The specific contribution of our research is to dismantle the theory that the rank and file of Solidarity had a set of limited trade-union objectives and that the movement was diverted from its proper course by a group of politicised intellectuals at the top. The opposite would perhaps be a little more true, although it is equally unacceptable. In reality, there was no difference between the rank and file and the leadership: the discussions between rank-and-file militants in the Szczecin and Wrocław groups were no different from the debates of the National Committee. At every level national consciousness, democratic aspirations and the defence of the workers are as inseparably linked as the domination of the economy, the monopoly of political power and subservience to the Soviet Union are within the Party. There is certainly an evolution to be seen in Solidarity, but its general nature does not change.

The factors of change lie elsewhere. Solidarity's success and the concomitant crisis within the Party had the effect of directly confronting the union with problems concerning the management and survival of the country, and with the conditions for its own existence. Is it conceivable that an organisation with ten million members should be denied normal access to the media? Is it acceptable that a Party which is rejected by the majority of the population and which in any case is no longer capable of exercising its authority and taking decisions affecting the economy, should still monopolise all decision-making? The very existence of Solidarity, the Party's inability to adapt to a situation going directly against its totalitarian aspirations, and the failure of its acts of provocation, all contributed to exposing the central problem of the relationship between society and the regime. All the collective actors in Poland had to confront that question.

It had of course been present since the very first day. At first it was experienced as the need to constitute a force through which society could express its views and its opposition to the Party. It then became evident to most people that, if the confrontation which the overwhelming majority of Solidarity members and leaders did not want was to be avoided, then public life must be freed, the Party must be forced to restore democratic institutions, neutral territory must be created in which decisions were made according to criteria of economic and technical rationality. The evolution of Solidarity, then, is a function of the general definition of its aims, and is not entirely determined by events; it constitutes an internal dynamic, made up of the changing relationships between the component elements of the action. More particularly, the same multiplicity of views as to the movement's aims, the same distance between radicals and moderates, recur at every stage, but each time on different ground and in the light of different objectives. The action remains faithful to a set of general principles, but takes on different forms according to the situation which is being faced.

SELF-MANAGEMENT

It was inconceivable that the creation of free trade unions would not have political and economic reverberations. Their existence had to be guaranteed by institutional reforms and by freedom of organisation and information. This in turn was a direct attack upon the PUWP, which had never confined itself to its leading role in the state and claimed the right to exercise its hegemony over every area of society. Moreover, Solidarity could not stop at its first victories but, as the movement took new initiatives, it found itself coming up against two sets of constraints: on the one hand Soviet domination, and on the other the economic crisis, which had been an important factor in sparking off the workers' movements of 1976 and 1980. The effect of these inescapable constraints was further to accentuate the tendency for each component element of Solidarity to become autonomous and to follow its own individual logic. Our research groups were very aware of the danger of the movement splitting as a result of this tendency, and there was a clear desire to find a new principle of unity for the movement. Figure 11 illustrates this search and shows the problems which were to be overcome.

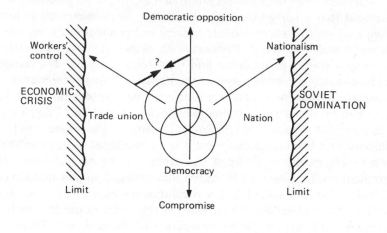

Figure 11

What was to be done to prevent the national element becoming a struggle for independence isolated from the social aims of the movement? How was a situation to be avoided in which the truly political action of those groups ironically accepting the Party's condemnation of them and calling themselves 'anti-socialist elements' might become separated from the mass of the workers, as was already the case with the students? And how could the movement resist falling back on a form of workers' control which would restrict Solidarity's action to the more militant of the large enterprises?

The first possible solution was an historic compromise with the Party, which was also suffering the consequences of the economic crisis and was ready to undertake some reform of the economy. Rakowski, the Deputy Prime Minister, and Barcikowski, a member of the Politburo, were the main advocates of this Hungarian-style realism which sought to use Solidarity as a means of putting an end to disastrous methods of management, thereby consolidating the Party's dominant position.

In fact this solution, which was defended for long enough by the DiP group, under the general leadership of Stefan Bratkowski and bringing together Party members, Catholics and some independent intellectuals, was never really accepted by the groups. The most that can be said is that a few militants, particularly in the Gdańsk group, wanted to see a complete transformation of the Party, which is a sufficient indication of the difficulty of this solution. The militants were in no sense hostile to ordinary Party members, of whom a significant proportion also belonged to Solidarity, but

93

they harboured deep hostility towards the Party leaders. They thought that a balance of power must be sought between Solidarity and the Party, but they did not believe in the possibility of any kind of political agreement between them, even with the mediation of the Church, because they were convinced that a party essentially totalitarian in character could never accept for long that society should become independent of the regime.

It was therefore within itself and through its own actions that Solidarity must find a way of maintaining and reinforcing its unity. The solution which gradually came to be seen as the right one may be summarised as follows: the movement must accept the geopolitical constraints which had been clearly restated by the rumours of Soviet intervention following the Bydgoszcz affair in March and the Soviet Communist Party's letter in June; Solidarity's trade-union action must also be combined with more direct participation in the economy if the crisis was to be overcome. The movement must not let itself be drawn into nationalism, nor into directly political action, nor indeed into a revolutionary movement of workers' councils; it must combine the strength of the social movement with an organised campaign for the reconstruction of the economy. These two objectives should be easily combined, since the first requisite of economic recovery was the elimination of the Party from the enterprise and a return to criteria of economic rationality. Trade-union and democratic action had to come together, not to push for a complete transformation of society, but in order to carry through urgent reform of the enterprise and the economy as a whole. Finally, the idea of workers' self-management defined the meeting point of trade-union and political action.

In May and June of 1981, the principal subject of discussion within Solidarity was no longer the recognition by the regime of the rights of the union, which had been established since 1980; nor was it the threat of counter-attack by the adversary; it was self-management. Many factories, and in particular one network of large enterprises, decided independently to set up self-management councils representing a complete break with the workers' councils established with high hopes in 1956 but now an empty husk. Debate began in the *Sejm* with a view to bringing in a bill on self-management, and conflicts broke out in enterprises, among them the airline LOT, in which the workers tried to elect their own manager.

What is the precise meaning of this term 'self-management', the connotations of which include the reforms introduced in Yugoslavia after 1950 and, in France, a current of thought having its origins in the CFDT? In Poland, those who speak of self-management have in mind their desire to free the management of industry from the hold of the Party and the *nomenklatura*. That being the common base, opinions then diverge, some imagining something akin to workers' control, others thinking more of the recognition of economic rationality on a less formalised and more pragmatic basis. The debate on self-management is practical and not ideological, and can only be understood as a desire to break with previous methods of industrial management.

Before 1980, the enterprise had practically no autonomy. However large, it was part of an industrial union (*Zjednoczenie*), and as such was under the control of a minister and was forced to operate under a pricing system which had no directly economic basis. Because of this, an enterprise manager – whose functions are far removed from those of the director of a Western firm – was not able to choose between different suppliers and customers, or between different products and production methods, according to criteria of economic viability or technical rationality. Admittedly, after 1956 and especially after 1970 the recruitment of enterprise managers did not take place exclusively according to the rules of the *nomenklatura*: the technical competence of applicants became more of a consideration. But the engineers, the technicians, the workers and probably to a large extent the managers as well, could not understand the working of the enterprise and the decision-making process. K. Pomian, in a brilliant article (in Kende & Pomian 1978), has shed some light on this matter. Investment decisions in Poland, he says, are not made on an economic basis: if money is invested in an enterprise, it is a reflection of political influence. A provincial official, for instance a Party First Secretary at *województwo* or town level, will attempt to obtain massive investment in local heavy industry because this will confer status on him; whereas a group of small factories producing consumer goods does not increase the prestige and power of the person who obtains the initial investments for their construction.

Self-management is seen by everyone as a break with such an economy run on non-economic criteria. This break has two sides to it: on the one hand, it will free the hand of enterprise managers and allow them to make rational choices; on the other, it will give the workers some kind of control over the running of the enterprise, allowing them to eliminate the waste, corruption and arbitrariness which proliferate in the grey areas which centralised economic management tends to maintain and even increase.

Within Solidarity, an emphasis placed on one or other of these two aspects of self-management was always a signal for animated discussion, in our research groups as well as at national or regional level. Some saw the most important thing as being the appointment of competent, honest managers, concerned to restore rational order to the enterprise and so to bring the country out of the crisis it faces. The trade union must not interfere in management: it must restrict its role to the protection of workers' interests, and must do so all the more strictly under effective and rational management. Others insisted on the central part to be played by workers' councils, which would define factory policy, leaving the manager to apply it: they would be the legislature within the enterprise, and the manager would only hold executive power. In Silesia, this function of the workers' councils was conceived as a form of workers' control: the organs concerned with self-management were hardly distinguished from the trade union itself. The 'active' strike was already an expression of this, with the workers continuing to produce but declaring themselves the masters of what was produced during the 'strike'. If they had produced tractors, they would go and sell them to the farmers or exchange them for food. If the miners worked a Saturday but declared it an active strike, the coal produced would be used to buy medicine or milk for the children. The first view, on the other hand, stressed the separation of the trade union and the self-management committee, within which Solidarity would obviously have a dominant part to play, but on which the Party committee within the enterprise, the Young Socialists and the official, sector-based trade unions would also be represented, the latter two being under the influence of the Party.

Finally, we should note a third tendency, midway between the other two, and corresponding more closely than either of them to the present situation in Polish factories. This gave the self-management committee a dominant role in the determination of the social policy of the enterprise; it took away from the Party committee the role which gave it its power, and to that extent was an affirmation of the leading role which the committee representing the workers must play, but at the same time it recognised that the workers' committee could hardly, in the present situation, take control of the enterprise's economic policy. This intermediate formula gave the union supervisory powers echoing the ideas of Wałęsa and Mazowiecki.

The idea of joint management was unanimously rejected. The union could not and did not want to share responsibility for the management of the economy as long as it was under the direct political control of ministries and sections of the Party's Central Committee. Solidarity has no more desire to share power than it has to seize it for itself. It constantly defines itself as a social movement, a force of resistance to the regime and to the external constraints under which the latter operates.

All the different versions of the theme of self-management were a powerful integrating factor bringing together Solidarity the social movement and Solidarity the agent of social liberation. Despite the different currents of thought on the subject, the idea of self-management had the capacity to unite the two tendencies within the movement. Only Solidarity had the political and social power to free the enterprise. But Solidarity did not wish to replace the Party as the power in the land: by freeing the enterprise, it sought to restore life to a vital sector of civil society. As a result, all the militants admitted that a point would come where they would have to choose either to continue their activity in the trade union or to take an active part in self-management. Jan Lityński, the editor of the newspaper

Robotnik, told us that it was already becoming clear which militants would follow these respective paths. Lityński, like everyone else, applauded this separation of functions, and considered it entirely normal that conflict should break out between the union and the self-management committee representing the interests of the factory. Stefan Bratkowski, the president of the Journalists' Association, expressed the same idea though a little less strongly: for him, the essential requirement was the creation of a real centre of economic power within the enterprise, and various forms of capital ownership had therefore to be defined. Solidarity members were as little convinced by this extreme managerialism as the Party leadership. In Solidarity, the theme of self-management is not part of any total model of economic management: it is simply a question – although this is in itself a considerable ambition – of doing away with the absolute power of the Party within the enterprise, seen as an extension of the liberation of the trade unions enshrined in the Gdańsk Agreement.

As the economic crisis deepened, Solidarity's action increasingly took place in the economic field. But Solidarity does not see itself as an economic actor. In its own eyes, it remains a social, democratic and national movement, whose role in the economy is to remove the omnipotent rule of the Party and to create a free space for the activity of economic agents, supported by the union but sufficiently independent to enter into conflict with it.

The notion of *Solidarity II* was our research groups' response to this phase of the union's evolution. The idea was introduced by the researchers and elaborated by the groups: following on from *Solidarity I* after this had attained its main objective, the freeing of the trade unions, Solidarity II was seen as being essentially a movement for self-management. The formula does not seek to imply that a different type of movement replaces the original one: the idea is rather that the same movement passes from one phase to another, extending its action from the trade-union to the economic field, but retaining its status as a social movement simultaneously trade-unionist, democratic and national in character.

The transition from Solidarity I to Solidarity II was speeded up by the Bydgoszcz crisis. The theme of self-management allowed Solidarity to regain its balance after a series of violent internal conflicts. Elements within the union wanted to prepare for direct political confrontation, and here was an answer to them: the union's action must continue to be based in the factory, while at the same time representing a more direct challenge to the regime's economic management and, by extension, to its economic policy. Solidarity II can therefore be seen as a new stage in the movement's action, in which old objectives and motivations remain but are adjusted to new conditions.

This step is not an exclusively positive one. The growing importance of self-management represented a step backwards at the level of mass action, since it did not have the same capacity for mobilising the rank and file as the issue of trade-union independence. Solidarity was now committed to an indirect form of action, the main aim of which was the rebuilding of social institutions rather than the defence of the workers' interests. There were different reactions to this: at one extreme, some members of the Gdańsk group quickly began to reach beyond self-management towards directly political action; in the Katowice group, on the other hand, the notion of self-management was interpreted as an active defence of the workers against the regime. It was in Warsaw that we saw the most solid alliance between offensive and defensive, between the movement forward to political action and a simultaneous search for institutional solutions avoiding the danger of direct confrontation between Solidarity and the Party.

ON TO POLITICAL ACTION?

By November of 1981 the theme of self-management was far less predominant than in May and June of the same year. Little was said of it at Łódź, and at Wrocław and Szczecin it was clearly associated with the most moderate elements of the movement. This was perhaps because of the compromise solution on the election of enterprise managers which had been adopted by the *Sejm* in September, and which had been accepted by Wałęsa but greeted with much hostility by the union's other national leaders: self-management was from now on seen as another compromise rather than the latest in a series of victories, and a compromise just as unsatisfactory as the Warsaw Agreement of the spring. Perhaps even more unsatisfactory to the extent that the economic crisis was deepening at the same time as the crisis within the Party, and the militants felt themselves being drawn into it. There was no sense of triumph at this time, no dream of conquering the seat of power itself. On the one hand, it was clear that militants, like the whole of the population, were being forced back upon immediate questions of physical survival, while on the other there was a realisation of open crisis within the regime and the knowledge that, since the population trusted Solidarity alone, the movement would inevitably have to extend self-management from the enterprise to local institutions and then to political institutions as a whole, which meant imposing and organising free elections.

We refer to these developments as *Solidarity III*. The aims are now manifestly political: freedom of information, and especially normal access to television for Solidarity; open nominations in the local elections scheduled for February 1982; creation of a second chamber within the *Sejm*, made up of the representatives of social and economic groups; creation of a social council for the national economy, a group of specialists with considerable powers of initiative; and, ultimately, free elections to Parliament.

The movement evolves

The gravity of the economic crisis made the need for a political agreement between Solidarity and the Party even more urgent than ever, and the Church used its offices to try to bring this about. But Solidarity militants were not disposed to enter directly into the political arena. They did not want Solidarity to become a political party in order to put up candidates for the local elections: the movement should continue to represent society in its opposition to the regime, and should not enter political conflict. However, as the central point of conflict came nearer and nearer to the centre of political power, it became more and more difficult for Solidarity to maintain its own unity. Certain minority factions were ready for political action, while at the other extreme many militants wanted to fall back on trade-union activity, some in order to deal with the immediate needs of the workers and in particular the food supply, others out of a desire to create more and more discontent among the rank and file as a way of resisting the manoeuvres of the Party and the government. The wildcat strikes which took place at this time in many factories and regions were a far better indication of the state of mind of the militants than the public statements of Marian Jurczyk or Jan Rulewski. The central tendency of this final phase was distrust of a Party which refused to negotiate and resorted more and more frequently to acts of provocation. Subsequent events showed just how justified such feelings were: even at the time, repression and the military takeover were being prepared inside the Party. More and more often, militants would say that the movement had to go the whole way to national independence and political democracy, although they still did not envisage the immediate imposition of free elections, and even less a break with the Soviet Union. Conscious of the breakdown of the whole economic system, they fell back on their base and reaffirmed the principles and raison d'être of their movement.

All the evidence points with equal force to two apparently contradictory conclusions. On the one hand, there is an indisputable escalation towards political action, culminating in the Congress of Solidarity and the decision in favour of free elections, which meant nothing less than a decision to overthrow the Party. This escalation can also be seen in the idea of the active strike, which would inevitably have led to the existence of two centres of power. But, on the other hand, there is an absence of any political mobilisation and the development of purely defensive action at rank-and-file level.

If we are to understand this apparent contradiction we must return to the idea that Solidarity is not and never was a political movement. Because its capacity for political action is strictly limited by Poland's dependence on the Soviet Union, and by the economic crisis, it is a conviction and a state of mind rather than an instrument of collective action. The corollary of this is that it is a social movement much more than a trade-union organisation. And as the crisis deepened and hostility to the Party became more explicit, so Solidarity moved away from its role as a movement for the liberation of society and fell back on its convictions, organising them into opposition to the ruling order. When it denounced Russian domination, the autocracy of the Party and the incompetent management of the economy, Solidarity did not want the Poles to take up arms, to demonstrate in front of Party headquarters or to form revolutionary workers' councils. It affirmed its defence of workers' rights and of national independence, but not for a moment did it repudiate a democratic programme which only appears intolerable to those for whom all dèmocracy is intolerable. When it called for elections, its aim was not to become a political party and win those elections, but to abolish itself in the multiplicity of political parties or to return to the more limited function of a trade union. Solidarity certainly entered into more and more direct conflict with the regime, but it was fighting not for its own power, and did not seek to seize control of the state; with increasing explicitness it declared that democratic solutions and elected leaders could lead the country out of the crisis. The absence of political mobilisation is clearly seen in the way in which the movement fell back on action of an immediately defensive nature, for instance the hunger marches, during the summer of 1981.

In this third phase, the most 'radical' action was directed not upwards in the direction of the seizure of power, but downwards, towards forms of rejection behaviour. When anyone spoke of radicals in 1980, the term referred to the KOR and above all to the tendency represented by Jacek Kuroń. He constantly repeated that the adversary was collapsing and that Solidarity, having already achieved a decisive victory, must continue to press forward and accept wide responsibilities in public life. Although he was in favour of caution and above all wanted to preserve the movement's unity, his analyses seemed to be a call to directly political action. Well before the creation of the union, he had clearly stated that any action undertaken in Poland could not but be ultimately political in nature: circumstances had placed the workers' movement in the forefront of the action, but the important thing was not the instrument but the job to be done, which was none other than the restoration of democracy and the creation of independence at least as great as that of Finland.

In the autumn of 1981 the term had taken on a completely different meaning. Now, it often referred to the enemies of Kuroń and of the KOR. The radicals were the populists and the nationalists, the 'true Poles' who were tired of fruitless negotiation and agreements which were broken by the regime, and impatient to bring into the open the contradiction between the social and national identity and a regime seen simply as a foreign agent. In Warsaw, these radicals were challenging the authority of political brains like Zbigniew Bujak, and in Wrocław they attacked the leadership of the MKZ. It would not be inappropriate to compare these tendencies to the most intensely nationalistic elements of Piłsudskism. Nevertheless, they did not become dominant within Solidarity, and especially in Silesia this withdrawal into the shell of radicalism more often than not took the form of defensive class action. But despite their differences, these two attitudes have important elements in common: both are anti-intellectual and anti-political.

On both fronts, then, the effect of radical tendencies was to incite Solidarity, not to become a political party, but to be more conscious of the political, economic and military dangers to which it was exposed. At the beginning of its life, Solidarity had put forward a set of principles regarding its conception of society; in its last weeks, it had to defend itself against the increasing militarisation of the regime and an economic crisis which left the population of the country hungry. The more extreme were the positions which militants adopted, the less they believed that their aims could be attained. Influential 'radicals' even began to move closer to Wałęsa and his readiness for compromise and negotiation. Even an act as spectacular as the appeal to all the peoples of the Soviet empire which was made at the end of the first session of the Congress must be understood as an expression of the militants' faith in the deepest forces of the national life, and not as a statement of intent to intervene politically in the affairs of other states. Solidarity did not move on to political action: this final phase should rather be seen as dominated by an awareness of the dimensions of the crisis, and fear and rejection of a Party which had lost massive numbers of working-class members and was no longer able to control or manage economic, administrative and social life.

But the growing importance of this tendency towards resistance should not obscure the fact that Solidarity was at the same time moving onto directly political ground. In the course of the Congress it issued a direct challenge to the Party and recognised, as the Party had already done, that it was difficult to be a member of both organisations at once. The idea that Solidarity should somehow intervene in the forthcoming local elections began to take shape. The appeal to the peoples under Soviet domination was taken as a provocation by the Party. Such agitation, which Wałęsa was sometimes unable to control and which originated above all in the National Committee, was a prelude to confrontation. Few people, however, wanted this, and the majority of militants and leaders thought that no unbridgeable gap existed between the solutions proposed by Solidarity and by the Party.

The series of three phases – Solidarity I, II and III – which we have distinguished in the evolution of our research groups, should be seen as part of our general analysis of the movement. Throughout its history, Solidarity remained simultaneously a trade union, a democratic force and a national movement. During each phase, it consciously challenged the total system of domination, but at the same time it remained convinced that it must limit itself and not become a political movement. The factor of change between the autumn of 1980 and the autumn of 1981 is the balance of power between it and the Party.

At every point in its evolution, Solidarity succeeded in reconciling its own internal dynamic, urging it on to conquer more and more ground, and, on the other hand, its desire to see the re-emergence of social and political actors entirely independent of its influence. The idea of self-management represents just such a reconciliation: the union has an important part to play in the economy, but industrial managers remain independent. In the same way, the more political orientations of the last few months went no further than the desire to create a political space which could be occupied by the most diverse forces. Closely related to this is the peaceful character of Solidarity: it never behaved like a political force seeking power, nor like a revolutionary trade-union movement, and the sense of shock which militants zealous to defend freedoms and the machinery of democracy felt when the regime resorted to violence against them was in direct proportion to the non-violent nature of the movement.

vv

The militants analyse their own action

SELF-ANALYSIS

It is now time to move on to the most important phase of our research. The early discussions which took place within the groups at Gdańsk, Katowice and Warsaw provided a basis upon which we worked out an analysis of the movement taking as much account as possible of written material and of the comments of Polish intellectuals. The groups' debates and, above all, their meetings with various interlocutors, provided the raw material for this analysis, which was then reintroduced into the groups. The preceding chapters represent the conclusions of this analysis.

We must now attempt to evaluate the use of such work: did the general analysis of the movement made by the research team prove to be an effective instrument for actors and observers alike to further their understanding of the movement? The analysis may be judged useful if it produces new knowledge, if it provides fuel for discussions which in turn ask new questions, and if it facilitates a better comprehension of historical events and of the movement's internal mechanisms. It is this principle which informs the work of the research team from this point on: the general analysis produced by the team together is now reintroduced into the individual groups and the militants are asked to take hold of it and use it as an instrument of analysis. As a consequence, the register changes: the groups become the analysts of their own movement. A 'conversion' occurs taking the groups further in the direction of analysis and requiring that they view previous debates from a certain distance. The following pages, therefore, are not so much an account of the struggles and hopes of the militants as of their own analysis of them. The reader will see that the workers of Gdańsk, Katowice and Warsaw have no difficulty in constructing interpretations which sometimes reach high levels of complexity.

This 'conversion' was all the easier to attain in that it corresponded to the expectations of the militants: just as Solidarity expected its intellectuals to operate as advisers and not as ideologists or a kind of political avant-garde, so our groups wanted the sociologists to place them in a situation of analysis, rather than behaving like group leaders, distributing the Word and collecting opinions and reactions in return. The researchers put forward and defended their analyses with the help of diagrams and tables; the militants reacted, drew other diagrams, added to or modified the tables. The groups were thus engaged in a joint enterprise in which the actual and potential meanings of the movement were gradually brought to the surface. The starting point of this long process of analysis was the image of Solidarity as a movement made up of three elements: the first hypothesis of the research team was that Solidarity was born of the integration of these three elements during the strike of August 1980.

At this stage in the research the groups were not asked to speak about their struggle or to debate with partners and adversaries: the work of analysis represents a break with former proceedings. The atmosphere in the groups changed immediately, becoming at once more reflective and warmer: everyone was keen to move on to ground which was unfamiliar to all of them, and our work moved into its central phase, in which workers, technicians and office staff, under the stimulus provided by the researchers, analysed their movement and more particularly its evolution. This took place in the spring of 1981, when the movement was conscious of its own power and had not yet despaired of reaching some agreement with a Party which was neither too strong nor too weak to negotiate. Solidarity had already ceased to be just a social movement, and was engaged in the reconstruction of society. Its action was progressing upwards from the defence of the union, through the reform of the enterprise, to the creation of democratic institutions. The three groups in question were aware of this movement of expansion, and also of the consequent difficulty of maintaining the integration of the movement's three dimensions – social, political and national – over an increasingly wide area of action.

The discussions which took place must be seen as part of the great debate within Solidarity on an issue of central importance: how could the movement expand its action without losing its unity, without being torn apart by competing objectives?

We shall look first to the Gdańsk group. Here there was a strong sense of identification with the August strike and the Gdańsk Agreement. In the first meetings the group was particularly insistent on the unity of the movement. The question which then had to be answered was this: how could this unity be redefined when Solidarity found itself in a situation in which it was clearly obliged to go beyond the Agreement?

The problem confronting the miners of Silesia who met in the Katowice group was a different one: here, working-class consciousness was stronger than the desire to rebuild institutions, and the question which arose was whether they would be able to transcend attitudes of resistance and rebellion. The hypothesis which quickly became established was that, as

Solidarity's action broadened, they would have more difficulty than other groups in finding a way of synthesising their different objectives.

At Warsaw, on the other hand, the militants had no trouble contemplating the extension of their action, perhaps because in the capital the intellectuals of the democratic opposition had enjoyed considerable influence ever since the birth of the KOR at the Ursus plant after the riots of June 1976. The question in this case was to know just how far the militants wanted to go, and how the unity of the movement was to be preserved.

Official union documents, news-sheets, speeches made by union leaders and even interviews with them do not give us access to the inner life of the movement. Such sources cannot tell us how it integrates the component elements of its action, how it extends its action, how it unites defensive and counter-offensive tactics, how it combines the driving force of a social movement with a programme for the reconstruction of democratic institutions. Only through group discussions provoked by the questions and the comments of the researchers, can we penetrate deep into the central area where the movement's policy is worked out and transformed.

GDAŃSK

The collective identity of the Gdańsk group was to be found above all in their very clear awareness of having been and still being at the centre of a struggle of the greatest historical importance. The group spontaneously identified with the initial image of the movement which researchers and militants together came to refer to as Solidarity I, symbolised by the Gdańsk Agreement. In August 1980 the fusion between working-class action, the affirmation of a national identity and the desire for democracy had taken place with little difficulty, because the point upon which all these were focussed was the limited objective of setting up a free trade union. The group did not see the agreements of August 1980 in a restrictive way: they never lost sight of the fact that these agreements 'between Poles' were the expression of a strong national consciousness, and they stressed their political just as much as their trade-union content.

But the spring of 1981 was different from the summer of 1980, and even if the Gdańsk Agreement had not been fully implemented, the movement had no choice but to move on to a different level. The economic crisis had deepened, the threat of Soviet intervention had been clearly felt in March 1981, and internal tensions had begun to appear between the leaders of Solidarity, Andrzej Gwiazda and Jan Rulewski criticising Wałęsa. Solidarity could no longer claim to be totally unified, and the theme of self-management did not provide the group with a road back to such cohesion. The group tended to split, occasionally re-establishing its unity by reminding itself that it was the figure-head of the Gdańsk Agreement, but soon losing it again. How then could trade-union action, the political struggle and the national affirmation be integrated at a new level?

The Gdańsk Agreement

In the first few minutes of the first meeting the Gdańsk group asked itself the question 'Can we be just a trade union? Are we not a political actor?' Jan and Zbigniew were among the first to formulate a reply to these questions which was often to be used by the whole group: Solidarity was a union, but had to move towards political action. As long as the political and economic crisis remained unsolved, members, rank and file and leaders alike, could not confine their action to the factory. Later Solidarity would be able to act as a true trade union, and follow the Swedish example which was often held up as a model of its kind. But for the moment the union had to ensure the political conditions for its own existence. The Gdańsk Agreement had freed the union, and its implementation had now to be ensured. The twenty-one demands had included the recognition of free trade unions, the guarantee of the right to strike, and an end to the repression of free speech. The Gdańsk group felt itself to be the bearer of these demands. It did not demand anything else, but it did insist that they should be met in their entirety. The long session in which the group met Andrzej Gwiazda gave it the opportunity to express very forcefully this desire to defend the Gdańsk Agreement, the whole Agreement – and perhaps nothing but the Agreement.

In discussion with Gwiazda, who was then the Vice-President of Solidarity, the group made a clear distinction between pure trade-union activity and political action. Bogusław thought that Solidarity should work as a trade union in the enterprise, and that the campaign for the implementation of the twenty-one demands of August 1980 should take place at the level of the National Coordinating Committee. Janusz explained how, from the point of view of political action, 'the KKP and the MKZ create the conditions for action and draw up proposals at national level which enable us to formulate opinions within the factory'. General political action, prepared at the top, must filter down into the factories to fuel the work of the militants. Everyone recognised the importance of applying political pressure in order to defend the ground won in August 1980, and that unanimity runs counter to the simplistic opposition between radicals and moderates. The group reminded Gwiazda that he was perceived as a radical: he was the one who, only three months previously, had publicly criticised Wałęsa. Did that mean that he was urging Solidarity on towards becoming a political party? Not at all: Gwiazda's 'radicalism' was above all the expression of his absolute desire to avoid retreat and to see that the agreements of August 1980 were kept. Gwiazda in turn reminded the group that he was responsible for the biggest compromises in the movement's history, and said that he thought he was perceived as a radical because the movement was weakening and not because he himself wanted to go too far. 'Over the last nine months', he said, 'we haven't obtained a single institutional guarantee. We haven't changed, but we have given in.' There was hardly any gap between his positions and those of the group, for no one seriously contemplated transforming Solidarity into a political party, or even, in the immediate future, establishing any new parties. 'It's just not possible at the moment', said Zenon, although he was undoubtedly extremely tempted by such a perspective. In this area, then, the group went no further than the Gdańsk Agreement. Gwiazda himself at the time had successfully insisted that a demand for the abolition of the Party's leading role in the state should not be included in the negotiating demands; in June 1981 the group held identical views, to such an extent that Jan could say 'We recognise the leading role of the Party.' Zbigniew went even further, maintaining that the Party's leading role was to represent the aspirations of the workers: if it behaved strictly according to its statutes, there would be no problem. In Gdańsk, the movement had obtained the right to organise free trade unions, and for the moment the group hardly envisaged going any further and seeking to liberate other areas of society. The militants wanted action at two levels: on the one hand the union should articulate workers' demands concerning working conditions, pay, the availability of goods in the shops, housing and health; on the other there must be a campaign for the defence of political prisoners, whatever their views, against censorship and, more generally, pressure in favour of freedom of speech and organisation. No one isolated these two sides of the action, and everyone considered that it was the combination of the two which allowed the movement to advance, by which they meant exerting pressure leading in the direction of national independence.

Should trade-union action in the factory be the union's central role, and political action be left to those higher in the union hierarchy? Or was it more important to refuse to dissociate the two, at every level linking the social struggle and the struggle for the liberation of society? It was the latter view which predominated in the group, and for two reasons. Firstly, the effect of the economic crisis was to weaken true trade-union activity by forcing the union to put off wage claims; and secondly because exclusively trade-union action might involve the union in a logic of compromise with the Party which no one thought realistically possible, however much certain members sometimes dreamed of it. The group was made up of people who saw themselves primarily as trade unionists, with a smaller section who considered themselves to be more political animals, but the desire to integrate the two dimensions was a permanent feature of the discussions, and anything which might threaten this fusion – pure trade unionism and cooperation with the Party, the rejection of the self-limiting function, or strictly political action – was rejected. The movement's unity was far stronger than differences of opinion within the group.

Was this stability the result of the movement's own self-control, or was it rather a manifestation of a limit inherent to Solidarity which meant that it was not capable of going any further than the demands of August 1980?

A long discussion showed first of all that the group could not contemplate either relaxing its pressure on the regime, or moving on towards directly political action. Janusz and Bogusław, who up to then had often been opposed, were in agreement over the idea of the 'imposition of democracy': Solidarity must seek to force the Party to accept some degree of democracy, perhaps, as Janusz suggested, by exerting pressure on the *Sejm*. At that point Zenon spoke of the formation of political clubs, an idea which appealed to several members, but Bogusław and Paweł quickly brought the group to order by reminding them of the limits: such a policy of pluralism meant changing the system, and the Soviet Union would not accept that. Zenon immediately insisted that within his enterprise he was a responsible trade unionist, and even presented himself as a moderate: the world of bus and tram drivers was a tough one, often very nationalist and inclined to favour an open break with the regime, and he often intervened to temper the mood of the most radical and prevent possibly catastrophic explosions.

For the first time, then, the Gdańsk group had allowed itself openly to express its desire for a political pluralism which was incompatible with the present limits of possible action; but Zenon, who was more tempted than anyone by political action, brought back the group's self-control with his appeal for realism. This episode marks the group's consciousness of the gap between the possible and the desirable; but it was followed by a much more spectacular event. As a more light-hearted conclusion to a hard day of analysis, one of the researchers suggested that the group might play at political fiction for a while. What would Solidarity do in the hypothetical event of a sudden hardening of position on the part of the regime and the rise to power of the hard-liners in the Party? The response was a unanimous and immediate explosion: a nationwide general strike. Suddenly, the group's identity had been defined as nationalist and anti-Soviet. In an imaginary mode, the desire for independence, which clearly represents the movement's ultimate horizon, had found expression. As far as its desires were concerned, the Gdańsk group did not stop at the liberation of the trade-union movement. It wanted much more, but there was a very strong internalisation of the constraints weighing upon the movement. The group had to live within itself the distance separating its aspirations from reality, and chose as a solid base and the essential aim on which to set its sights, implementation of the Gdańsk Agreement.

The militants analyse their own actions

The liberation of the enterprise

Once the trade union has been liberated and the right to a free and autonomous existence obtained, is Solidarity's next step the liberation of another space, the enterprise? There was clearly no very strong commitment to this path in the Gdańsk group. Every member felt the consequences of the economic crisis and could describe its manifestations, but no one seemed really capable of adopting a clear position on what was to be done. In discussion with the *wojewoda*'s assistant, Zenon and Janusz observed that an attempt was being made to involve Solidarity in various forms of dialogue and joint management, and made it quite clear that there could be no question of accepting: to do so would be to accept responsibility for the crisis without having the power to run the economy.

Perhaps the road forward lay in a different direction: should Solidarity become the agent of a parallel economy working on the basis of direct relations and agreements involving no third party? This idea developed in the group during the meeting with the leader of Solidarity of Individual Farmers. Tractors could be repaired at the shipyards in exchange for meat or potatoes. But Jan only had to relate the difficulty in which the workers at the Paris Commune shipyard had found themselves the day they were faced with a thousand chickens to be killed and distributed, for everyone to feel that solutions of that kind simply disorganised work and production and could not solve the economic crisis. As far as the Gdańsk group was concerned, then, it was not Solidarity's job to have any direct responsibility for the management of the economy, either through joint management or in the form of some kind of parallel economy.

The group in fact was never inclined to spend much time on the question of self-management. But when the manager of a large enterprise in the region came as an interlocutor, the idea of some kind of collaboration between the union and management at factory level came spectacularly to the surface. The manager put his cards straight onto the table. He wanted efficiency, authority, a job well done, and tended to be autocratic; he proposed an alliance between Solidarity and management in which they would oppose the paralysing influence of the central authorities and planning ministries in the name of the efficient running of the enterprise. When he pointed out that the renewal of his post as manager was to be decided by a vote of the workers' council, Zbigniew unhesitatingly replied: 'You're a good manager. As far as external problems are concerned, you're no different from the rest of the workforce. Inside the factory, any conflicts which might arise would be about the idea of democracy . . . We hope the vote goes your way.'

As we said, the group never spent much time on the question of self-

109

management. It simply thought that the enterprise had to be freed from the stranglehold of bureaucracy, and was prepared to back anyone who, like this apparently efficient but authoritarian manager, shared that goal. But this aim was clearly not high in the group's priorities, and did not represent the stakes of an important stage in the struggle.

When a problem as central as self-management was not spontaneously brought up by a group, the researchers introduced it. In this case, they put to the Gdańsk group the following question: could they not accept the idea which was predominant in the Warsaw group of a movement which, once it had obtained the recognition of free trade unions, moved on to a higher level of the struggle and set as its objectives the freeing of the enterprise, and perhaps ultimately of the whole of the economy, from the grip of the Party? The group's first response was to look at the distance separating Solidarity, the workers' councils and enterprise managers, and the relations between them. The workers' councils owed their continued existence to Solidarity, which guaranteed the political conditions in which they could develop; in Zbigniew's words, 'the workers' council rests on the union'. There was a distance between the two institutions, but the group sought to minimise it. Jan insisted that the people who were elected to the workers' councils should be people 'who fight for the cause, for workers' problems'; he thought that Solidarity should control the councils. Gradually, however, the image of a greater distance between the two began to emerge: the workers' council was the expression of the interests of the enterprise as a whole, while the union was concerned with defending the workers' interests, and between the demands of economic rationality and the claims of the workers there could be contradiction and conflict. The idea of workers' councils truly independent of Solidarity began to gain momentum. Marian pointed out that such autonomy would only be acceptable if the Party played no part in the workers' councils. What happens to management in this view of the workers' council as the body responsible for the running of the enterprise? The answer is simple: directors would be chosen by the councils and not nominated by the authorities, and should base their policy on the council's directives. But we must emphasise that when, at the request of the researchers, the group did approach the question of the enterprise, it did so without any enthusiasm, and never defined the enterprise as a social space to be liberated. The *nomenklatura* did not represent a problem for the group, as if a question which was important in the Warsaw group no longer needed to be considered in Gdańsk. For this group, it was more important to fight the economic crisis by introducing some degree of rational management and by loosening the grip of the Party, defined as external to the enterprise. There must be an end to the power of centralised administration, the ministries, and the management of the great industrial unions (*Zjednoczenie*), an end to methods of management which had led on the one hand to the economic crisis and on the other to economic dependence on a foreign power. The enterprise must be allowed to make its own decisions regarding its economic policy, particularly in its trade with abroad.

Such an argument was not confined to the enterprise, and could only be meaningful when integrated into a wider view of the economy as a whole, but this wider view was hardly sketched in, and then only by Janusz. The group recognised that the rescuing of the economy from the paralysis inflicted by centralised institutions had recently become an important task for the movement, but it was unable to see this as an area in which the movement could make significant advances. The economic crisis meant that some form of intervention was necessary, but the group contemplated this without enthusiasm.

Internal tensions

The Gdańsk group, then, did not see the struggle for self-management as a means of reuniting the different component elements at a stage beyond the Gdańsk Agreement. But neither could it continue to fall back on the stable and well-integrated positions of Solidarity I; the group was now marked by increasingly acute tensions, mainly between those who clung to a social definition of the movement's action and those who wanted to draw the movement onto a more clearly political path. It was in fact even clearer than that: in the space of three successive sessions the whole group went through a series of violent transformations, beginning as an actor defined essentially by its trade-union orientations, then becoming decidedly more political before returning to its original identity but at the expense of a growing feeling of anxiety, and an awareness that it had lost some of its strength and unity in this series of changes.

The first of these critical phases took place when the group met two union leaders, one from the sailors' union and the other representing the dockers. These officials from the old sector-based official unions, who had lost much of their former power but were still active, were at first taken to task by the members of the group; then they began to explain their positions, and the tone changed, with both sides trying to find out what they had in common and in which areas they were opposed. Jan, immediately after he had denounced the working of the sector-based unions, went on to say: 'The situation is such that we ought to reject everything which sets us apart, and look for any grounds for unity . . . We should leave all the old grudges until later.' What exactly was it that the militants had against the old unions, and which was preventing them from sitting down at the same table, and on the same side? Was it that these unions were seen as the agent of the Party and the civil service? The interlocutors replied that they were far less dependent

111

now than before. Was it that they were perceived as hostile to the movement of August 1980? They said that they had supported the strike from the very beginning! Was it the undemocratic nature of the unions? The bad leaders had gone, they said, and they had become more democratic. Were they seen as lacking the national unity which Solidarity could claim? But a new national structure was being formed. Adopt a coherent position on all the big issues, said Jan and Zbigniew, try to be worthy of our trust, support some kind of renewal, suggested Krystyna, show some altruism and try to see further than the defence of the selfish interests of your own members, said Mirosław, stop these deals with the authorities which can only divide us, and then we can compete with each other in an honest and democratic way and build up an effective cooperation.

The effect of this meeting was spectacular. The group had shown that it was prepared to occupy the same ground as the sector-based unions, the economic defence of workers' interests in the factory. The group mistrusted them as long as they had links with the regime, but their justification of their objectives was a great success with the group, which, more emphatically than at any other moment, now defined itself as fundamentally working-class and trade-unionist in character. At the end of the session Marian said that he 'would like to see goodwill and cooperation between Solidarity and the other unions, so that the problems of the workers can be properly represented'.

The next day, all this had changed: the second critical moment had arrived. With Adam Michnik as interlocutor, the group expressed much more hostility towards a purely trade-unionist attitude. The dominant register was now one of democracy, and Michnik had first to answer a number of questions about the KOR. The atmosphere was not entirely favourable to the KOR, which Jan defended stolidly but which was the object of some mistrust on the part of others. Marian expressed fears that the KOR tried to interfere in the affairs of Solidarity, while Zbigniew and Krystyna spoke of Bogdan Borusewicz, a member of the KOR of whom it was said that he was seeking to be elected as a delegate to the Congress of Solidarity: he did not work, and therefore had no right to represent the rank and file. Bogusław compared such behaviour to the tactics of the Party, imposing its delegates on the rank and file; he attacked 'outside ideologies' which were trying to infiltrate Solidarity, whether it was the KOR, the PUWP, the KPN or the Church, and he became involved in a polemic with Michnik, who forced him to admit that he was criticising the ideology of the KOR without knowing anything about it.

This mistrust of the KOR was founded on a real lack of information; it was rooted in the fear of manipulation and a reluctance to see a repetition within Solidarity of the workings of the PUWP. It did not imply any hostility to the democratic ideals which inspired the KOR, indeed it was perhaps the expression of a desire for internal democracy which was felt by the whole group. For the moment at least it had nothing to do with the populist and anti-intellectual tendencies which were to develop later, particularly after the Congress. What Michnik had to say produced a very clear effect, which Zbigniew summarised when he said: 'Some of us, including me, had our doubts about the intentions, the means and the origin of the KOR. Now I know that Solidarity came out of the KOR. They said it before, now it's us who are saying it.' The group had for the first time recognised the important contribution of the KOR, and Michnik's visit had re-established the balance by putting more stress on the democratic element within the movement. With the exception of Bogusław, the group had been convinced by Michnik.

But this renewal was not to last: we come now to the third in this series of critical moments. Next morning Paweł complained that we had spent too much time talking about politics, and, together with Zbigniew and Bogusław, expressed regret that insufficient attention was paid to problems concerning the factory and everyday life. Teresa went even further. She had said nothing the previous day, and said that Michnik had frightened her, but now asked how we dared put so much stress on politics when material problems such as food and housing were so crucially important. At her factory she had been asked to defend a prisoner, somebody called Moczulski about whom she knew nothing, and all the while nothing was being done about the lengthening food queues . . . The group's reaction was to return to its economic concerns and to repress its project for political liberation.

The group was now in a state of anxiety. The series of oscillations from a trade-unionist orientation to a political one and back again had brought home to it its increasing inability to unify the component elements of its action.

The meeting which took place on 1 July 1981 between the Gdańsk and Warsaw groups confirmed the fragile unity of the former. Under the influence of the dominant preoccupations of the Warsaw group, the discussion abandoned all reference to trade-union action in favour of political themes. As if it was swept along by the logic of an inevitable political advance, the Gdańsk group became weak and fragmented, with many divergent positions emerging. Janusz, who from now on ceased to be the spokesman for the whole group, took up a position on the political side, wanting Solidarity to guarantee the existence of a multiplicity of parties which would emerge as a result of the liberating work of the social movement. More realistically perhaps, Zenon repeated his attachment to a multi-party system, but said that leaders, programmes, political groups or circles would have to form first. Mirosław placed himself firmly in the exclusively political camp. On the other side, and receiving much criticism from the Warsaw group, Bogusław and Zbigniew let it be known that their dream was for a single party, but one really representative of the interests of the working class; they added, in more strategic terms, that any idea of putting an end to the PUWP could only lead to Soviet intervention. Paweł, still more moderate and ready for compromise, thought that the Party's base was healthy and very close to Solidarity: 'It's fighting for the same things as us, and it contains a lot of Solidarity members.' There was no more unanimity within the Gdańsk group, which had again shown that, once the core of the discussion had ceased to be the implementation of the Gdańsk Agreement, its unity fell apart. Jan, who had been the clearest expression of this constant reference to the Gdańsk Agreement, had resisted as well as he could this political surge, which was to remain strong. He was reduced to despair by the experience of this crisis.

The conclusions to be drawn from that day's discussions are clear. The Gdańsk group had not moved on from Solidarity I to Solidarity II. It had experienced a powerful surge towards political commitment, which might have placed it at the level of Solidarity III and made it the agent of the political liberation of the country. But this surge was premature, for, rather than leading to a unification of the members' attitudes and an integration of the different dimensions of the action, it tore the group apart.

Free elections

The Gdańsk group met for the last time on 30 October 1981. Between this meeting and the previous one, Solidarity's Congress had been held, a great strengthening of the movement's political dimension had taken place, and the economic situation had grown considerably more serious. A general strike of one hour had just taken place, called by Solidarity to press its demands and to channel popular discontent of which it was beginning to lose control.

The group was in a state of anxiety. Trade-union action was becoming less and less possible: the general positions of the national leadership had to be followed, and in any case the defence of individual interests would only mean a headlong rush towards deeper economic crisis and further disorganisation of production. The formidable sense of unity which had characterised the movement at its inception had disappeared. Teresa related how her factory had only followed the strike call after one of the leaders of the MKZ had intervened. The workers were weary and no longer mobilised, not calling union policy into question, but simply finding it far removed from their immediate concerns. Zenon added further details to the picture: everywhere in offices and administrative services people were leaving the movement, while a desire for complete rupture and extremist action was being more and more strongly voiced. In his own workplace he was having increasing difficulty in restraining such attitudes. He added that the regime's propaganda effort was having its effect – he was very worried by anti-Semitic tracts which were circulating – and Marian noted that acts of provocation were on the increase.

Was the movement about to disintegrate or, at least, weaken? Certainly not. At the same time as it reviewed a disquieting situation the group insisted not only that what had already been won should be defended, but that new aims must be set. The government had adopted a threatening position; there was talk of a state of emergency; the economic system was totally disorganised; there were shortages of everything. No one in the group except Zenon saw the widespread desire for rupture as a cause for dismay, and Janusz spoke for nearly everyone when he said that hunger and anger were a greater danger for the regime than they were for Solidarity, as long as the movement managed to keep control of dangerous actions like hunger marches, and to avoid riots. What else could be done? Zbigniew clung to the principle of the movement's self-limiting function and said that there could be no questioning of the leading role of the Party. Geopolitical considerations made it impossible to think in terms of changing the political system, and he thought that a single Party, as long as it was a 'truly Polish' one, was more than acceptable. Janusz did not miss the opportunity to say that he should stop daydreaming, that a Party which was in essence totalitarian was incapable of change.

The argument between these two militants was dramatic: Zbigniew, who was above all concerned to defend what had been won in August 1980, was extremely worried by the swell of opinion represented by Janusz and by the group's desire to move on to new ground and undertake the liberation of a political space. It was a brave position, but an untenable one: the whole group now thought that the Party was in a state of complete disintegration, with the exception of its most hated hard-line elements, and it could hardly be persuaded to respect the leading role of the Party and confine itself to the implementation of the Gdańsk Agreement. Only an authoritarian leadership would have stood a chance of keeping Solidarity strictly to the agreement, which was why Zbigniew, now more than ever, defended Wałęsa and maintained that in the present situation, centralised leadership was indispensible. Janusz replied that the very nature of the movement was to function democratically, and even to give the greatest possible autonomy to its local and regional organisations. Democracy was vital, said Janusz; it was fatal, replied Zbigniew, for it would push the movement to its ruin. Surely Zbigniew would not be able to hold out for long in the group?

At this point an unexpected change took place. The researchers had just reminded the group of a general analysis of the movement based on the idea of the successive steps of a staircase. The first step, in August 1980, Solidarity I: the liberation of the union; the second step, from the spring of

1981 onwards, Solidarity II: the liberation of the enterprise through self-management. The Gdańsk group had always been the representative of the struggle for the acceptance of the agreements of August 1980, and had recognised, without any particular enthusiasm, the need for a campaign in favour of self-management. But if this struggle was restricted to the enterprise, not only would it not solve the country's economic problems: it might, as Paweł pointed out, increase them, by giving the large enterprises an advantage over the small ones. Was it not essential to climb one more step, and undertake the liberation of economic policy as a whole? And if so, how? In a real expression of collective will, the group replied: yes! The movement must now liberate the country's political life, force free elections and have done with the Party's monopoly of the media. By moving on to this new ground the group was reunited, and even Zbigniew, although he resisted for a long time, finally followed the general movement. Janusz then proceeded to temper the tone of this spectacular surge forward, trying to present it as a more controlled process. They would have to proceed by stages, he said, rather than immediately demanding free elections to the *Sejm*: they should press for a second Chamber for economic affairs, or a Council for social and economic affairs, and free elections at local level . . . So the Gdańsk group, which for so long had been the representative of the first form of the movement, and which had shown a relative lack of interest in the second phase, self-management, so strong in the Warsaw group, had now decided to liberate the political field from the Party's grip. And yet no one in the group thought that the movement should seize power: they sought to give new political forces the means to organise themselves and play their part in a democracy.

The story of the Gdańsk group finishes here. The group seemed to have re-established its unity by adopting a political definition of the stakes of the conflict. But that unity remained fragile. It had only been reached after a long duel between Zbigniew and Janusz, and if the latter had not been there it is a matter for conjecture whether the group would not have fallen back on trade-unionist attitudes, perhaps more defensive than offensive. But the principal weakness of this new unity was that it had been achieved by sacrificing the movement's nature to its desire for solidarity: it would surely be an exaggeration to say that the exclusively political register of the final meeting represented the fusion of Solidarity's three component elements. By agreeing to question the leading role of the Party, the Gdańsk group had found some kind of balance, but it was no longer the guarantor of the Gdańsk Agreement, and its cohesion was certainly less than in August 1980. The change was indicative of a wider development: from now on, throughout the country, the main drive within Solidarity would be towards political liberation, and references to trade-union action and the national dimension would become relatively artificial.

SILESIA

A working-class community in rebellion

The miners of Silesia did not attain the fusion of trade-union action with democratic themes which took place in Gdańsk and at factories like the Ursus tractor plant. As a group, they were dominated by their consciousness of being exploited by masters who were themselves under foreign orders. Under these conditions, how could their action go beyond a purely working-class dimension and become a movement for the liberation of society? As the situation in the country made such an extension of the movement's horizons more and more inevitable, was there not a danger that the three elements of the movement – trade unionism, democracy and national feeling – would fragment in Silesia? And if anything could prevent such a disintegration, was it a desire for political intervention, the hope that a whole range of problems could be solved through negotiation, or, finally, the constant affirmation of the impossibility of any compromise between the regime and the working class?

The Katowice group recognised and indeed spontaneously spoke of a conception of the movement as simultaneously specific and general, a working-class movement which sought the liberation of the whole society. But from the first meeting it was clear that the group was inclined to emphasise the national struggle on the one hand and, on the other, the working-class struggle against exploitation. These two dimensions were, respectively, the group's ultimate horizon and the base of its action, and democratic themes were seen as a kind of intermediary stage, a transition between the two.

Like most miners, Silesians often spoke of themselves as different from other categories of workers. But this sense of being apart was not based on any hostility towards the world outside the mine: it was directly linked to a sense of national identity. The Silesian miners constantly refused to separate their action as workers from their action as Poles. The group's meeting with a priest provided an opportunity to define more clearly this sense of community and nation, the astonishing sense of national unity upon which Solidarity relies even today.

We have already seen that the Katowice group identified itself as a trade-union actor, violently opposed to the exploitation of the miners. It also defined itself as a national actor, and passed easily from one theme to the other, from working-class revolt to the affirmation of national identity. But it was indeed more a movement from one to the other than an integration of the two, and the democratic dimension, as we have said, seemed less central. The group's reactions to the researchers' general analysis only

117

served to confirm these first impressions. Krystian immediately signalled his disagreement. In his view, Solidarity was not a fusion of its three component elements, and the movement's history proved it. August 1980 had been an explosion of national feeling, 'the mouths and the minds of the nation opened'; in December 1980 the movement had started to think about democracy; now, it was just beginning to turn towards trade-union action. 'You lump it all together', he told the researchers, 'but I distinguish. Each element has its own place, and one implies the next. I believe that national affairs led to trade-union affairs, not the other way round.' The image of Poland surviving through the ages and today living under the thumb of a foreign master was deeply rooted and often repeated; the national dimension occupied the foreground of the group's discussions, while the very idea of a movement was questioned: according to Krystian, for instance, a national awakening had entailed a democratic one, which in turn had led to trade-union action. The researchers defended the idea that Solidarity was a movement, and had been integrated from the very beginning, but the militants rejected the idea, even when they were reminded of the historical development of the action in Gdańsk and Szczecin. For Krystian 'the national problem is why Solidarity was founded' and many people agreed with him, including Józef, who had often stressed the importance of political action but who spoke of 'the nation's anger at the beginning'. Democratic ideas only followed. A similar argument, rejecting the idea of the total integration of the movement's elements, was sometimes used, this time defining the original awakening in social rather than national terms. Stanisław and Mirosław thought that at the beginning all sorts of actors, workers and others, had begun to fight for their rights and that only afterwards, when people were better informed and educated, had questions of democracy arisen. Most of the group maintained that the nation had come first, others said it was the union, but in both cases democracy was relegated to the background. The group had no trouble accepting the idea of interrelation between trade unionism and national action, and Krystian thought that Wałęsa was a perfect example of that interrelation: 'the way he brought national and workers' problems together was very good, but he didn't get involved in politics'. It was only at the end of the session, after the researchers had gone over the history and Józef had spoken of the importance of the democratic and political elements of the action, that a noticeable shift took place within the group and it accepted the need to fuse the various elements.

Managing the enterprise

The working-class consciousness of the group was not just a rejection of the productivity motive, or the defence of a community. It was also the positive awareness of being a source of wealth for Poland, if that wealth were not squandered by bad management, appalling planning and poor equipment. The miners maintained that the extraction of coal depended simply on physical effort, but that modern machines could increase output and make the job easier. They were resolutely in favour of modernisation, and criticised all the tricks, like the invention of non-existent stocks, and the adding of stones to the coal, which management used to make it seem that the Plan was being met.

If, as we have seen, one effect of the economic crisis was to make trade-union action more difficult, another of its effects was to broaden the scope of such action. This mechanism was clear in the group's meeting with the vice-president of the National Commission for Mines, whose job it was to coordinate Solidarity's policy in the mines and negotiate with the ministry. 'We are on the edge of disaster', he said: the industry owed so much money that equipment could no longer be serviced, investment had completely stopped and production would soon fall disastrously. The interlocutor claimed to be apolitical, but it was clear that in his view the crisis must have the effect of extending trade-union action into the area of economic responsibilities, since its immediate claims could not be met.

This view of the economy was already part of the militants' general vision, and the call for the acceptance of some responsibility was heard. Everyone wanted to see the economy rebuilt, and believed that prices must be set by the market and not by bureaucratic decision. Mirosław thought that Solidarity must make a clear stand for responsibility in the economy: in the absence of any initiatives coming from the government, it must make its own proposals for reform. Krystian added that Solidarity already enjoyed considerable *de facto* economic power, since 'there is an official government but Solidarity is the real one'.

The field in which Solidarity's action must be constructed could only be the enterprise, and the central actor in the struggle could only be the working class, even if, in order to perform that role, it had to speak a universal language. While remaining within tolerable limits, trade-union action broadened out into political action in two ways. Firstly, and least importantly, the effect of Solidarity's internal democracy was to create a centre of political life which the authorities could not ignore: public opinion was created, said Stanisław. The other extension towards the political dimension was the creation of forms of self-management. For all the militants, radical and moderate alike, self-management represented a fusion of many important elements and a consistent continuation of the founding spirit of the movement. Such action was democratic, and it involved first and foremost the workers; more simply, it represented workers' control of liberated territory, the enterprise. Self-management did not mean any change in the nature of Solidarity. By expelling the bureaucrats from the enterprise and replacing them with competent executives and specialist advisers, it simply extended the power of the nation at the expense of the Party. The nation was still defined as an integrated community rather than a set of social relations to be liberated.

The researchers said to the militants that self-management also meant the appointment of new managers, perhaps more efficient, who would stand out against trade-union demands, especially since the economic crisis would leave them very little room for manoeuvre. At that point, Solidarity would change in character, in the sense that it would no longer be just a popular working-class movement, but would be involved in the creation of a new field of social relations. This gave rise to a long argument between the militants and the researchers. With the exception of Mirosław, the miners opposed this view, saying that conflicts between the councils managing the enterprise and the trade unions could only be of secondary importance. The militants believed that workers' councils would set the economy on the road to recovery, and at the same time would prevent unemployment and reduce inequalities between profit-making sectors of the economy and less profitable ones. They refused to imagine that they might end up striking against the councils which ran the mine. The discussion was extremely tense, and throughout the militants constantly affirmed their faith in their ability to control the management and, essentially, to set up a form of workers' control.

A duel began between the researchers and the militants. What was at stake was the recognition that the field of trade-union action could be divided in two: on one side was a conflictual area in which the union's job was to make demands and defend its members' interests; on the other side was a managerial area in which the union had to follow essentially economic criteria. The researchers maintained that the economic crisis forced the union in two directions, towards sharing or taking over responsibility for management, and towards an extension of its demands, and that the effect of this was to create an even wider gap between the two aspects of its activity. The group did not want to accept this. Only next day, towards the end of the morning, did the idea of a new kind of action gradually begin to take shape.

First of all it was the more moderate, trade-unionist members of the group, Stanisław and above all Mirosław, who thought that the councils would be a place for negotiation with the authorities, and that this would imply alliances but also conflicts with the union. In Stanisław's case the image of conflict was masked by an appeal to the idea of community and national unity. It was Józef who made the break, saying that Solidarity must form management councils made up of honest and competent people, and that their job would be to define and carry out policies which would not necessarily coincide with the immediate interests of the workers. He admitted that the process of self-management would not be under the complete control of the union. Krystian went further along the same line: the work of economic development must be seen as separate from the union, because it would entail not only criticism of the economic policies of the adversary but would involve proposing new economic policies inevitably requiring sacrifices, unemployment, increased output . . . In the end no one believed that there could be an easy way out of the crisis, and the militants admitted that 'what is good for the enterprise will not necessarily be good for the nation'.

Workers' control

Nevertheless, the reservations which were expressed show that, as far as the militants were concerned, the economic responsibilities which were accepted would have to be of a 'working-class' nature. After all, the extent of the crisis was deliberately exaggerated in order to force the miners to give up their free Saturdays. And what was really known about these engineers who ran the Commission for Mines? Józef's scepticism was based on the idea that self-management in such serious circumstances could be a trap: 'If they allow us to run the mine, we'll be finished, nothing could be worse.'

The group's meeting with B brought out even more clearly this desire for workers' control within the economy. B was a miner who had worked with the network of seventeen large enterprises set up in April 1980 to work out a plan for self-management, in which the mines at Wojek and Katowice had been involved. B thought that the workers had to take control of the enterprise and manage the marketing of the coal. Already a race to set up workers' councils had started between the Party and Solidarity. The regime must not be allowed to recuperate the idea of self-management as it had done in 1956. The enterprise had to replace bureaucratic directives with rational economic criteria, and workers' control was a way of ensuring this: if the mine was handed over to the miners, everyone would have a stake in the success of the enterprise. The miners did not see unemployment as a threat, and Mirosław even thought that the workers would accept sacrifices: 'If they agree with the union to work Sundays, then they'll work Sundays.' The militants in this group saw the job of the workers' councils as being to reconcile a new economic logic of openness and rationality with direct workers' control of production. They believed that democracy and economic rationality could coexist. This session was an expression of a working-class utopia which the militants did not dare to call a reconciliation of the productive forces and relations of production, for to say that would have been to use the language of the adversary. The group set up an opposition between the infinite wealth of nature and the egoism and incompetence of the ruling class. The miners were sure of their economic power and their central importance, and the West seemed to them to offer an insatiable market and a rich source of foreign currency. Whereas at the beginning of the meeting a militant like Henryk could insist on the distance between the aims of the enterprise and the logic of the trade union, by the end the whole group was carried away by this utopia of the reappropriation of wealth and infinite development: 'The experts and technicians have failed, the workers must take over the helm.'

As far as politics were concerned, the militants declared that they did not believe in the democratisation of the Party, which according to Krystian was no longer legitimate and would be incapable of mobilising the nation. The Party and government had to be separated. Above all, the militants were 'against the single-party state'. The PUWP was by its very nature undemocratic. The temperature began to rise. Franciszek catalogued the failures, the successive betrayals and crimes of the Party. It was not Polish, it did not represent what Poland wanted, the principles of Leninism were foreign to the country. The Party was under the thumb of the Soviet Union.

The group's demands at union level were relatively moderate, but there was a progression towards far less conciliatory democratic criticism of the regime, and finally to an increasingly radical nationalism. Throughout its existence the group of Silesian miners alternated between a rising tone of rupture with the status quo and a return to moderate and 'reasonable' positions. This of course corresponds to Solidary's double nature as a simultaneously radical and conciliatory movement.

Probably because a sense of community identity was a strong dimension, the Katowice group was relatively homogeneous, and its tendencies towards outright rebellion were transformed into the political and trade-union radicalism which we have described. But at the same time the group was clearly aware of the limits imposed by the situation. Would it be able to manage this tension between its rebellious urges and the limits of possible action? Would it be able to define a field of possible action as a continuation of the victories of Gdańsk, or would it instead choose to follow the path of rupture with the regime?

The triumph of the 'radicals'

It very soon became apparent that the militants wanted to go beyond the limits which up to then they had respected. Józef pointed out that Solidarity was not succeeding in obtaining the implementation of the agreements which had been signed, and that the Party was putting more and more obstacles in the way. For him it was clear that Solidarity would split into a party and a union, since it was obvious that 'the PUWP cannot be both Communist and democratic. If we stop now, the Party will recuperate everything.' Even at the trade-union and economic level the conflict with the bosses was 'insurmountable'. The voice of the moderates was heard less and less. Henryk hoped that the Party would finally expel the hard-liners and treat Solidarity as a partner in dialogue and not an 'enemy of socialism'. But Mirosław had no illusions about the direction in which the Party was going: the fact that the Party Congress was going ahead showed that it was taking things in hand. The militants therefore had to cling to the union and try not to lose too much ground. There was always the hope that the Party would see that it had to reckon with Solidarity's ten million members.

What would these militants do if repression became more severe and if, for instance, the regime arrested Kuroń? The first reactions were lukewarm and somewhat mistrustful; after all Kuroń wasn't a worker, he went too far, and people were tired of all the tension and more and more taken up with immediate problems of survival. But all that was needed was a passionate plea from Józef in favour of the right to strike and freedom of speech, and the group came round to his opinion.

When they met the Gdańsk group, the more radical members of the Katowice group took centre stage and reaffirmed social and political aims which left little room for the more shaded opinions of the Gdańsk militants, and reduced the more moderate Silesian militants to practical silence. Jan led the group. He accepted that 'the managers should not be under the orders of the workers, because conflict between the bosses and the workers is bound to exist'. But self-management institutions, like the union, must be guaranteed by political action against the Party, because the PUWP was in no sense a workers' party. This phrase found an echo with Mirosław, who said that it was the party of the intelligentsia. While Zbigniew, from Gdańsk, called for greater moderation, Jan went on: conflict was inevitable, the Party would never let go of its enterprises, and the embryo of a political party had to be created now. Józef added that several parties should be formed, since it would be 'madness' to replace one single party with another.

Jan thought that the PUWP, apart from not being a workers' party, was not Polish either. The time for moderation was past: 'Wałęsa has said that we shouldn't be a political party. Let him get out then.' Jan explained that they must begin political action immediately, print pamphlets about Katyń, fight for the teaching of a real version of history which would include 'extraordinary things, like for instance the fact that in 1939 *Pravda* was full of friendly greetings to Hitler'. Mirosław and Henryk said nothing. Only Stanisław held out, calling for an alliance between Solidarity and Party moderates. The Gdańsk militants seemed to have been carried along by the storm. Janusz was the only one to declare that a struggle for the application of all the agreements signed in September was the strongest and most realistic platform for action; he reminded the groups of the international limits which everyone had to respect, and recalled Bogdan Lis's view that the militants of the PUWP should not leave the Party because it was still, despite everything, a protection against Poland's neighbours.

The first part of the meeting between the Katowice and Warsaw groups was similar to the meeting with the Gdańsk group which has just been described. The meeting was at first dominated by the radicalism of the Silesians, in the form of a long speech from Józef. His discourse was that of class struggle. He made a violent attack on the absurdity and foreign domination of the organisation of the economy: the coal which they mined disappeared 'we know where'. The Party was an obstacle to all significant change. Jan continued on a more nationalist register: war had now been declared between the Russian empire and its oppressed peoples. The Communist ideology was a creation of the Russians, who had in their cultural make-up certain Asiatic features. Self-management, in so far as it freed the enterprise from the monopoly of the Party, was widely accepted, but the Silesians thought that the Party would emerge strengthened from its Congress and would proceed with a more clearly defined offensive against Solidarity. Similarly, they thought that the Party would seek to maintain its grip on the media. The dominant image, then, was one of inevitable conflict. Once again the more moderate members of the Katowice group had remained silent, and felt that they had scarcely received any support from the Warsaw militants whose ideas were often close to theirs.

Rupture and retreat

On 30 October 1981 we had another meeting with the miners from Silesia. They expressed a desire for rupture with the regime and withdrawal back to the basic principles of the movement. How are we to explain this 'fundamentalism' of which there was much talk at the time of Solidarity's Congress? Does it indicate a change in the movement's stakes, brought about by the economic crisis, or should it be seen as a sign that the union was being transformed into a revolutionary political force?

The militants said that in a few months the climate had changed. It seemed clear to them that the regime had no desire to negotiate and that its positions were even hardening with the worsening of the crisis within the Party. In Katowice itself there were more and more acts of provocation against the union, the work of 'uncontrolled' groups who were in fact manipulated by Party hard-liners. Many people were tired and were finding the shortages harder and harder to live with. Some said that Solidarity's popularity was on the wane, since the union had not shown itself to be capable of improving living conditions. Signed agreements had not been applied and the free Saturdays had been withdrawn; 'with the Saturdays of law 199 and Wałęsa's Saturdays, we work every Saturday'.[1] The strike of one hour called a few days previously had been observed, but with none of the enthusiasm of previous strikes.

Jan, who before had seemed a strong and optimistic leader, was now hesitant and discouraged: 'We no longer know what to do.' The working class must set itself an objective', said Krystian. Solidarity felt simultaneously strong and paralysed, no longer having clear aims. The exhilarating atmosphere of June was much changed. Most of the group rejected the theme of self-management. Franciszek was very clear: 'Self-management is the self-exploitation of the workers.' It was a trick, said Krystian, for it had created the impression that it was the union which was to blame for the crisis. Furthermore, the economy was so disorganised that there was nothing left to manage at enterprise level, and self-management could only be meaningful if it was extended to the whole of the economy. Since June, in other words, the central stakes had ceased to be self-management: economic reform was now the issue. The regime seemed incapable of carrying such reform through without the support of Solidarity or recourse to violence, and Jan, Karol and Krystian thought that the main question was therefore Solidarity's participation in the running of the economy. The group did not see this shift in the field of action as a victory, a natural step forward: it was something which had been forced on the movement by the regime's alternation between weakness and aggression, and by the catastrophic effects of the economic crisis, and it was a source of anxiety. Even Mirosław, who had been the group's most consistent supporter of the idea of self-management, admitted that it was no longer important. He had defended a moderate strategy, but he no longer had any faith in the 'moderates' within the Party. He clearly felt impotent and sad, and said very little.

Amidst the general feeling of weakness and virtual paralysis, Franciszek was the only person to maintain that Solidarity should now become an insurrectional revolutionary force. No one went along with him. It was no longer easy to find forms of action and organisation corresponding to the radicalism of the group's principles. According to Krystian, since the essential problem was the economic crisis, Solidarity must begin to develop the active strike as a means of autonomous production. If the regime did not carry out acceptable reforms, the union must go further and keep 50% of production for itself. Such a step was necessary because it was feared that the authorities were deliberately allowing the situation to deteriorate in

1 Law 199 obliged the miners to work on certain Saturdays because of the central economic importance of coal. It prefigured the militarisation of the mines which was to follow the military takeover of 13 December 1981. During the summer of 1981, Wałęsa had asked the miners to work one Saturday a month in order to avoid worsening the economic crisis.

order to 'starve' the movement into defeat. The active strike was seen as a survival measure, the mining community falling back on its own resources to protect itself. It was a strengthening of the capacity to resist rather than a step in the direction of setting up an alternative centre of power and, ultimately, taking power within the state.

Extremely violent attacks on the regime and its domination by the Soviet Union were associated with this strategy. Never had the movement's underlying working-class and national values been so forcefully affirmed. Did that mean that the limits of possible action were breaking down and that Solidarity was considering a seizure of power? Certainly not: at the same time the radicals in the group stated more clearly than ever their desire to compromise and negotiate in order to avoid a military coup. Negotiation was necessary because the militants 'could not see where their action was leading'. Negotiations had to be imposed, if necessary by a general strike, and the movement had to speak more and more firmly and accept no compromise on its basic principles. But Jan admitted that he felt paralysed at the prospect of this double orientation, and, knowing that the rank and file was more and more radical and explosive, he called for caution and calm. Karol, who had become much more radical since June, also related how he was preaching patience to the rank and file. On the other hand, action of considerable dimensions was needed to channel militants' anger and reunite the movement, although this did not exclude the idea of compromise: the militants had already agreed to considerable compromises over their free Saturdays.

The militants were conscious of the ambiguity of their position: their appeal to the founding principles of the movement was not leading to action, and they wanted their leaders to reinforce the union's capacity for negotiation and its political influence. Since June there had been a spectacular change in the group's tone: then, they had felt that they were in charge, that they were forcing back the limits of their action; today they felt that they had been checked, and that they were the victims of factors beyond their control. Their reaction was to take refuge in their identity as workers and Poles, and to try to reproduce the warmth and conviction of August and September 1980.

During 1981, Wałęsa was much criticised by radicals in the movement and the example of the miners proves that this was not simply the work of intellectuals or small political groupings, but that, on a mass scale, Solidarity bore within it a desire for rupture. Nationalist groups like the KPN had little influence, but the workers' movement contained a strong element of political criticism and desire for national independence. Solidarity's radical face must not be obscured by the limited objectives and the more moderate language of the union's leaders.

The miners, with their class and national consciousness, were in a state of constant rupture with the regime. They wanted to reorganise the economy, starting with the enterprise, but they did not believe that such an objective could be attained by negotiating with the authorities. They did not consider political action, not to mention resorting to acts of violence, but they were nevertheless far removed from the simultaneously audacious and cautious strategies of opposition intellectuals. This explains the fact that this was the group which changed the least; the tone became tougher and hope gave way to bitterness, but in the autumn just as in the spring the dominant note was the rejection of the Party as incompetent and corrupt, the party of local tyrants and foreign domination. As Solidarity's action progressively extended from the trade-union field towards the management of the enterprise and the reform of institutions, this rejection became increasingly uncompromising.

WARSAW

The Gdańsk group had accepted the hypothesis about the nature of Solidarity which had been presented to it by the researchers without difficulty. The Gdańsk Agreement, after all, was a perfectly conscious expression of the interdependence of trade-union action, democratic aspirations and the assertion of the national identity. At Katowice, the miners were firmly rooted in a consciousness of themselves as a class which was inseparable from their national consciousness. In their case the democratic theme might have disappeared, but the group's hostility to the dominance of the Party was such that it did not. The Warsaw group, on the other hand, was dominated neither by the historical experience of the strike of August 1980, as at Gdańsk, nor by the strong social experience of a community of workers conscious of being the country's principal source of wealth, as was the case with the Katowice miners. The group's progress in the direction of analysis was consequently slower than the other two groups.

Conversely it was in this group that the movement's transformations found their most active expression. In the course of its work, the group moved from trade-union action to a more general struggle for the liberation of society; at this point the theme of self-management became predominant, which never occurred in the other two groups. But gradually, especially in the autumn, this theme began to weaken, and desire for rupture, in particular a violent nationalism, came to the fore. The group lived these transformations quite consciously. It had quickly recognised that Solidarity was built on the fusion of social, political and national aims, but its main preoccupation lay elsewhere: how could this social movement rebuild society and create free institutions, particularly in the economy, and what were its chances of overcoming the hostility of the Party? The group did not, however, become a political actor in the strict sense of the term: it wanted to unite trade-union activity with general democratic action, especially in the enterprise. This proved to be a limited and fragile synthesis. The story of the Warsaw group is above all one of the search for, the discovery and the progressive abandonment of this central objective. It is a story which helps us to understand the evolution of Solidarity and the debates which took place within it.

Workers' rights

At the beginning, during its meetings with interlocutors and its own discussion sessions, the Warsaw group constantly returned to the problem of the enterprise, even though class consciousness was in no sense as dominant an element as in the Katowice group. The group considered that the essential objective was to free the workers as completely as possible from the domination of the Party, and to obtain institutional guarantees for that freedom. No member of the group showed a highly elaborated concern with political problems comparable to the preoccupations of Janusz or Zenon in the Gdańsk group. Krystyna, who was the most radical, rarely spoke and never sought to play a central role.

All the militants saw themselves as shop-floor activists; none of them had any responsibilities or influence within the MKZ. They were strongly aware of the gap between the level at which they operated as trade unionists and the more political level of their leaders.

There was a very wide range of opinion within the group, and discussions were very open. There was no leader. Jerzy, who talked a great deal during the first sessions and who might have been taken as expressing the views of the whole group, quite soon lost his central position, and his views became increasingly those of a minority. The group defined itself as belonging to a social movement, but it was convinced that once the movement had established its own existence, it must liberate society, starting with the enterprise.

Differences of emphasis within the group between the various objectives which the union should set itself were of minor importance. The essential point was that the union was a social movement which had grown up from rank-and-file level, and that it was therefore somewhat mistrustful of strictly political ideas and, to an even greater extent, of plans for reform. One of the print workers, Eugeniusz, reacted in a way which was reminiscent of the Katowice miners. He was immediately hostile to anything political, and wanted more than anything else to drive the party out of the enterprise and to defend the workers and their capacity to produce.

During this first phase of its work the group showed great respect for the views of Staszek. He had been one of the leading figures in the Ursus strike, and he was a popular figure within his enterprise; he wanted to remain one of the rank and file, being highly suspicious of the way in which the authorities promoted people to positions of authority where political concerns effectively diverted them from the everyday problems of working people. This was a criticism he made of his friend Bujak, who had come from the same factory and who now, as the leader of a trade-union federation with nearly a million members, was fascinated with the abstractions of political debate. Staszek saw the movement as much more than a trade union: it was for him an expression of faith in humanity in the face of the ruling class and its apparatus, an affirmation of honesty over corruption and of the values of Christian Poland over a materialism which had been brutally imported from abroad. The strike, and the birth and formation of the union had been a form of redemption for him. He wanted to abolish all forms of social and political organisation which seemed to him to be foreign to the world of truth and justice. He saw in Solidarity a return to reality, to the people's faith, to the desire for a national existence, to respect for work. At the same time he took great note of the material demands of his comrades, and few people in the group were less inclined towards adventurism than him. Listening to him, one thought of some of the leaders of the Lip strike at Besançon;[2] but there is no public political debate in Poland, and in Staszek's case an appeal to moral values replaced the reference to Marxist political analyses, which are the language of the regime.

Jerzy was the complete opposite of Staszek: an engineer, and still close to a Party which he had wanted to join after some years in the Young Socialists, but which had refused him entry, he too saw things predominantly in terms of the enterprise, but this was because he thought as a manager and because the workers seemed to him not to see far enough in their demands. The thing which Jerzy and Staszek had in common was that they constantly brought the group back to the everyday experience of a working community. The group was dominated by a combination of the positions which these two individuals symbolised: the moral affirmation of the workers' movement, and the defence of the enterprise through the trade union. Sometimes these preoccupations would come closer together, and sometimes they were opposed one to the other; but they both meant that the centre of gravity of the group was nearer to the social movement than it was to action for the liberation of society.

Industrial democracy

The Warsaw group nevertheless quickly realised that it was not enough simply to affirm the rights and the values of the Polish people and Polish

2 The strike at the Lip factory in Besançon in 1973 provided a focus for thought about self-management in the French trade-union movement. Opposition to redundancies began in April, and led to the occupation of the factory in June. The strike and occupation were led by Charles Piaget of the CFDT. The 'affaire Lip' was concluded in January 1974. (Tr.)

workers. It knew that despite the victories of Gdańsk, Szczecin and Jastrzębie, Solidarity's action was strictly limited, on the one side by geopolitical constraints and on the other by the worsening economic crisis. The group also accepted the view that the movement's component elements tended to separate and move apart: in some quarters there was a tendency towards a full-blooded nationalism well represented by the KPN; elsewhere, priority was given to political problems; while others thought that the movement must maintain or return to true trade-union action. Finally, the group was sympathetic to the offers of agreement or alliance which were being made by Party liberals, in particular Stefan Bratkowski, at a time when Solidarity's influence within the Party also seemed to be growing. At Katowice, the dominant response of the workers to this new situation had been a purely trade-unionist one, but of a very radical nature, reminiscent of the revolutionary trade unionism of the early twentieth century; at Gdańsk, we had witnessed a long and rich debate between the trade unionists and the supporters of political action. In Warsaw the theme of self-management developed in place of pure working-class trade unionism, although it shared the latter's mistrust of strictly political action.

The Warsaw group saw very clearly that the future of Solidarity depended on finding a new synthesis between the defence of workers' interests and the reform of economic institutions. It believed that only self-management provided such a synthesis, although this was admittedly partly because the idea of self-management could be interpreted in various ways. Staszek and Grzegorz believed that self-management had to remain close to trade-union action, while for others it was above all an extension of democracy into the enterprise. A third sub-group half way between these two saw it as simultaneously trade-unionist and political in character. The majority were however in agreement that self-management had to be Solidarity's principal objective during the second phase of its action.

Only Krystyna and Eugeniusz wanted the union to enter directly into the political field; Jerzy and Tadeusz, at the other extreme, thought that the ordinary members were only interested in the defence of their immediate material interests, and feared that the self-management theme would leave them cold. Even these two minority groups did not really question the importance of self-management: rather, they wanted respectively to speed up and slow down Solidarity's development into a movement for the liberation of society. Everyone wanted to protect the unity of the movement, under threat from the tendency for trade-union and political action to go separate ways. Hence their reticence in the presence of political interlocutors, of whatever political shade; they welcomed them warmly and sometimes enthusiastically, but they wanted little to do with political action, feeling that it would divide them.

But despite this desire to maintain the unity of the social movement, the group eventually came to put greater emphasis on the ways in which the reinforcement of the social movement was related to the liberation of civil society. It was at this point that the group was at its strongest. It was conscious that this represented a step forward, and saw the eclipse of Jerzy and the rise of Grzegorz as an expression of this. During the meeting with the Gdańsk group Jerzy could even refer jokingly to his defeat, observing that his friend Teresa now preferred to sit next to Grzegorz. From then on he no longer came regularly to the group, and he was absent from our last meeting at the end of October.

Several members of the group came to take up stronger positions than they had at the beginning; in every case the evolution was towards a greater emphasis on the interdependence of trade-union and political action. Those who were reluctant to follow this movement, Tadeusz for instance, in general claimed that this was a reflection of limited aspirations on the part of the great mass of workers.

Whereas at the beginning the group had been concerned with principles and rights, it now spoke in strategic terms. It sought to define a programme. Grzegorz was the most important figure during this phase. As a young technician he was above all concerned with the absurd management of the economy. He knew that the tractors which he helped to produce were unsellable because they did not correspond to the needs of Polish agriculture with its predominance of small family farms. Self-management for him had to represent a return to rational economic criteria, although it was also a way of defending workers' interests and, of course, a means to drive the Party from the enterprise. His positions were moderate, less politicised than those of his friend Kazimierz, but less defensive than those of Jerzy. The group saw itself as moderate, and gave an increasingly central place to Grzegorz, as well as to Andrzej, another great proponent of self-management. It nevertheless continued to affirm its attachment to the national consciousness and to its religious foundations.

At the outset the group had found it difficult to accept the idea that Solidarity was a fusion of different elements, but it now settled itself much more firmly than the two other groups in the centre of the ground which we have defined as Solidarity II. The Gdańsk group remained too attached to the spirit of the Gdańsk Agreement to accept without much reluctance that the movement should move on from that phase to another, while some members simply leapt forward to more immediately political positions. The Katowice group, for its part, was too rooted in working-class consciousness to see the transformation of economic institutions as centrally important. The Warsaw group, on the other hand, took hold of the idea of self-management and placed it at the centre of its preoccupations, in order to avoid the threat of being split between a base completely taken up with the most immediate material problems and a leadership predominantly political in character.

This reticence to contemplate political action was very noticeable during the group's meeting with the Gdańsk militants. A long discussion took place between Jerzy, the least politicised of the Warsaw militants, and Janusz and Zenon, who were defending the need for political action. The other members of the Warsaw group remained silent and when, much later, they spoke up and recognised the importance of such action, they simply said that Solidarity had 'exposed the Party for what it is' and that the PUWP's monopoly of all areas of public life had to be broken. When they were asked what would incite them to go on general strike, the only reason they gave was the suppression of the union's press by the government. If the leaders of the democratic opposition like Kuroń and Michnik were arrested, they thought it unlikely that the majority of the workers would come out on general strike. In their view, political action was only justified as a way of repelling the enemy, which in turn was the first condition for the rebuilding of the country. That reconstruction had to be carried out by a combination of mass union action and rational economic management.

Their main aim, obviously, was not to seize power, but to create a pluralist society. Andrzej expressed it in the following way: 'Before, there was only the Church to limit the power of the Party; now there is Solidarity too.' The next step was to create consumer groups and above all self-management committees, the influence of which the Party would be unable to ignore. It had to be forced to give a voice to all the actors in public life. Not everyone agreed with Teresa when she repeatedly insisted on the need for free elections to the *Sejm*: the majority saw the independent existence and activity of a growing number of actors on the social scene as the essential priority. As a social movement which sought the liberation of society, Solidarity was more directly concerned with the rebirth of social forces than the reconstitution of political machinery. Democracy certainly presupposed certain institutional guarantees, but the courage of social actors was fundamentally more important. For the members of the Warsaw group, public life was more a matter of convictions than of institutions.

Does this continued desire for the democratisation of society stand a chance of being heard, or will it be destroyed by the Party?

At the end of the meeting between the Warsaw and Katowice groups on 3 July 1981, the researchers asked the militants to choose between three hypotheses concerning the possible course of action which the Party might adopt after its forthcoming Congress. Would it accept compromise with Solidarity? Would it go as far as undertaking economic reform and leaving Solidarity a free hand? Or would it counterattack?

The second hypothesis was too optimistic to be taken seriously. The first had certain attractions for those who wanted compromise with the Party. And yet all the members of the Warsaw group who spoke believed in the third hypothesis and expected the Party to return to the offensive. They did not envisage the worst, but thought that Solidarity would have to confine itself to a very strict definition of trade-union activity. Only Krystyna believed that a further counter-attack on the part of Solidarity would follow. Others spoke of the union's strength, of its membership of ten million, and said that any project for economic reform would have to enjoy its support. But everyone repeated that the Party would try to regain control of social and economic life, and reimpose its power everywhere and on everyone. One of the Polish researchers from the Katowice group gave his reasons for pinning his hopes on the first hypothesis, but no one from the Warsaw group was convinced.

Action

When we met the Warsaw group again, a short time before we moved on to work with other groups, there seemed at first to have been little change. Andrzej had become president of the self-management committee of his enterprise, and was devoting himself to this work with great enthusiasm. He opened the meeting with a repeated statement, supported by Grzegorz, of his belief in the central importance of self-management and, by extension, of a gradualist approach. And yet the tone quickly changed. Several members of the group described how they had become more radical over the past few months. Wacław, who worked in the same enterprise as Andrzej, expressed his doubts about the effectiveness of the self-management committee. In his view the struggle had now to be taken to a broader and more political field, which was the position Krystyna had defended from the beginning.

But in what sense was this term 'political' to be understood? In fact, the group gave little time to strictly political problems like local, regional or even national elections, or the freedom of the press. Nothing was added to the position which the group had already adopted on the creation of a second chamber of the *Sejm*. 'Political' in this context might be defined as the expression in a much more direct way than before of the fundamental and insoluble conflict between society and the regime. The phrases used to refer to the adversary became tougher. Never before in this group had anyone spoken of 'Reds'; never had it been said that the Russians had become used over the centuries to living in slavery and could not understand the Poles' love of freedom and democracy. Neither had there ever been such a strong feeling that the adversary would reject any idea of compromise and would use any means to re-establish its absolute power. Such radicalisation did not mean that the militants wanted to capitalise on their gains and go onto the offensive against the Party: it was simply the expression of their awareness of the gravity of the situation. Proof of this can be seen in the fact that those who had not become more radical were the ones who recognised that the economic crisis weakened the will to fight.

Rather than speaking of the workers in the factories, many spoke of the consumers in the food queues, who were criticising Solidarity in practically the same way as they criticised the Party. Tadeusz went further in his pessimism, speaking bitterly of Solidarity's weaknesses and its lack of internal democracy. Eugeniusz, who up to then had been highly politicised, now combined extreme radicalism with deep pessimism, and pinned his last hopes on a possible uprising of the nations under Soviet domination.

Staszek seemed oppressed, and spoke much less frequently than before; he was haunted by the image of possible confrontation and bloodshed, and wanted to do everything possible to avoid such an outcome. Those who still had some faith in Solidarity's capacity for action spoke above all of the rank and file's determination to defend themselves, and said nothing about any kind of political offensive. No mention was made of a seizure of power by Solidarity, or of any significant change in the nature of the regime.

The group was turning in on itself and on the movement's internal strength, feeling that its ability to transform institutions was under threat. Despite the fact that, as a group, it had frequently been exposed to the action of intellectuals from the democratic opposition, it had returned to defensive positions. Only Grzegorz and Andrzej now spoke of self-management; the others no longer seemed interested. On the other hand, the group was more conscious than ever of the geopolitical and economic constraints under which it was operating. Some were sure that they could resist them, others were almost discouraged, but no one was unaware of them or thought that they could be overcome by determined action.

The evolution of the Warsaw group is sufficiently clear to support the idea that Solidarity's action went through three phases. Those phases can now be better defined. The first was the one in which the movement stated its values, its motives and its objectives, in which, buoyed up by the successes of August 1980, it extended its influence in society. During this phase, which extends up to the Bydgoszcz affair, Solidarity was identified with society, and can therefore easily be defined as a social movement, at once trade-unionist, democratic and national in character. In the second phase the movement, feeling the direct threat of foreign intervention in the wake of the Bydgoszcz affair, and seeing the economic crisis going from bad to worse, tried to consolidate its gains, seeking through institutional reform to find some ground for compromise with the Party, which was weakened but which was attempting to change and said that it recognised the existence and the rights of the free trade unions. From the summer onwards we are in the third phase: here, Solidarity defines itself less and less by its hopes and its values, and sees itself increasingly as a force of resistance to threats and provocations.

The movement's radicalisation is a sign of its desire to defend not only the rights which it had itself acquired, but also the national identity, and the degree of social democracy which had already been restored. While the union's leaders sought to open new areas of negotiation or to take counter-measures to government action, the militant base, less closely linked than before to the population as a whole, adopted a tougher stand and affirmed its will to act. But throughout this evolution Solidarity, as seen through the Warsaw group, never ceased to be faithful to the main principles of its action. At each moment, the movement was just as conscious that it represented a challenge to the whole system as it was of the need to control and limit itself. The movement's continuity runs deeper than any changes in strategy.

CONCLUSIONS

A comparison between the three groups shows how Solidarity responded to the changing political and economic situation and managed the transform-ations which it underwent itself. Everyone agreed that action could no longer be confined to the organisation of free trade unions, and that Solidarity must play a central part in economic recovery and in the reform of all aspects of the national life; everyone, finally, accepted that the action had to respect certain limits and avoid direct confrontation with the Party and its powerful ally. But beyond these clearly stated positions, Solidarity had to face great internal difficulties. Unity between a social movement of a predominantly working-class character and a more general campaign for the liberation of society became increasingly difficult to maintain. The first of these two elements tended to retreat to the defence of workers and consumers, while the movement for the liberation of society tended to become a radical challenge to the very basis of the state. At the same time the effect of the economic crisis was to increase the gap between the rank and file and the union leadership.

The Gdańsk group envisaged Solidarity more as a social movement, while the Warsaw group saw it rather as an instrument for the liberation of society. The opposition between the Gdańsk and Katowice groups was of a different order: the movement represented by the Gdańsk group was one which clearly affirmed its values and its objectives; the other group was more defensive, making its demands in the name of the exploited workers and the subject nation, and hardly believing in the chances of establishing political democracy.

But these differences must also be transcended. Comparison of the three groups shows the usefulness of our hypotheses: whether they were united or not, the movement's three dimensions were present everywhere. In each case, also, Solidarity was at the same time a social movement and an action for the liberation of society. Finally, in all three groups, the movement's action can be seen to have two sides: one is offensive and reforming in character, while the other is more defensive and bears a greater desire for rupture. The movement never lost control of itself. It seems difficult to say the same of the Party: and we may wonder whether the growing political tensions of 1981 cannot be explained by the growing imbalance between, on the one hand, a weak and divided Party, and, on the other, a movement widening the scope of its action but never allowing itself to be carried away by this process of extension or by the internal divisions which it provoked. Is this not a more satisfactory explanation than the view which sees developments in Poland as an escalating conflict setting the two adversaries on a course of increasingly violent and global confrontation?

PART THREE

TOWARDS RUPTURE

The problem of political power

In the middle of 1981 the worsening economic crisis which steadily brought the country nearer to the edge of bankruptcy was not Poland's only problem. Despite its attempts to stem the tide, the Party was unable to govern, to negotiate or even to maintain its own internal cohesion. In such circumstances, how could Solidarity's action be limited to the creation of free unions, or even of self-management committees within the factory? The crisis was a national one, and Solidarity, as the representative of the nation, could not remain just a trade union, whether it wanted to or not. The country's future was in the balance, and the question of political authority was on the table. Solidarity knew that there could be no question of taking power itself: it had no more ambition to be a political party than it had had on the first day of its existence. And the international parameters had not changed in the slightest; the union knew that its continued existence depended on respecting two conditions: the maintenance of Poland's military alliances and the preservation of a Party sufficiently strong for Moscow not to feel obliged to intervene directly.

Solidarity was drawn towards political action, but at the same time had to resist the tendency to overstep the boundaries of the possible. Its more moderate members felt the desire for greater confrontation with the authorities, while the radicals were increasingly aware of the danger of going beyond the limits. Solidarity had come a long way from August 1980 and the triumphant affirmation of its aims as a trade union and a democratic and national movement. How did it manage to respond to so many contradictory pressures, maintaining its unity and its capacity for action? Could it go beyond the Gdańsk Agreement and step directly into the political arena without upsetting the delicate balance which had allowed it to survive and develop?

On 5 September 1981, when Archbishop Glemp celebrated a Mass in Gdańsk to mark the opening of Solidarity's first Congress, no one knew whether the movement was going to choose the path of rupture. But very soon the Congress was to reveal in a most spectacular way the force of the political drive at work within the movement, and the consequent tendency towards fragmentation. The time had come for Solidarity to be clear about the direction which the liberation of society was to take, and to tell the Party the kind of relations which it envisaged with the regime. Solidarity's Congress should therefore be seen not only as a spectacular event unique in the history of the Eastern bloc; it is also a moment of crucial importance in the history of Solidarity. For, in becoming a political rather than a social actor, did Solidarity not lay itself open to increasingly intolerable tensions between its desire to act legally, through negotiation and a search for agreement and compromise with the regime, and, on the other hand, an urge for complete rupture with the regime, provoked, or at least exacerbated, by the economic crisis?

THE CONGRESS AND THE POLITICISATION OF THE MOVEMENT

The first thing to strike observers of the Congress was a formidable political upsurge, of great power but at the same time extremely calm. In the space of one day, 8 September 1981, everything, or almost everything, was said. The Congress began by passing a motion on self-management denouncing the *nomenklatura* and the 'selfish interests of the bureaucratic apparatus of the Party-state', and declaring that if Parliament did not organise a referendum on self-management, Solidarity would. This amounted to a declaration that the movement was prepared to take exclusive responsibility for the development of self-management: it wanted agreement, but if obstacles were put in its way, it would take direct action. Solidarity sought a negotiated settlement, but it represented the will of the whole society, and was strong enough to act as an alternative centre of power.

The motion was passed unanimously. The Congress then proceeded to ratify the principle of free elections to the *Sejm*, and to pass a series of motions which caused Moscow to describe the Congress as an 'anti-socialist and anti-Soviet orgy'. An open letter to Poles living abroad but which was obviously meant for those living in what is now part of the Soviet Union, stated that 'Solidarity is not only a trade union, but also a social movement of thinking citizens wishing to work for Poland's independence'. It was decided that Solidarity would publish a series of booklets for the teaching of Polish history and the Polish language. Next, the Congress delivered the famous 'Message to all the workers of Eastern Europe', telling 'the workers of Albania, Bulgaria, Hungary, Rumania, Czechoslovakia, the GDR and all the nations of the Soviet Union' that 'our aim is to fight for a better life for all working people'. What a challenge! The message went on: 'We support those amongst you who have decided to choose the difficult path of fighting for a free trade-union movement. We believe that in the not too distant future our representatives will be able to meet in order to exchange our experience as trade unionists.' Finally a motion was passed demanding free elections to the Regional Councils and to the *Sejm*.

Without the slightest hesitation, then, the Congress gave free expression to the urge towards political action which had for so long been contained by the leadership. Was this the end of Solidarity's self-limiting function or rather, as the correspondent of *Le Monde*, Bernard Guetta, thought, the end of self-censorship? The Congress stated openly what had never been made explicit. And by doing so it marked a great step forward: as the struggle with the authorities developed, the movement could not but extend the immediate stakes of its action. 8 September 1981 showed the world that Solidarity sought much more than the implementation of the Gdańsk Agreement; it wanted to free industry and political life as a whole from the grip of the Party. It showed also that, without calling for a struggle for national independence, Solidarity no longer wished to remain silent about its feeling of solidarity with the other oppressed workers and nations of the Soviet empire. By rejecting the Party's monopoly of Polish political life, the Congress denied its leading role in the state and, verbally at least, exploded one of the limits which it had set itself in August 1980. All this it said aloud; some caution was, however still exercised, to the extent that the Congress rejected several attempts by a Gdańsk delegate, Sobieszek, to have a motion passed explicitly demanding the abolition of the Party's leading role in the state. Furthermore the Congress respected another limit in the sense that it never questioned Poland's place in the Warsaw Pact.

If the Congress gave spectacular expression to the movement's desire to end the oppression of the peoples of the Soviet empire, nothing was said about the political means to be adopted in the fight against Soviet domination. Here, the distance between the desirable and the possible was maintained. The movement had not ceased to limit itself, but it had reduced the range of that self-limitation and had taken a step towards its horizon, national independence. Later we must analyse whether this step was a real one, whether it was a prelude to action or simply a verbal gesture made in the excitement of the Congress. But at the time no one doubted that the movement had taken a considerable step forward.

INTERNAL DEMOCRACY

The effect of this advance towards the political front was at first to make attitudes to democracy a central criterion of differentiation between militants. On one side were those who, in the name of democracy, wanted to leave considerable freedom for initiatives at local and regional level but to impose strict control of the rank and file; on the other, a concern for effectiveness in negotiations led to a defence of continued strong and centralised leadership.

The whole Congress was organised in such a way that no infringement of democratic procedures was possible; the contrast with the political mores of the Communist bloc was striking, and had indeed been consciously intended by the organisers. It was even the occasion for a joke: when the time came to elect the president, the ballot boxes were held aloft upside down, to show that they were really empty and had not been interfered with. A complex procedure had been adopted, whereby any delegate could intervene, ask for a vote to be taken, and in certain cases have extra time to speak. At the same time the organisers had taken steps to prevent the Congress from deviating too much from the agenda. This meticulous formal democracy was a guarantee of the movement's legitimacy and put the Congress's decisions beyond all possible dispute. Obviously it also had its disadvantages: it was cumbersome and often slow.

The demands of action were, however, a potential threat to the transparence of democratic debate, as the Congress was to realise on two occasions: the first arose when the militants were trying to define the kind of leadership which the movement should have, and the second occurred between the two phases of the Congress, when a group of leaders took a much disputed decision.

The delegates were presented with two options concerning the composition of the future National Committee of Solidarity. The first would lead to the creation of a Committee which was centralised and united, and probably more effective than the second option; this envisaged a decentralised Committee with no special place for veteran figures within the movement, and would probably give greater weight within Solidarity to the regions than to any central authority. After extended debate the principle of centralised leadership was adopted. Karol Modzelewski, in particular, had supported this option, saying that Solidarity was at war and that decentralisation could represent a death-blow. Lech Wałęsa said: 'Democracy will come when the principle problems we now face have been solved.' The governing bodies of the union were given legislative and executive powers, and the position of Wałęsa, who wanted to have a free hand in his negotiations with the regime, was strengthened. In the same spirit it was decided that it should be possible to hold more than one office – at national and at regional level, for instance.

There were, then, two opposing tendencies at the Congress. The first included most of the 'barons', who decided to follow the advice of experts like Kuroń and form a group around Wałęsa; here, priority was given to the imperatives of action, and to the need for an agreement with the regime. The second, which undoubtedly reflected the strong view of the rank and file, called for more internal democracy and for the decentralisation of the decision-making process. Beneath the debate about democracy there lay another: was the movement to proceed to a centralised offensive, capable of forcing the regime to retreat, or should action proceed from the rank and file, in which case it would sometimes be extremely vigorous, would necessarily be less controlled, and might lead either to the defence of particular interests at regional, local or trade level, or indeed to revolutionary rupture.

The other occasion for prolonged discussion on the democratic life of the movement was the compromise which was reached between Parliament and a few of the union's leaders, including Wałęsa, in the period between the two phases of the Congress. Jacek Kuroń had put all his weight behind this compromise. The Congress had decided that no law on self-management would be accepted as it stood without society as a whole being consulted. And here was the leadership flying in the face of that decision and committing Solidarity to a compromise which, to make things worse, was significantly less radical than the union's agreed position. There were cries that democracy had been ridiculed, that Wałęsa was behaving like a dictator; others added, in the anti-intellectual accents of workers' power, that Kuroń was a manipulator. The leadership explained that this compromise had been absolutely necessary and that it had allowed the *Sejm* to win a certain amount of autonomy by confronting the government head on. Finally, the Congress passed a vote of censure for the way in which the compromise had been forced on the movement, making no reference to the actual content of the compromise. This did not prevent the Congress from giving a vote of approval to the retiring leadership.

But, once again, underneath the debate about democracy, and partially obscured by it, lay the growing gap between the supporters of limited action, negotiated step by step and progressively forcing the adversary to retreat rather than seeking to overthrow him, and, on the other hand, those who, because of the worsening economic crisis, because they felt the strength of the movement and because in any case they hardly believed any more that it was possible to negotiate with this regime, wanted to see a tougher attitude which might lead to acts of rupture.

A CRITICAL MOMENT

This gap should not be seen as meaning that the movement was splitting and that the leaders were becoming cut off from the base; it simply indicates tension between the tendency towards rupture or a withdrawal of the movement into itself, and the desire to find some kind of negotiated balance with the authorities. Within this tension, it was always the latter desire which was the stronger. The force which might have drawn the movement into a drift towards revolution did not tear it apart, indeed it rather served to give weight to those who sought political and institutional solutions. Wałęsa was surely in a much better negotiating position if he was seen by the authorities as the only moderate element capable of preventing a social explosion.

Nonetheless, this tension was going to take on more complex forms as it began to separate elements which up to then had been highly integrated.

The Congress represents the moment when Solidarity openly and sometimes dramatically experienced the growing difficulty of managing the
different elements of its action, which were starting to become antagonistic
rather than complementary.

The trade-union element of the movement was in itself hardly represented at the Congress: Solidarity appeared much more as a movement for
the liberation of society. The reason for this was a general realisation that,
because of the economic situation, traditional industrial demands and strike
action were impossible, and that the movement had now to fight for the
political conditions of its existence. Taking this logic to the extreme, one
might claim that Solidarity was almost ready to accept price increases and
unemployment, and to take the responsibility for these, in exchange for
political guarantees. In this situation, traditional industrial action tended to
withdraw into its shell, and a number of speeches showed how trade
unionism, when it was deprived of an adversary and of ground upon which
to act, could become a discourse of workers' power. Hence the occasional
expressions of rank-and-file aggression towards advisers, intellectuals and
scientists. Denied the prospect of trade-union action, the working-class
component of the movement deteriorated, falling back on a kind of
defensive populism directed at the upper reaches of the movement, seeing
the leaders as manipulated by their advisers and blind to the frustrations of
the rank and file. Only 'Leszek' (Wałęsa), despite a decline in his charisma,
was spared such attacks.

The nationalist component of the movement also tended to break away
and enter into conflict with the democratic element, which remained close
to the positions which the KOR had defended for years. The conflict had
started to emerge in the first few days of the Congress, but it was when the
dissolution of the KOR was announced that it exploded into the open. That
morning, 29 September 1981, the aging Professor Edward Lipiński had read
a statement explaining the reasons for the disbandment of the KOR, and
then, in a personal capacity, he had launched into a violent attack on a
regime which was the direct negation of the ideals of socialism for which he
had been fighting for sixty years. It was this that sparked off open conflict:
that afternoon a delegate proposed a motion thanking the KOR for all that it
had done for the movement, at which point a delegate from Masovia, the
region around Warsaw, proposed a counter-motion in which the part
played by the KOR was reduced to one of many different contributions to the
birth of Solidarity. The Niezgodzki motion was a clear expression of
nationalism hostile to the KOR, and was understood as such by everyone,
especially since it was widely known that Masovia had been the scene of
various violent arguments between 'true Poles' and militants close to the
KOR. It was asked why both motions could not be passed, and the delegates
from Radom, who knew better than anyone what the workers owed to the
KOR, proposed a third text in which the KOR was thanked even more

warmly than in the first. Jan Józef Lipski, a delegate to the Congress and a member of the KOR, collapsed with a heart attack just as he was about to speak. In dramatic circumstances, the Congress had become aware of a split between nationalists and democrats, between 'true Poles' and the supporters of the former KOR.

This split should not be exaggerated. Perhaps it concerned above all a highly politicised fringe, a set of activists present at the centre of some of the union's large regional organisations but not in the factories. But it was nevertheless clear that active nationalism did exist and had a tendency to split away from democratic action. That even the most extreme expressions of this nationalism did not cut themselves off from the movement was due to the fact that they were the extension of anti-Soviet and national feeling which remained very strong. Still, this militant nationalism with populist overtones must be seen as distinct from the national feeling expressed in the emotive speeches which had drawn rapturous applause from the Congress.

The democratic component, then, was weakened by an upsurge combining nationalism with the discourse of workers' power, having fundamentalist tendencies, and representing a populist appeal to both national and class identity. These forms of disunity are a marked contrast to the other image of the Congress, which shows a political drive of irresistible strength, calm and sure of itself. These opposing tendencies were both present and equally real, but openly and in front of the whole Congress the movement fought for control over its own internal conflicts, and elected as president the man who best represented the integration of the movement's three component elements and symbolised the desire not to give in to populism and to stick to a strategy of counter-offensive whereby the movement continued to seek the path of negotiation and institutional solutions. Wałęsa was elected with 55% of the vote, while Marian Jurczyk, representing working-class populist tendencies, received 25%. Andrzej Gwiazda, for a long time a central figure in the democratic opposition but now increasingly drawn towards a populist sensibility, received only 9%, and Jan Rulewski, whose main feature was his hostility to the Soviet Union, received 6%.

FIVE LEADERS

The Congress provides us with an opportunity to introduce four of the union's leaders in more detail: each candidate for the presidency made a long speech of introduction to the Congress before replying to delegates' questions. We shall add a portrait of Zbigniew Bujak, who was not a candidate, but whom we came to know well when he met the Warsaw group in his capacity as president of Mazowsze, the Solidarity organisation in Masovia.

These men, each in their own way, illustrate the movement's central problems, in particular the opposition, which never became a schism, between the search for agreement with the authorities and the affirmation of populist feeling which always threatened to lead to rupture.

Andrzej Gwiazda

Gwiazda is first and foremost a man of August 1980. He was one of the group which had for a long time been thinking through and preparing the movement's action, and he played a very important part in organising the strike and working out a strategy for negotiation with the government.

An engineer at the Elmor factory, he symbolises the link between the working-class and democratic elements of the movement. In 1968, almost alone, he tried to mobilise working-class support for the student movement; in 1976, together with his wife Joanna, he sent a letter to the *Sejm* expressing his support for the KOR, and subsequently he was involved in every movement which prefigured a coming together of working-class and political action.

From January 1981 onwards he moved away from Wałęsa and was presented as a 'radical'; while not believing in the feasibility of seeking to seize power within the state, he agreed with those who had no faith in the Party and therefore refused all concessions. In his view, concessions led to confrontation. The movement should rather aim for an ambitious compromise reflecting society's aspirations. In this toughness verging on intransigence, Gwiazda, the man of conviction, resembles those who tended towards defensive attitudes, although they were very different from him in other respects. These militants considered that the possibility of an institutional settlement of the conflict was increasingly remote, and at the same time tended to move away from the democratic elements of the movement; and as the tension within the movement between populism and democratic action became stronger, so Gwiazda was increasingly torn between a desire to reach a compromise and a conviction that the regime was doing everything it could to frustrate that end. That was the reason for his low score in the presidential election, despite the sympathy which he received from those who were irritated by Wałęsa's autocratic tendencies and above all from those who recognised him as a real democrat, much closer to the KOR than to the 'true Poles'.

Marian Jurczyk

The Szczecin leader was an experienced fighter. He had led the struggle in 1970, and in 1980 he had been elected leader of the MKS in his region. He belonged to the top level of the union's leadership, and was often considered to be Wałęsa's number two. But he lacked Wałęsa's ability to bring together the various meanings of the movement and appeared above all as a strong and resolute trade unionist.

For Jurczyk, there were no concessions to be made to the regime, and no compromise was possible. He had followed the Ninth Congress of the PUWP, advertised as the congress of renewal and democratisation, and had seen no change from previous attitudes. He therefore considered that the movement must fight to impose its demands. This refusal to believe in negotiation and the institutional mediation of the conflict was accompanied in Jurczyk by a constant return to the affirmation of working-class identity, which defined and gave strength to the movement. This withdrawal, as we have seen, pointed in only one direction – rupture – and yet that was not what he wanted. But Solidarity's roots lay in working-class trade unionism, and Jurczyk expected the movement's leader to be permanently in touch with the base, and not to cut himself off by taking questionable decisions. The world of the workers was good, and the world of the intellectuals was suspect, and Jurczyk saw himself as the leader of a movement which he feared might be manipulated by overly politicised or intellectual leaders. This rank-and-file approach should not necessarily be seen as implying a commitment to an ideology of workers' control, to the extent that it is the expression of a desire to act as a responsible trade unionist. But in a situation in which classic trade-union action was increasingly meaningless, Jurczyk found himself becoming the symbol of a working-class essence rather than a man who could lead the union in its involvement in social conflicts. He represented working-class identity on the defensive, centred upon itself. He was a worker, and also a Pole.

It was difficult to reconcile trade-union and national action at a practical level. Jurczyk managed to achieve this in a defensive and populist speech. Convinced that Poland was rich but badly managed, and speaking in the name of the exploited workers, their wives who had to carry on in dreadful conditions and their friends who died in 1956 and 1970, Marian Jurczyk was the perfect expression of the defensive side of the movement. To the extent that this defensive aspect had become more marked at the time of the Congress, it was not surprising to see him collect nearly 25% of the votes.

Jan Rulewski

The name of Jan Rulewski is primarily associated with the extremely tense situation of March 1981: he was the union leader of Bydgoszcz, and was severely beaten up by the police, as a consequence of which he became a national hero. He was an outspoken figure in the movement, known above all for his energetic hostility to the Soviet Union. He never said that Poland must break the Warsaw Pact and leave the Eastern bloc, but his whole action was directed by the idea of refusing and no longer being afraid of Soviet domination.

He often gave the impression of wanting to have done with the self-limitation of the movement, and let the confrontation take place. Solidarity must understand that it must go well beyond trade-union action and define the stakes as the control of Poland's foreign relations: that was the key, he said; once Poland was in control of its relations with abroad it would be able to choose the direction in which the economy should go. That was why he sympathised with an economic programme for the complete abolition of the present system and the establishment of a liberal free market economy with a dominant private sector: he wanted to break all Poland's ties with Moscow, and he knew very well that an unplanned economy enjoying independence in its foreign trade policy inevitably meant withdrawal from Comecon. He was dominated by a nationalism based on rebellion and rejection of foreign dependence, but when he sought to define himself positively he still saw himself as a Pole rather than a worker or a trade unionist. His anti-Soviet stance was accompanied by an emotive moral appeal to the notion of Man, an appeal for constructive personal relationships, and a struggle against all the evils which corrupted the nation, beginning with alcoholism. Rulewski was always applauded when his subject was the Soviet Union, but he gained little support when it came to electing a president. His vote, the lowest of all, clearly shows that the movement still distinguished between its convictions and the real possibilities open to it.

Zbigniew Bujak

Bujak had no reason to stand, and lose, against Wałęsa in the presidential election; he preferred to move closer to him with an ultimate view to becoming his successor.

A young man, born in 1954, he was the president of one of the two largest regional unions, Mazowsze, with over one million members. He was in a sense the movement's favourite, and many thought that he had not yet reached the peak of his trajectory as a leader. Others, more hostile towards him, stressed that he had not had to fight to impose his authority, and thought that he was fragile.

Bujak was a political leader rather than a grass-roots trade unionist. After August 1980, he could have continued to run the union at Ursus, where he had been in joint charge of the strike committee with his friend Zbigniew Janas. But he preferred to work from the top, where it was possible to use a global vision of problems to determine action of a general kind, and where one had to be able to negotiate with the authorities. Bujak's actions suggested that he saw Solidarity as a social liberation movement rather than a social movement. An organiser and a political strategist more than a factory leader, Bujak was keen to see political forces emerge within the movement, and favoured the formation of 'workers' clubs' as a means to this end. More generally, he was sympathetic to anything which might bring forth new social or political actors, and also to anything likely to relieve the union of responsibilities which he thought it should not have to bear.

As a leader at Ursus, a centre of rebellion in 1976 and of KOR action, Bujak owed his political education to the intellectuals of the democratic opposition. Kuroń and Michnik, in particular, were his friends first, and his advisers second. For this very reason Bujak's position within the increasing internal conflicts of the Masovia region was becoming less central than at the beginning: he was increasingly seen as a 'man of the Left', a democrat, as opposed to the 'true Poles' like Antoni Macierewicz who formed the nationalist 'right', while, in the centre, Seweryn Jaworski was assuring himself a solid power base by his constant presence in the factories.

Lech Wałęsa

Lech Wałęsa is not only the charismatic hero of Gdańsk, the star surrounded by journalists. He is, above all, the central figure of Solidarity, the man who brings together its different elements and symbolises its unity.

A worker with a large family and a practising Catholic strongly marked by his peasant origins, he was one of the founders of the free trade union and had for a long time been a democrat convinced of the importance of political opposition. And yet it was precisely on this score that he was widely criticised by those who thought that, after a few months of the movement's existence, he behaved autocratically and did not care sufficiently about internal democracy. The reason for this was that apart from being the movement's spokesman, he was also its main negotiator. In that capacity he had to act as a politician, a man of action, a formidably wily and intuitive tactician rather than a long-term strategist, far removed from the internal debates of Solidarity and totally absorbed in the task of defeating the adversary.

Lech Wałęsa constantly spoke in the name of the workers and the whole of Polish society, but he never behaved like a revolutionary leader. He repeated again and again that Solidarity did not wish to seize power, that it wanted to introduce democracy into the country, freeing institutions and organisations from the grip of the Party, but not taking control of them. He was above all the man of the Gdańsk Agreement, and he sought to resist the forces which tended to push the movement forward towards more political objectives, thereby separating elements which had been strongly integrated at the beginning. He was, for instance, clearly not on his favourite ground when self-management was under discussion, and he was not one of the group which made free elections one of the movement's aims. But he enjoyed the support of a very good set of advisers, and he was always able to take advantage of the whole range of their political preferences in order to keep in touch with any theme which became central to the movement's preoccupations.

Solidarity, as we have seen, was on the one hand a political counter-offensive and, on the other, a defensive action with populist overtones. Wałęsa obviously continued to seek negotiated solutions, but he never lost touch with the rank and file as it became increasingly angry and more and more tempted by a populist withdrawal. He knew how to find the right words to turn a situation round and persuade strikers who were determined to push their claims through to the bitter end, that they should go back to work in the interests of Solidarity and society as a whole. As far removed as it was possible to be from the 'true Poles', he believed that the movement could reach agreement with the Party on the basis of 'Poles speaking to Poles'; and while the partisans of workers' control denounced the intellectuals and the top of the hierarchy, he enjoyed the trust of the rank and file, whose emotions and convictions he knew how to share.

If he was never questioned by the rank and file, his position was challenged by some of the leadership, although many 'barons', when faced with a choice, preferred to support rather than oppose him: he was the only leader who could negotiate from a position of strength and at the same time enjoy the continued support of those who were becoming more radical. Everyone was aware that he was just as clever within the union as he was in his dealings with the authorities; he could get his decisions through, but he also knew how to isolate his opponents and win over the most implacable of them. One of the reasons for the relatively low 55% vote which he received at the Congress was that many delegates, as well as being attracted by the tough stand of Jurczyk or the other qualities of Gwiazda and Rulewski, wanted to give a lesson in democracy to the leader who sometimes abused his position as the movement's symbol.

ECONOMIC REFORM

The meaning of the idea of self-management was now clear. The Party was to be driven from the enterprise, and management was to be handed over to a new actor, relatively independent of Solidarity, who was capable of establishing economic rationality in the place of waste and incompetence. This represented a politicisation of the struggle, and the compromise around which debate had centred for so long had now been accepted by the movement, even if it was not seen as entirely satisfactory. But the movement did not stop at self-management in the enterprise: what use were workers' councils if the decision-making process was dominated by a rigid and ineffective system of central planring, if decisions regarding prices, wages, customers and suppliers were all made elsewhere and the council's room for manoeuvre amounted to little or nothing? Freeing the enterprise would mean nothing unless general economic reform quickly took place. But what was to be the substance of such reform? Here again, the movement was torn between two attitudes.

One current of thought emerged, led by Professor Kurowski, which called for a clear break with the present economic system. Government policies had to be decisively rejected, said Kurowski: there must be a massive shift of investments from the public to the private sector, in industry but above all in agriculture, where nationalisation had led and always would lead to catastrophic results. Kurowski added that investment in the armaments industry must be stopped, and international trade agreements revised in the light of their profitability. In short, this was a programme for a return to economic liberalism and market forces, representing a complete break with centralised planning. Poland's economic independence was frequently referred to.

This programme also included various measures for the improvement of productivity, in particular the reintroduction of Saturday working; but it was opposed not so much from a trade-union point of view as on the grounds that it was too clear a threat of rupture with the regime. The other current of thought, represented by economists like Ryszard Bugaj and Andrzej Wielowiejski, favoured a much suppler attitude and measures which did not represent an immediate abolition of all planning. '

Although the delegates had no particular experience of economic discussion, there was protracted debate on these questions. And, once again, the reason was that beneath the economic debate lay the fundamental opposition within the movement between the partisans of a strategy of caution and the proponents of rupture. The Congress finally preferred not to make a clear choice between the two: the programme which was adopted included a series of appendices in which the various economic proposals were simply set out.

At the height of its trajectory, then, Solidarity was still driven on by a powerful social movement, and was clearly engaged in political action. The strength of the social base gave it a power which was necessarily a challenge to state power. But such action was badly defined. That its aim was not the seizure of power is self-evident; but there was hesitation between a constantly disappointed hope for negotiation and reactions of rebellion and rupture which were particularly strong among the rank and file. Was there not a danger that Solidarity would disintegrate, no longer able to control popular discontent and despair, would wear itself out in increasingly difficult negotiations, and might even lose the sense of its own limits?

AUTUMN 1981

The ambiguity and hesitation which were evident at the Congress can be seen, after the end of the Congress, within both Solidarity and the Party, even if we now know that martial law was already being contemplated. On the one hand General Jaruzelski, who had replaced Stanisław Kania after his defeat and resignation on 18 October, spoke of the government's willingness to engage in dialogue, and seemed to be looking for some formula of 'national consensus'. On the other hand, the statements and actions of the authorities displayed real firmness and a refusal to concede any ground. Up until the middle of November there was a double movement within the PUWP. Its leaders sought to negotiate with Solidarity and the Church, but at the same time they allowed the hard-liners to become a centre for hardening attitudes. Simultaneously, massive numbers of rank-and-file members were choosing to leave the Party, as were moderates at the top, more reticently and sometimes under duress. In a few weeks the Party lost hundreds of thousands of members, a large part of its working-class base. At the same time it expelled Bogdan Lis, the last major Solidarity figure to remain a Party member, then Stefan Bratkowski, the president of the Journalists' Association and one of the main proponents of renewal within the Party.

And yet it seemed that some kind of front of national unity was being contemplated. Not only did General Jaruzelski suggest that he wanted some such solution: he made the first overtures and, on 4 November, he met Archbishop Glemp and Lech Wałęsa to prepare the way for dialogue and cooperation. Agreement was far away and there was no indication that the positions of the different sides were reconcilable, but the meeting of 4 November was seen as a historic moment which might well justify Wałęsa and his supporters who were holding out for a political agreement. This was the beginning of dialogue, and towards the middle of November the three parties began to work out the procedure by which national consensus was to be reached.

The Party also seemed to be losing control of the *Sejm*. Parliament had, for several weeks, been displaying some independence of mind and on several occasions had rejected attempts by the Party to impose authoritarian emergency measures. The peasant and democratic parties and the Catholic groups in the *Sejm*, previously under the complete control of the Party, now showed that they wanted to disengage themselves and join society in the struggle for democracy. The PUWP's system of political control was

152

considerably weakened, although its leading role was not effectively challenged.

On the Solidarity side, the tension between the desire to reach national consensus at any price, and the tendency towards rupture, was steadily growing. It demanded a democratic system but did not seek direct access to power. It was pushing for a social council for the national economy with powers of control rather than decision-making, and made up of people chosen for their competence and not their political sympathies; although it perhaps thought that the great majority of competent people were on its side. The National Committee followed Wałęsa in his calls for calm when it felt that real negotiations had begun, which was the case after 4 November; but when agreement seemed impossible, the Committee, which often tended to be angered by Wałęsa's autocratic behaviour, showed its disapproval and wore itself out in wrangling and indecisive voting.

So, just as the regime displayed two faces, one closed and authoritarian and the other open and conciliatory, so Solidarity had to face the intense contradiction between the need for conciliation and the impossibility of giving any ground. The general strike of one hour on 28 October had a double meaning: it was a reminder of the union's political demands and of the urgent need for economic measures, but it was also a sign of good will towards the regime, in the sense that Solidarity was pointing to the efforts it was making to channel and defuse the wild and undirected anger which was sweeping the country, and which was encouraged by confusion at the top. There was an unparalleled growth of strikes and demonstrations, in particular at Żyrardów, Tarnobrzeg, Sandomierz, in the Zielona-Góra region and at the Sojnowiec mine in Katowice. Such wildcat action was nearly always of a defensive nature, provoked by food shortages or designed to reinforce a local political demand such as the resignation of a particular Party official. Solidarity wanted to show that it could stop this.

The disintegration of the Party occasionally led to the existence of alternative centres of power. The active strike was the main manifestation of this. The rank and file only rarely understood that such action often served only to disorganise production even more, driving the country, and the union with it, deeper into crisis; and it took all the conviction, experience and maturity of the militants at the Huta-Warszawa factory to persuade the workers to call off a sale of clothes at the factory. These initiatives, the ultimate logic of which was the setting up of alternative centres of power, were an affirmation of working-class identity, in turn the expression of a social movement on the defensive. They took place in a complete political vacuum: rather than conflict, they represented the occupation of the ground by the union. They were not confined to the factories. They occurred in other areas of social life: some teachers, for instance, took it upon themselves to ignore official programmes and instructions and to teach Polish history and literature which the authorities had eliminated from the curriculum. But the crucial point is that such initiatives were now present in the National Committee itself: appeals for democracy and local or regional autonomy were frequently accompanied by proposals for the union to organise the production of tractors in armaments factories, or to take over from the official administration responsibility for the distribution of coal and food. The most radical members of the Committee were saying that the government remained deaf to their demands. The conclusion was to say that the union should organise its own programme, boycott official elections and encourage active strikes. Yet such discourse can be seen in two ways. In the case of those who were most firmly set on a complete break with the regime, it meant that there was no longer any prospect of agreement with the authorities; but for others, and they were a majority, such discourse was still perceived as a means of pressuring the authorities into the negotiations which they seemed to be running away from. These hesitations and disagreements weakened the movement, although there was still great faith in its strength.

The most concrete demands made by Solidarity were still directed by general principles, as one example will show. In November the eighty delegates at the Nowa Huta steelworks were holding their monthly meeting. First they heard Adam Michnik, the union's adviser in that particular enterprise, analyse the political situation and explain what choices seemed to him to be necessary in the light of the movement's democratic aims. Then the discussion turned to demands concerning the workers more directly: food and rationing. Suddenly, the discussions with Michnik seemed a long way away. And yet, after a long debate at which rank-and-file activists were present, the delegates decided, in the name of working-class solidarity, not to use the economic importance of their enterprise as a weapon to press for increased food rations. For the same reason they also decided to give the office workers the same ration tickets as the manual workers, even though the latter were a large majority in the enterprise and in the union. Despite being weakened by tensions, Solidarity was not in danger of splitting, and remained committed to its general aims. But how did it respond to a situation in which everything seemed possible but nothing in fact was, in which production was collapsing and severe shortages setting in, in which the Party was disintegrating and the direct or indirect threat of Soviet intervention was always present? Did Solidarity prepare to advance and take power? Or, on the contrary, did the militants fall back on acts of uncontrolled rebellion? Or did the movement still seek a political compromise?

These questions are not the same ones which were asked at the beginning of this work. The answers are not to be found in written documentation. If we are to know how these problems were experienced at grass-roots level, we must turn to the actors in the struggle and analyse with them their capacity for dealing with the problems which they encountered. That is why the research team decided to move on to a second phase in their sociological intervention. This took place in Łódź, Wrocław and Szczecin.

vv

Radicalism and compromise

LIGHT AND SHADE

We have already seen that each of Solidarity's three component elements has two sides: working-class consciousness is concerned with the defence of workers' interests, but it may also take the form of a populist defence of the weak against the strong and consumers against the monopolists; national consciousness involves the affirmation of a cultural identity, but it may also become an aggressive nationalism; the desire for democracy, finally, is almost always associated with the defence of freedoms, but it can be transformed into an appeal to the people, the base, against all leaders, and an insistence upon an almost military discipline required to save the threatened nation. The question which now arises is this: is the effect of the dramatic situation of the autumn of 1981 not to extend the area of the movement which is in shadow at the expense of the lighter areas? Do we not see a strengthening of the most defensive reactions, and a weakening of plans for the reconstruction of society? At the same time, it becomes more and more difficult for Solidarity to define itself exclusively as a social movement: it is drawn into political action. The next question is therefore this: is it not true to say that the aspect of the action which is most strongly reinforced is the one which combines a political orientation with a defensive, populist, aggressively rank-and-file tone, while the one which suffers most is the one uniting a truly working-class movement with the desire for a general democratisation of society? In short, are not the forces which were in the ascendant in the autumn of 1981 the ones furthest away from the spirit of Gdańsk?

These forces took as their base the discontent of a population exhausted by shortages and interminable queues. As the chances of a compromise grew more remote and the grip of Solidarity – and of the Party – on a worsening situation became less firm, popular reactions became sharper: the nation felt threatened, its enemies were felt to be preparing for attack, and the result was a tendency to find conspiracies to expose. There was increasing mistrust, not only of the Party leaders but of anyone at the top, with the exception of Wałęsa, who never ceased to be seen as the man from the bottom who had risen to the top but had remained a man of conviction and cunning. Intellectuals, even those who were most closely linked to the union as its advisers, were the objects of a suspicion which had always been present but which became stronger. There was even a search for scapegoats, and in a country where the Jewish population had almost entirely disappeared the voice of anti-Semitism was heard, and not only among the hard-liners within the Party.

Anti-Semitism raised its head in our research groups on two or three occasions. It was to be seen, beneath the surface, in a few local Solidarity news-sheets and was given much more explicit form by Marian Jurczyk in October 1981, when he spoke publicly of having done with the Jews and Communists who were running the country. It was a minor theme, but, leaving aside meaningless clichés, it became more widespread as the democratic element of the movement weakened and was replaced by a populist exaltation of the Polish nation and the virtues of the working-class base. Rooted in a thousand years of history, anti-Semitism at that point was above all the expression of the movement's inner crisis and of hostility towards militants who were political rather than trade-unionist, intellectual rather than working-class, and whose national consciousness was questioned. One member of the Warsaw group, for instance, suggested that the leaders of the KOR were the sons of a Stalinist Jewish bourgeoisie. Was Kuroń a Jew? he asked Zbigniew Bujak, who immediately replied that the question should never have been asked. Similarly, two members of the Gdańsk group, outside working sessions, criticised the KOR which they said was dominated by Jews. A mixture of increasingly harsh nationalism and of fear that the movement was being manipulated by politicised intellectuals, this anti-Semitism was in general repudiated by Solidarity, more often than not in the most forceful way. Our groups refused to identify with Jurczyk's statements, and no one ever made directly anti-Semitic comments; at a more public and official level, the union's position was that anti-Semitism was a weapon used by the regime, and it was publicly denounced. And how can we fail to see that the very reason for Solidarity's existence was a desire for the liberation of areas of democracy within society, and that the only possible effect of this could be to reduce the space available to anti-Semitism, which was indeed fuelled by the regime?

This can be applied more broadly. The strength of the 'true Poles' movement, nationalist and hostile to the intellectuals of the democratic opposition, was increasing, but nowhere did it obtain victory. The great mass of militants continued to entertain a set of positive projects, at once ambitious and moderate. At Lublin we visited an enterprise where the militants proudly proclaimed themselves as radicals. They had won power in the enterprise and had, in reality if not officially, eliminated the Party. They were taking all sorts of initiatives in the region, helping farmers and taking part in the building of churches. They did not accept the authority of the union's regional leadership. They had erected in front of their factory, at

157

the side of the main road which crosses the country from East to West, a monument with a worker standing, his arms raised and his chains broken, before a cross. But were they revolutionaries? Certainly not. They were firmly behind Wałęsa and intended their action as a means of exerting pressure on the Party to force it to negotiate at regional and national level, and they were careful to avoid any adventurism. They were simply enthusiastic about their responsibilities, their freedoms and their desire to contribute to the recovery of the country and the restoration of justice.

If one looks only at militants' feelings, it does appear that the movement in the autumn was, on occasion, close to rupture. But the image of an escalation towards confrontation is dangerously false, since it prevents us from seeing clearly that the effect of the political and economic crisis was to encourage the disintegration of Solidarity much more than to drive it forward.

At Łódź, Wrocław and Szczecin, the tendency was for the movement to split: on the one hand, increasingly aggressive discourse, and, on the other, withdrawal back to the problems of the factory and everyday life. Union officials were hardly ever tempted by the urge to press forward with inflated demands towards what both sides called confrontation. On the contrary, their desire was to find a new balance for their action by giving it predominantly democratic aims: shared responsibility in economic reform, free elections, normal access to the media. But as the crisis worsened, the Party felt less and less able to overcome it by its usual methods. Solidarity, for its part, was losing the ability to unite its diverse tendencies: populism of a nationalist, workers' control variety spoke more and more strongly; there was an increase in strikes provoked by deprivation and exasperation, while the 'radicals' began to be divided amongst themselves, some of them wanting to make a last attempt at negotiation, others being ready to launch into political action.

In the autumn, then, Solidarity was in no sense moving forward on a wave of attack. It was the victim of the crisis far more than a force capable of imposing its will, and the experience of the tension between its desire to change Polish society and the effects of the economic and political disintegration of the Popular Republic of Poland, was an increasingly painful one.

ŁÓDŹ

Populism

At Łódź, the capital of the textile industry, the economic crisis drove the workers to demonstrate in the street. It also made trade-union activity within the enterprise increasingly difficult, and the union's role was reduced to a kind of social work in which the militants expended all their energies. Production became more disorganised, and self-management in this context was a dangerous illusion: what purpose could it serve when everything that was needed to carry on the work was missing? Solidarity could no longer act as a trade union, and the discourse of action gave way to that of conviction and principle. The struggle came increasingly to be seen in moral terms as a fight against Evil, and more precise reference to work and production disappeared.

But the dominant tone was nationalist and even, for the first time in our research, patriotic. At the beginning, the group seemed to be carried away by nationalism, but at the same time it turned away from ambitious and far-reaching plans, confining itself to the immediate defence of the workers and sometimes even imprisoning itself within a discourse of rebellion. Between this trade unionism of survival and the nationalism of the group, which tended to drive it in the direction of political rupture, there began to develop an enormous vacuum. Would the group choose between these two forces? How could it maintain the movement's unity in the face of such a threat? Was it heading for rupture, or was it capable of resisting that temptation?

Genowefa had come to the movement through patriotism, and it was on that basis that, for a very long time, she was to have considerable influence within the group. She wanted an end to the silence surrounding Polish literature, an end to the history books in which Kościuszko merited half a page and Lenin a whole chapter; she would speak of the victims of Katyń, and Moscow's domination of her country was a constant source of anguish to her. The group as a whole spoke in nationalist terms: 'Poland is and will remain Poland.' 'If Poland was free, we would have enough to eat', said someone else, adding that 'Solidarity is truly Polish.'

The initial atmosphere, then, was populist and defensive, and it was difficult to open up a breach in this enveloping discourse. But a visit by Józef Srcniowski, a member of the now disbanded KOR, started the group on the long road which was to lead it almost entirely away from its early populist preoccupations. The interlocutor gave a long account of the KOR from its creation, and although he did not indulge in polemic, the story which he told was sufficiently persuasive for populist criticisms to lose their power. Genowefa exclaimed: 'The KOR made us think, the Pope gave us courage', and Alojzy observed that the KOR could be disbanded, but 'society, and Solidarity, will continue your work'. A crack had been opened in the discourse of populism, and the whole group recognised that the very existence of Solidarity was partly due to the fact that one of its dimensions was the democratic one symbolised by the KOR.

The third step

The group then began to change rapidly, and the researchers actively urged it to define its view of the future course of action. At that point, it put forward the idea of the movement progressively climbing the steps of a staircase, at each stage liberating another area of social and political life. This upward progression was a necessity, said Genowefa, and if the 'third step' leading to the struggle for the liberation of political life was a high one, there could be no question of not trying to reach it. 'We must fight our way upwards to free elections to Parliament and, ultimately, to national independence.' The government would like to 'make us climb back down to the first step' – the recognition and continued recognition of a free trade union – and there was an idea abroad that such a return to the first step would lead to an economic miracle which would magically fill the shops with goods; but Genowefa saw the whole drive of the movement necessarily aiming at a 'fourth step' of national independence, which could only be reached via the third step.

Alojzy, too, thought that the problem of free elections was crucial. In his view the 'second step', self-management and the loosening of the Party's hold on the enterprise, was not of central importance. The union did not have sufficient competent people to replace the *nomenklatura* in the enterprise, and in any case self-management 'isn't Solidarity, it's another movement'. This extreme view was later accepted by the whole group; it shows the degree to which the economic actor inherent in the institutions of self-management was seen as external to the movement.

Like Józef at Wrocław (Figure 10), Andrzej even proposed to reverse the representation which had been put forward by the researchers. Instead of seeing the movement ascending the steps of the staircase, he said, one should start at the top: 'Without the third step, it's impossible to speak about the first and second', and in the same way the third could not be conceived without the fourth. The movement's meaning lay in its consciousness and its convictions, and they knew no limits, but the movement began its action from the bottom and limited itself.

At this stage, the group was firmly installed on the third step of our diagram. But did it conceive this step in terms of negotiation and agreement? Everything pointed to the fact that the group felt impelled towards rupture, or even that it actively sought confrontation. But in fact that was not the case. As soon as the discussion took as its starting point the idea that the point of rupture was not far off, Kazimierz said that he was strongly in favour of a national consensus being reached between Archbishop Glemp, General Jaruzelski and Lech Wałęsa. He even thought that it was time to silence the impulsive elements who had started the movement, and that they should hand over to more 'moderate' people. Agreement with the Party was urgent. Alojzy was convinced that the Party had no other choice but national consensus, and the group seemed to agree.

Very precise proposals were made, not without a touch of irony: the PUWP should be allowed to stand in free elections, said Alojzy; those Party members with some technical qualifications should remain in the government, suggested Andrzej; why not leave the Party with responsibility for the Ministries of Defence and Foreign Affairs, asked Ryszard and Andrzej, who thought it only fair that the Party should be in charge of relations with Moscow: 'Let them sort it out on their own . . .' The discussion showed that there was a real desire to work out a formula which would guarantee the democratisation of political life while leaving the Party with an honourable way out. The group was, then, very far from wanting rupture.

Reversal

It even sought agreement with the Party. When it met one of the Party leaders, who was admittedly a liberal, it began by attacking the Party's mistakes and its autocracy. Then it suddenly adopted a conciliatory tone with its interlocutor. Alojzy, who up to then had been highly critical of the Party, was the originator of this reversal, which was followed by the whole group. He asked whether meetings should not be arranged between people of goodwill. Andrzej, having noticed that the interlocutor was sympathetic to the idea of self-management, began a very detailed discussion with him which showed that on this precise point, some agreement was possible. Kazimierz, overwhelmed by the interlocutor's commitment to democracy, joined with him in the evocation of Poland as a second Japan, a dream dear to Wałęsa. In short, the atmosphere was one of 'Poles speaking to Poles' and the tone was almost one of euphoria; the group had just shown how passionately it wanted agreement with the Party. It no longer approached the Utopian need for a juster society exclusively through pure conviction: it was prepared to reason in terms of processes and institutional mediations. Once again, it had moved away from the rank-and-file populism which had dominated the early part of its life as a group.

The Łódź group was now very different from its initial image. It had left populism far behind, and rejected all appeals for nationalist rupture. Genowefa, who had dominated the early sessions, was now isolated, but she tried once more to lead the group towards a rejection of all compromise with the regime: 'Just think about the PUWP's patriotism. It never has existed and never will exist.' Anna seemed at first to support her, but she quickly added: 'National consensus is necessary. Agreement between the Church, the authorities and Solidarity is our only hope of avoiding a catastrophe. We must use all our desire for the destruction of this regime as a means of pressure to force the enemy to negotiate with us.' The active strike was not an end in itself, but a tool in the hands of the movement, whose action therefore fell short of being revolutionary. 'There will be active strike after active strike to back our negotiators', said Ewa; but there was no question of seizing power and taking the place of the state.

161

What had the impressive hunger march of the previous summer been like? Genowefa had taken part in it. She said that she had thought of the children who went hungry when she was sure there were stocks of butter and sugar in official buildings, and if she had had a child she might have set fire to the Party's committee offices. But she was the only one to adopt such a tone. Anna said that the MKZ had organised the march as a 'necessary evil', a means of resisting the desire for rupture which spread through the movement as the regime's attitude reduced the hope of successful negotiations. 'They're trying to force us to seek a break', said Alojzy, 'they're forcing us' to accept the responsibility of being an alternative centre of power. This idea was widespread in the group: everyone rejected the crisis behaviour which would be the result of rupture.

We are very far, here, from the image of war between two implacable enemies. The group sought a political solution through negotiation with the regime, and did not really imagine that the latter could resort to any other solution. Mistrust of the authorities was real and deep, but the group doubted whether the state could rely on simple violence. The army was on the side of the people and society, and Solidarity's membership was so massive that the prisons simply could not hold all the people who would have to be arrested for the movement to be paralysed. The group did not want rupture, and did not even conceive of it, and its initial populist discourse disappeared when agreement with the authorities became a feasible possibility. When that prospect became more distant, the actor withdrew into himself, into defensive discourse; when it became clearer again, the group declared itself ready to take some responsibility for the country's economic problems and to take part in the construction of political democracy. Never, even in a position of withdrawal, did the group envisage the use of violence.

In this way, positions which seemed at first to lead directly to rupture in fact led the group to two alternative positions of a very different kind: hope for a negotiated solution, and withdrawal back to the radical discontent of the rank and file. More directly than in the spring, the movement affirmed that the struggle had no limit other than the democratisation of society and the independence of the country; but, just as consciously as in the spring, it refused confrontation and accepted that the results achieved fell short of its ultimate desires. The movement remained doubly radical by virtue of its long-term aims and its rejection of the regime, but its action was not revolutionary.

WROCŁAW

The history of the Wrocław group, like that of the Łódź group, gives us some insight into Solidarity's evolution during the last phase of its legal existence.

Radicalism and compromise

In both cases there was a strong upsurge of nationalism and of ideologies of workers' control, and this was particularly pronounced in Silesia. The radicalisation of attitudes is clear, but was this likely to lead to confrontation? Did the militants seek rupture? From the very beginning, the Wrocław group was dominated by violent nationalism, but after many conflicts and long reflection, it moved beyond such reactions and finally defined a course of action very different from its original positions.

Nationalism and workers' power

Here, as elsewhere, the idea of self-management was on the wane. In the spring it had been a progressive step forward, but now it represented a moderate and defensive position. Only one member of the group, who was in charge of the self-management committee at his enterprise, still held to the point of view which had been defended by Andrzej and Grzegorz in Warsaw. The desire to share in the management of the enterprise was now less strong than the urge to drive the Party from the enterprise and from the economy as a whole. Rather than liberating society and rebuilding economic institutions, the militants wanted to be amongst their own and to be rid of this foreign body, the Party and its *nomenklatura*. This was admittedly the principal meaning of the idea of self-management in the first phase of our research, but now the tone was more conflictual. Many workers spoke of the fights they had had with a factory or department manager, and their tone was the same as that of the miners from the Katowice group, two of whom came to spend a day with the group. Everyone wanted a truly working-class movement, and complained of useless office workers and state administrators, and of incompetent managers whose criteria in making decisions were purely political. On the other hand they got on well with an enterprise manager who came to talk to them, who had been appointed because of his technical competence and was not the Party candidate for the job. The group was perfectly ready to accept that this interlocutor state his beliefs: he was a member of the Party and intended to remain so, above all because he was the son of a militantly atheist doctor, was himself anti-religious and believed in progress through science and technology. Once again it was confirmed that the rejection of the hegemony of the Party did not in the least exclude an ability on the part of the militants to accept Party members and to envisage cooperation between Solidarity and the Party in the enterprise, provided that professional and economic criteria came first and that the rest was considered to be a matter of private opinion.

In a situation of serious economic crisis, Solidarity members acted first and foremost as workers and wage-earners. But it was the government and the Party whom they considered responsible for the collapse of production.

163

This falling back upon the working-class base was not only an expression of the conflict between the producers and the *nomenklatura*; it was also a powerful expression of the fundamental opposition between the interests and feelings of the people and their masters. The life of the group was dominated by its rejection of the Party and its violent hostility towards the Soviet Union. And when the researchers introduced the idea that Solidarity was made up of three elements – trade unionism, democracy and national feeling – which were interdependent and of equal importance, several members of the group proposed changes. Three new images of the movement were suggested.

All three tended to reduce the importance of the democratic dimension and to place national feeling in a central position. In the first case, trade unionism and democratic concerns were seen simply as pockets within an essentially national movement; in the second, the movement was simultaneously totally working class and totally national in character, defined, in other words, by the twin popular realities of work and national identity: here, the democratic dimension was only introduced afterwards, and it remained peripheral. The third image was a variation on the first: the trade-union and democratic elements were partly subsumed under the national dimension, but their partial autonomy was also recognised. Such representations of the movement would have been inconceivable at Gdańsk and Warsaw, and even at Katowice, where the second would have been more easily accepted, the democratic theme was of more importance.

Similarly, the group modified the images of the movement's evolution which had been proposed by the Warsaw group. As we have seen, the Grzegorz theory (Figure 9) saw the movement rising by stages from the recognition of free trade unions, through the establishment of self-management in the enterprise and general economic reform, towards the restoration of national independence. The Wrocław group preferred the Józef theory (Figure 10), which reversed the above view and maintained that the movement's principal aim, from the very start, had been national independence, which, regressing down the ladder, in turn presupposed free elections, political democratisation, and the democratisation of the economy; the creation of free trade unions had been a first step. In this sense, the Wrocław group agreed with the Łódź group.

At Wrocław, in the autumn of 1981, national consciousness dominated working-class consciousness, relegating the aim of democratisation to a secondary level. Strong words were used: the Party and the regime were nothing but the agents of foreign domination; the Reds ought to have their necks wrung. Some even thought that Poland could leave the Warsaw Pact, and that nothing more serious would happen to it than had happened to France when it left NATO. A referendum had taken place in a local enterprise, and had been much talked of in the region. The results had been published in a factory newsletter under the headline: 'Workers of the world, forgive me. Karl Marx.' Three questions had been asked: should the present *Sejm* be dissolved and a new one elected? Yes: 88%. Should the leading role of the Party be deleted from the Constitution? Yes: 90%. Do you have confidence in Jaruzelski and his government? Yes: 82%. The third answer echoed a survey done in the spring which showed that, apart from the Pope, Wałęsa and Jaruzelski were the most popular figures in Poland. Jaruzelski was seen as a general, a leading figure in the army, which was in itself a powerful national symbol. The approval of Jaruzelski and the rejection of the Party expressed in the other two replies are consistent if they are seen as an affirmation of popular nationalism hostile to the political apparatus of the country.

There is nevertheless ambiguity here. There are echoes of what in France would be called Bonapartism, or even Boulangism,[1] in the simultaneous support for one charismatic figure and rejection, not just of the dictatorship of the Party, but of the whole political and social system. This is part of the widespread popular hostility and disdain towards the 'red' aristocracy, resting above all on a real hatred of the Russians which was part and parcel of opposition to the Party in moderate and extreme militants alike. Several members of the group spoke of the possibility of popular uprisings in the countries living under Soviet domination. For others it was so patently clear that the main conflict was between Poland and the Soviet Union that they counted above all on the Pope, the United States or even West Germany to stop the Russians invading their country. Everyone in fact considered such an invasion a possibility, and most members of the group said that it would result in civil war and a popular struggle against the foreign invader. It was all part of the same problem: if the Party's management of the economy was so scandalously absurd, the reason was that it was the agent of foreign domination. The Party was destroying Polish culture; one of the participants spoke emotionally about the destruction of crosses and other religious symbols in the countryside and in the factories. One went as far as to conclude: 'The Party wanted to turn the Poles into Russians.'

'True' Poles

This nationalism had been present in the Gdańsk, Warsaw and Katowice groups, but never with the same violence and never so centrally. The miners from Katowice worked with the Wrocław group for a day, and their tone was more political, more concerned with the democratisation of

---

1 Georges Boulanger (1837–1891): a charismatic French general who, between 1886 and 1889, provided a somewhat nationalistic focus for popular discontent with Republicanism. (Tr.)

institutions. It was at Wrocław that the voice of those who called themselves the 'true Poles' was heard most clearly. Militants from the town's transport system and an electrician from a firm supplying the railways violently expressed their rejection of the entire political system and their desire for rupture, even dismissing the majority of Solidarity's leaders as bureaucrats and politicians, although Wałęsa escaped such condemnation. One of them attacked both the KOR and the idea of the active strike. We are at war, he said, and Solidarity must demand of its members the same discipline which an army would. When the group met one of the leading figures in the MKZ of Lower Silesia, the transport workers attacked him with great violence, reminding him that the MKZ had not supported them when they were on strike and criticising his admittedly strong attacks on Wałęsa. Another of the 'true Poles' would have liked to see all political parties done away with in order for Solidarity to take power. Even those who disagreed with this extreme minority recognised that union members in general were becoming more radical. But, here more than elsewhere, this development did not represent a greater degree of politicisation; on the contrary, it was an intolerant, populist appeal to rank-and-file identity, fuelled by economic difficulties, the absolute loss of faith in the country's leaders and the fear of foreign intervention. Even the moderates admitted that more and more of their energy was taken up by immediate material tasks, above all the obtaining of food, and that as a result they were being drawn away just as much as the 'true Poles' from grand plans for the democratic transformation of society.

The violence of these feelings led to a rupture in the group. After their confrontation with the Solidarity leader, the two transport workers stopped coming to the group, despite our repeated insistence and their promise to do so. They seemed to want to shut their minds to everything but a defensive struggle within the enterprise, and to have nothing to do with a general reflexion on the movement's aims and forms of action. In fact they had broken with the movement, as the serious confrontations which took place at the same time between 'true Poles' and the union leadership in Kraków and especially in Warsaw showed. But their extreme behaviour must not lead us to conclude that the ideas which they held were those of a minority. At Bielsko-Biała we witnessed the split within the Presidium of the MKZ between the president, who was extremely nationalist, and another group, concerned to maintain a democratic orientation more in tune with the movement as a whole. In Upper Silesia, the president of the MKZ, representing more than a million workers, also defended very nationalist positions. Finally, the expressed opinions of the president of the Szczecin MKZ, Jurczyk, a leading figure within the movement, were, as we have already seen, sometimes close to this nationalist, populist and anti-intellectual sensibility.

At the very moment when the Szczecin group manifested forms of radicalisation which in no way represented a rupture with the plans for the democratisation of society in the spirit of Gdańsk, the Wrocław group revealed to us the importance of this working-class nationalism tending more towards rupture than towards negotiation, and towards the defence of the interests of the people rather than the reconstruction of society. At the end of the third day of work, the group was asked to reply to a questionnaire which had been devised a few months earlier by Solidarity's Research Centre, but which we had slightly modified at the suggestion of the group. The questionnaire asked respondents to class the aims of Solidarity in order of decreasing importance. Everybody, with one exception (the transport workers were no longer taking part), put national independence first, followed by the defence of workers' interests. Economic reform and self-management came significantly lower down the list, and were seen as having roughly the same importance as the restoration of national history and freedom of the press. Negotiation within the workplace, the central aim of Western-style trade unionism, was considered least important by the whole group. The main tendency of the group must, then, be seen as popular nationalism with an element of workers' control. We should, however, add that the most extreme nationalism was expressed by men whose professional level was above the average, while the two women members of the group put more stress on immediate popular demands.

Caution

Such feelings would suggest that the group might tend to demand of Solidarity very militant, perhaps even aggressive action. This was not, however, the case. When it came to defining a course of action, those who were closest to the ideas of the 'true Poles' were somewhat eclipsed by Edward, a moderate within the group, although he was a nationalist to the extent that one would expect of anyone whose father had been killed by the Russians in the Lwów region. He was followed by others when he said that all confrontation must be avoided, that Solidarity was not ready to, and perhaps should not, transform itself into a political force, that the principle of free elections had to be maintained but that they should be postponed until later, and that at the economic level the movement should seek an agreement with the representatives of the Party in order to get industry working again. A former member of the Party, he thought that it was capable of change, and that its complete collapse would inevitably mean foreign invasion. He repeatedly referred to the Helsinki Final Act, and above all appealed to the Church as a political force capable of defending the interests of the Polish people against the Party. He placed his hopes in an alliance between Wałęsa and Archbishop Glemp to resist pressure from Jaruzelski and negotiate with him. He did not convince all his comrades but he was given a hearing. Awareness of conflict did not lead to a desire for confrontation: the main enemy was the Soviet Union or, as the militants said, Russia, and between it and the Polish people it was important to maintain a national political system in which the influence of the Church would act as a counterbalance to that of the Party.

The 'true Poles' tendency and the moderation represented by Edward did not enter into open conflict; but how can one avoid the conclusion that disagreement between the two camps was an indication of a weakening within the movement, of internal struggles and perhaps even of contradictions? These had already been brought into the open by the obvious conflict between the leaders of the transport workers and the MKZ. Later, many members of the group described them more directly. Everyone recognised the waning influence of Wałęsa and of the union's advisers, the latter symbolised by Geremek's failure to gain election to the National Committee. One or two were in favour of a multi-party system being established, with Solidarity returning to a strict role of trade unionism; but the majority were behind Wałęsa, both because he was most representative of rank-and-file feeling and because he was a good negotiator, and they condemned the political ambitions of the many leaders who were prepared to put their own rivalries before the common interests of the movement.

And yet, in the last hours during which it was together, the group insisted on the limits of these divisions. In moments of danger, they said, the union closed ranks. In the spring, during the Bydgoszcz crisis, Wałęsa had been criticised, but the warning strike had been unanimously followed. In the autumn, the national strike of one hour had been massively observed. Asked by the researchers to judge how important their movement would seem to their grandchildren, the members of the group not only stated in simple terms their certainty of the great historical importance of Solidarity, but above all expressed their confidence in the future. They felt that they were being attacked, but they thought that a solution would be found, so convinced were they that the Polish people was united in its resistance to domination, and that its determination was its best protection against external threat. At no point did the group show any fear that Solidarity would be attacked from inside the country. The Party appeared to be disorganised and Solidarity was strong enough, with the help of the Church, to negotiate a compromise with the Party and the government. The meeting between Jaruzelski, Glemp and Wałęsa had not produced any concrete result, but it had taken place, and no one was conscious of rupture, imminent or already decided.

SZCZECIN

Trade unionists and politicians

The starting point of the Łódź and Wrocław groups was a defensive position of a nationalist and popular complexion. The Szczecin group was at once more complex and less defensive. The working-class dimension of the movement remained very much to the fore, which was only to be expected in view of the fact that since 1970 Szczecin had played an extremely important role in workers' struggles. After the repression of that period, clandestine free trade unions had been organised in several enterprises, particularly in the docks and at the Warski shipyard. As a seaport, Szczecin had also maintained relatively free access to information and contacts with the outside world. In August 1980, the Szczecin Agreement had been signed a few hours before the Gdańsk one. It was therefore no surprise to find the workers in the group testifying to this tradition of struggle against a Party defined as the enemy of the working class and of democracy. August 1980 and the Szczecin Agreement were still very present to them: there was strong resistance to a purely defensive action, and a lack of identification with the radicalism of the hunger marches. This predominantly trade-union orientation was not, however, the unanimous position of the group.

Two militants, Krzysztof, a seaman, and Mieczysław, a lawyer in an enterprise, clearly situated themselves within the movement for the liberation of society which is the other side of Solidarity's action. They called for the formation of democratic political parties on a national level. They wanted Solidarity to liberate political life in Poland. Krzysztof wanted to join a socialist party and Mieczysław a party of Christian-democratic sympathies.

The third element within the group was also situated on the political side of the action, but nearer to its defensive pole. The nationalism of Bożena and Luiza, whose families were from the Eastern territories, was particularly uncompromising. The horizon of their struggle was the liberation of Poland, and they made clear that for them, trade unionism and self-management were only steps along a road at the end of which 'Poland will be Poland'. But this nationalism was never entirely dissociated from democratic aspirations, and bore no resemblance to the 'black' nationalism which Party propaganda was keen to denounce, although the same Party tolerated and protected it when it was articulated by the Grunwald group.[2]

The group was conscious of being built around these three poles: on the one hand a social movement, with which the more trade-unionist members of the group identified most strongly, and on the other an action for the liberation of society with its twin orientations of political democracy and community-based nationalism. But the representatives of all three tendencies shared a sense that an impasse had been reached: negotiations were dragging on with little result, strikes in support of local claims were threatening rather than strengthening the movement's unity, and tensions within the movement were on the increase.

---

2 For more information on the Grunwald Patriotic Union, see Ascherson 1981: 268. (Tr.)

Towards rupture

The impossibility of compromise

This was the initial situation into which the researchers injected a new element. One of the researchers, Jan Strzelecki, also an adviser to Solidarity, and Krystosiak, the president of the Szczecin MKZ, proposed to the group that compromise had to be sought and reached. They were critical of the National Committee for opposing such compromise in the name of purity of principle, and so obstructing Wałęsa's work. They defended a policy of negotiation involving the renunciation of unrealistic principles, and called for the movement to give its backing to the leadership. In a dangerous situation, they said, what was needed was the courage to negotiate compromises and then to respect them.

The three tendencies represented in the group reacted differently to these proposals. The more trade-unionist among the members accepted them at first. They believed in a return to the forms of action of August 1980, when working-class mobilisation in the enterprises reinforced the movement's capacity for negotiation and was prepared to accept compromises. They thought that Wałęsa had to be trusted. But at the same time these militants wanted to keep up the pressure on the authorities. They all thought that the rank and file was more radical than them, that the workers were tired of waiting and wanted a general strike, although at the same time the immediate problems of personal survival often meant that they were becoming less mobilised. Even the institutions of self-management were beginning to lose control, with the development of more or less unofficial networks of distribution which only served to exacerbate the disorganis-ation of society and of the economy. Although these militants were in principle in favour of negotiation, they recognised that it was more and more difficult to achieve, and that their own position corresponded less and less to the attitudes of the rank and file, who perceived all compromise as retreat.

As expected, it was the defensive element within the sub-group favouring a movement of social liberation which was most hostile to the point of view put forward by Jan and Krystosiak. Luiza and Bożena fell back on the affirmation of irreconcilable conflict between Poland and a Party represent-ing the interests of the Soviet Union. Their militancy was close to the nationalism of the KPN; they wanted above all to distribute books in the factories, telling the 'true' history of Poland. They recalled the crimes of the Soviet Union, defended the memory of Piłsudski, and painted a picture of irreducible struggle against Soviet domination. The conclusion to which such convictions led was the refusal of compromise, because they defined no political strategy. Luiza and Bożena did not want and were not preparing for confrontation any more than the others; they did not for a moment envisage armed struggle or insurrection, and they realised that their nationalism and their preoccupation with Polish history could only be translated into a capacity for rejection and resistance, and not into action.

Finally, the supporters of non-populist democratic action also criticised the proposed compromise. They wished for negotiations, but said that they would only be made possible by a strengthening of the movement's action. They therefore proposed a general strike, although for them such action was above all an instrument of social and democratic struggle, and for that reason it was rejected by the trade unionists within the group. Here, the reference to August 1980 was absent, and self-management was simply seen as a step towards political struggle. Where the moderate proposals of Jan and Krystosiak had appealed to the movement's general principles, these militants wanted to proceed to free elections so that Poland could become a 'normal' country. Such talk might suggest a revolutionary movement within Solidarity: the intermediary stages have been left out, there is no more room for pretence, the time has come for the final confrontation. And yet, these militants refused to be defined as radicals; they referred to themselves as realists, and the appeal to principles alternated with an awareness of the limits of possible action. Mieczysław and Krzysztof lived simultaneously at two levels: a pragmatic one, and one of principle. The obstacles which the Party put in the way of progress seemed to them so great that they could imagine no form of action which could reconcile these two levels of consciousness. These militants spoke at great length in the group, but never managed to reach a stable position: they constantly oscillated between two poles. The desire for the liberation of society, and the existence of limits to the movement's action, remained unreconciled. Their democratic and national aspirations had been too great for them now to accept a retreat which would leave the Party in control of society, but neither could they set about building a revolutionary force for the seizure of state power.

In short, all three tendencies simultaneously rejected the solution which was put to them and failed to commit themselves to a course of action in direct contradiction to it. The more trade-unionist of the militants seemed to accept compromise, but said at the same time that no one was ready to support it; the more politically minded could only conceive of negotiations on the basis of far more radical positions; and conversely, the nationalists, whom one would have expected to reject any idea of negotiation, sought to avoid rupture. The group was still inspired by the hopes of August 1980, and did not know how to react to a crisis situation. Strictly trade-union action was too limited, it was unrealistic to think of taking power, and the enemy was too hated for the group to trust it to respect any agreement which might be reached.

Fate

As the meetings continued, the group seemed more and more paralysed. Many members felt that they had reached the end of the road. If there was

171

no compromise by February of the following year, said one militant, confrontation would be inevitable because the economic crisis would reach intolerable proportions. But such confrontation was at no point conceived as a seizure of power by Solidarity, and recourse to strikes was only proposed as a means of exerting pressure in favour of negotiations.

The group consistently failed to move beyond judgements to action: the strongest possible pressure had to be applied, but then the aim of such pressure was negotiation, and the enemy was not interested in that. The group rejected confrontation but believed it inevitable because the adversary could not accept compromise. Several members of the group thought that Jaruzelski was already preparing for military rule and was deliberately sabotaging the negotiations. On the other hand, no one called for the movement to prepare for open conflict.

It was as though the group felt that it could not escape the course of history. Wiesław again recalled the repression of 1970, and Krzysztof said that he felt ready to die, but not in some desperate insurrection with a gun in his hand. The group felt that it was being driven towards rupture; but radical statements and the total rejection of the system were not the expression of a revolutionary movement: they reflected, rather, the contradictory feelings of individuals who felt that they were the victims of fate.

A meeting at the Warski shipyard between the researchers and the militants of the workers' council was a last opportunity to throw light on the actors' feeling of paralysis, of having lost control of events and being at the mercy of destiny. The self-management committee, in the view of its own members, had no reason to exist now that the Party no longer dominated the enterprise, since no real decisions could be taken without economic reform. The militants accepted the representation of the movement progressing upwards through the liberation of the trade union, the enterprise and the economic system as a whole, but they did not believe that the Party could accept compromise at the highest of these three levels. They too felt that repression was on the way, and could find no political strategy to set against it. No one thought that a military coup was imminent, but when the militants took us back to where we were staying that November night, it was clear that in their eyes the movement was close to rupture. They rejected a strategy of violence and civil war, but at the same time they spoke with Jan Strzelecki, who was older than them, of the people who had fought in the Warsaw Rising for the working class, for national independence and for democratic freedoms.

CONCLUSIONS

As we leave the groups, we must ask whether the general hypotheses concerning the nature of Solidarity around which this book is built take adequate account of the diversity of the groups and of the debates which took place within them. It is relatively easy to show that Solidarity is on the one hand a workers' movement and on the other a national one; neither is it difficult to demonstrate how the movement manages to integrate and unify its widely differing elements. But it is far harder to justify the pertinence of the hypotheses which we have put forward, and to show that all the tendencies which are present in Solidarity at different times and in different places, make up a coherent whole, defined as all the possible combinations of the action's component elements. Here the national aspect is foremost, and there it is the trade-union element; at one moment defensive reactions are stronger, and then plans for a social or political offensive become dominant. In each case, the reasons for these differences must be found, and the explicative value of such notions demonstrated.

Ideally, we would have set up a larger number of research groups. Nevertheless, in our meetings with militants in other towns, we did not identify any themes or reactions which were not present in our formal research groups. It is, admittedly, possible to find within Solidarity more narrowly economist and more purely nationalist tendencies; but it is not coincidental that these played a minor role in the movement.

Before proceeding to a general interpretation of each group, let us briefly recall the three principal ideas which have guided the research up to this point.

The first is that Solidarity is simultaneously and indissociably a trade union, a democratic and a national movement. If just one of these elements disappears or becomes separated from the others, the movement will disintegrate and its capacity for action collapse.

The second is that Solidarity is at the same time a social movement and an agent of the liberation of society, seeking to restore autonomy to civil life. The liberation of society involves free elections, universal freedom of expression, and proper management of industry. This distinction between the two sides of the movement's action leads us to see its evolution in three phases. At first Solidarity is a social movement founded on the hopes generated by the success of the Baltic strikes; then the social movement combines with the movement for the liberation of civil society, and the result is a greater emphasis on reform of the enterprise and the economy, implying in turn change in the *Sejm*. In its third phase, carried forward by its own momentum but driven on also by the worsening economic and political crisis, Solidarity enters more directly into the political field, proposing institutional reform and even broaching the question of political power within the state. Our analysis shows the difference in atmosphere between the spring and the autumn of 1981, and sees this as a progression from what we have called Solidarity I, through Solidarity II to Solidarity III.

Finally, this distinction between the two sides of the movement must be combined with a distinction between two different tones, one more defensive, tending to fall back on the affirmation of the collective identity and rights of the social actor, and the other more offensive, aiming to transform given situations. Combining these two sets of distinctions, we arrive at the four main tendencies described at the end of Chapter 2. The following table sets them out clearly:

	Social movement	Liberation of society
Defensive action	workers' control (1)	defensive populism (3)
Counter-offensive action	spirit of Gdańsk (2)	political democracy (4)

The first tendency is close to revolutionary trade unionism. Its base is a truly working-class movement which sometimes retreats to a purely economic defence of the workers but more often affirms the complete rupture between the working class and the political and economic regime which dominates it. The second is more faithful to the spirit of Gdańsk: it unites a strong social movement and the desire to obtain the legal and political conditions for trade-union freedom. The third tendency is diametrically opposed to the second. We have often referred to it as populist, not in the sense which the term has taken on in Russian, North American or Latin American history, but in the sense which was commonly attributed to the term in our groups: the defence of ordinary people against the bigwigs, of the rank and file against the leadership, with workers' control and nationalist tendencies which are exaggerated in the case of the 'true Poles'. The final tendency is carried forward by a desire for fundamental change in society: for some, a stable compromise with the Party would suffice; others go further, and seek to disengage Poland, if not from the Soviet empire, at least from Communist society.

The closer a tendency or an individual leader is to the centre of the above table, the greater their influence may be considered to be. Wałęsa, whose dominance was challenged by a significant part of the union's leadership, nevertheless received massive support from the rank and file, because of his peculiarly complex position: he was both the figure-head of the social movement – it was he who defined Solidarity in that way – and the man who negotiated a general agreement with the government; both the working-class leader of the Gdańsk strike and a votary of the Black Madonna.

The richness and complexity which characterise the work of each research group make it impossible to identify each one exclusively with one stage, one form or one tendency. But it is important to show that a limited set of hypotheses can account for a considerable corpus of results, and in that way increase our understanding of the life of each group and the oppositions within it.

We propose therefore to consider in turn each of the three hypotheses which have been outlined above.

In the spring of 1981, there was unanimous agreement that Solidarity was at the same time a trade-union, a democratic and a national movement. The researchers had no difficulty in convincing the groups that this hypothesis should be the starting point of their analysis. At most, the Katowice miners put more stress on the inseparability between their working-class consciousness and their national identity; but if they placed less emphasis on their democratic goals, these nevertheless represented a dimension of their thoughts. The difference between the spring and the autumn was that these elements had separated out, and in some cases entered into opposition with each other. At Wrocław, for instance, a violent nationalism was in conflict with the search for negotiated solutions and a desire for free elections. This group seemed to be pulling simultaneously in various directions, and the same was true, in different ways, of the Łódź and Szczecin groups. This justifies the claim that Solidarity drew its strength from the fusion of its three dimensions. A purely nationalist movement would not be stronger, would not concentrate everyone's energies in one direction; on the contrary, it would become isolated and weak, whereas the specificity of Solidarity is that it is a movement of the whole nation, bringing together ten million Poles who share neither the same political opinions, nor the same professional interests, nor even similar conceptions of the movement's proper relationship with the Party and the Soviet Union.

Solidarity's evolution may be seen as the transformation of a social movement into a movement for the liberation of society, passing through an intermediary phase dominated by the idea of self-management, conceived in both trade-unionist and political terms. This view enables us to situate the groups in relation to each other, although it must not be seen as a stable and definitive interpretation: each group had to manage the sometimes difficult relations between the respective preoccupations of these three phases. The Szczecin and Gdańsk groups, understandably attached to the agreements which had been signed in their respective cities, had great difficulty in moving on to a subsequent phase, particularly as the agreements were far from having been implemented. In these groups, the failure to proceed regularly from one stage to the next created increasing tensions between the original social movement and the inevitable step into politics which many members resisted and which as a result took extremely radical forms.

The miners of Katowice were more attached than any other group to a pure social movement, and this was their strength. But it was also the cause

175

of the tensions which increasingly plagued the group: the shared class consciousness led some to seek compromise with the Party to avoid politicisation of the struggle, while it led others to a total rejection of the regime.

The Łódź and Wrocław groups took a clear step forward into political action, despite the resistance of a few moderates; but the price which was paid was a considerable weakening, of which the groups were conscious. Had not Solidarity's strength from the very beginning been the fact that it operated outside the Party's territory rather than seeking to invade it, and therefore appealed to a legitimacy completely separate from the Party? If the movement were to define itself primarily by reference to its hostility to the Soviet Union, would it not be putting its very existence at risk? The Warsaw group was more conscious of these problems, so much so that it had some reservations about the idea that the movement passed through three successive phases. It recognised that the movement's logic was a de-mocratic one, but never abandoned the idea that such political action must remain linked to the movement's trade-union activity.

With these remarks we are already entering the third part of these conclusions. Does the notion that the life of Solidarity is constituted by the relations between four main tendencies help to throw light on the internal debates within the groups and the differences between them?

Not all the groups contained all four tendencies, but neither was any one group totally identifiable with one tendency alone. The work of the six groups considered as a whole may be seen as a general process of discussion and debate centred on the four tendencies. Two tendencies stand out as being stronger than the others, and the opposition between them was the central axis of discussion: the spirit of Gdańsk and defensive populism. The latter was relatively weak in the spring, but by the autumn it had made up a lot of ground. The idea of workers' control, which was firmly rooted in Silesia, must finally be seen as closer to the spirit of Gdańsk than to defensive nationalism; and the aspiration for political democracy, because it never took a revolutionary form, can easily be recognised as a desire to extend the Gdańsk Agreement.

The Gdańsk group for a long time defined its goals in the formula: the agreements, all the agreements and nothing but the agreements. But there then began a slow process of disintegration, each element of the action becoming stronger and more autonomous: some members became more political, while others fell back on a programme of specifically trade-union action.

In the case of the Katowice miners, there was a spontaneous integration of all the movement's tendencies around a strong sense of community identity and the idea of workers' control. But some saw this as a political programme, whereas for others it was closely related to the idea of revolutionary workers' councils. There was never any direct expression of defensive populism, for the group was consistently carried beyond such a position by its desire for trade-union independence, which had the effect of directing it towards democratic action. After the declaration of martial law, this spirit of community was to be the basis for the miners' resistance to the military takeover of the mines, carried out courageously and at considerable cost.

By the autumn, the Łódź and Wrocław groups had become much more defensive, falling back on an affirmation of working-class and national identity. Some of the members even identified with extreme forms of nationalism. The spirit of the Gdańsk Agreement was already further away, and the desire for democratic action had more difficulty in finding expression. These groups were inclined to identify with one tendency alone, and this weakened their capacity for action. The movement now seemed to be losing its grip on what had given it its strength and its faith: its only definition of itself was by reference to an enemy which it knew it could not defeat, with the result that it did nothing more than hope for a compromise which, if it came, would have disappointed the groups' real aspirations. These groups were aware that they were losing the initiative and that the only role left for them was one of protest.

At Szczecin, on the other hand, the spirit of August 1980 was still very much alive; but at the same time the other tendencies were more in evidence than they had been a few months previously in the Gdańsk group, and were simply juxtaposed. There was no longer any synthesis between the different orientations. The group was conscious that it was no longer in control of the situation, and its response was to fall back on the spirit of Solidarity at its birth, which in no way corresponded to the circumstances of autumn 1981. The affirmation of the principles of August 1980 had turned to nostalgia; it was with great pessimism that the workers of the Szczecin group recognised the growing gap between their hopes and a social crisis whose dramatic consequences they foresaw.

The Warsaw group was the one which took furthest Solidarity's progression from a social movement to a movement for the liberation of society. But it was never prepared to set political action against trade-union action, which is why it established itself more firmly than the other groups on the ground which we have defined as Solidarity II, represented here by a central concern with the reform of industry and the creation of self-management committees. The position of the Warsaw group at the centre of the movement's constellation explains the weakness of its analyses at the beginning, when the object of analysis was Solidarity I, and the weakness which it showed again in the autumn, when it had to realise that its hopes had been disappointed. But it proved extremely strong in the early summer, when it met the Gdańsk and Katowice groups. At that point it was clear that all its different elements tended to come together in a broad conception of self-management, both trade-unionist and political in character.

This brief recapitulation has, we hope, at least served to show the usefulness of our hypotheses: however different were the circumstances in the spring and the autumn of 1981, and however diverse were the groups, they all belonged to the same movement. The parameters within which they worked were those of Solidarity as a whole: a movement representing the nation and the working class in the face of a common enemy, and which attempted to avoid the twin danger of confrontation and retreat in its search for democratic solutions to the crisis of society and government.

ᴠᴠᴠ

Resistance

BEYOND THE LIMITS?

As we have seen, the image of a movement mounting one by one the steps of a staircase leading to national independence was the source of much discussion in our research groups. We must now attempt to come to some conclusions about Solidarity's historical evolution. Does this image reflect the reality? Did the movement gradually cease to limit itself?

The three limits to its action which Solidarity had set itself were: the leading role of the Party in the state, which was explicitly guaranteed in the Gdańsk Agreement; Poland's place in the Eastern bloc; and finally, trade-union demands were to be moderated in order to take account of the economic crisis. At the movement's Congress, the first of these limits seemed to be exploded: the union's declared aims of organising free elections to the *Sejm* and obtaining normal democratic access to the media were a challenge to the Party's leading role.

These aims were unanimously approved, but they do not signal an end to the movement's self-limiting function. Firstly, there was no question of making Solidarity into a dominant political force which would use the elections to seize power from the PUWP. On the contrary, there was a readiness to seek a formula reconciling the democratisation of public life with the preservation of the Party's leading role. The movement wanted an end to the Party's monopoly of public life, but did not lose sight of the fact that there came a point beyond which enormous problems would arise. The movement consciously pushed its action to the limits, but it did not really go beyond them, for it met an insurmountable obstacle in its way. Secondly, nothing was done to put into practice the movement's democratic plans. Solidarity spoke of a referendum and of the possibility of taking the initiative with the creation of certain institutions to replace official ones, but it never acted on these proposals. As for those who considered that the time had come to undertake political action, they met outside Solidarity in political groups and clubs the existence of which had been known for months; it had been predicted for a long time that these groups would transform themselves into political parties, but this hardly occurred, if at all.

The two other limits which the movement had internalised were questioned even less. Nationalism had indeed become stronger in Solidarity, and anti-Soviet discourse was more frequent and more explicit; but this was talk which hardly became translated into action, and those who wanted priority to be given to nationalist political action did so outside the movement, going to swell the ranks of the KPN. Finally, on the economic front, Solidarity never doubted the need for economic reform the result of which would be considerable sacrifices on the part of the workers, and the attitude of the leadership in consistently calling for the avoidance of local strikes of an economic nature was clearly perceived by the rank and file.

So the movement continued until the very end to be torn between its principles and its praxis, between a set of far-reaching aims and a reality which imposed limits which it was unthinkable to overstep. In certain cases these tensions gave rise to spectacular reversals of attitude. At the beginning of October 1981, Jacek Kuroń repeated that the idea of free elections seemed to him premature and dangerous, and at the time he was practically alone in such moderation. A month later he was the founder of a political club one of whose immediate aims was to put up candidates in the local and regional elections and thereby to impose, by its very presence, a degree of political pluralism. This extreme case clearly shows the immense space covered by the movement, which continued to exercise a self-limiting function but which was condemned to living in permanent tension between its desires and the real possibilities open to it.

THE REJECTION OF CONFRONTATION

At every level there came a time when the movement was aware that the authorities had chosen the trial of strength rather than negotiation. Even Lech Wałęsa, who could never be accused of not having sought agreement by all possible routes, said that confrontation was now on, but that there could be no question of the movement allowing itself to be led into 'areas of confrontation which are not of our choice'. Like its leader, the movement was now seemingly paralysed: like it or not, it now faced an enemy who sought confrontation. On 2 December, for the first time since the creation of Solidarity, the authorities used force to stop a strike: the cadets of the Warsaw Fire Officers' School were evicted by the police in a spectacular operation. After the first reactions had died down, there was consternation in Solidarity. Wałęsa declared a 'state of extreme emergency', but asked everyone to wait for instructions from the Presidium.

The union leadership met at Radom on 3 December. Many of them were aware that a response based on legalism and a refusal to resort to violence might be interpreted as a sign of hesitation and inability to act. Wałęsa was against the idea of a general strike, but with the leader facing a confrontation which he did not want, proposals for the first time began to emerge suggesting that the movement should prepare for direct military or political action. Pałka, from Łódź, proposed the creation of workers' militias; Bujak, from Warsaw, suggested that 'a sort of provisional government' be established, and Rulewski, from Bydgoszcz, added a proposal for elections. After a night of discussion the leadership published a statement taking note of the regime's refusal to conclude a national agreement and making clear the union's intention of calling a twenty-four hour general strike in the event of Parliament giving the government emergency powers.

But these words were not to be acted upon, and in reality the movement's leaders continued to resist the revolutionary tendencies which the situation only helped to reinforce. While the movement threatened strike action, Wałęsa twice visited Archbishop Glemp to examine the possibility of compromise with the authorities.

On Friday 11 and Saturday 12 December, the National Committee met at Gdańsk. Resolutions were passed indicating a real hardening of attitudes on the part of Solidarity. But there was still no question of the movement imposing its demands by force: the idea was rather to show that the demands which the government was refusing to negotiate echoed the desires of the whole country. Up to the very end, the movement refused to constitute itself as an actor seeking to take power: rather, it proposed a referendum on the government's record, economic reform and the principle of free elections, as a way of showing the legitimacy of its demands. The Committee approved in principle a 'day of national protest against the use of violence in social conflicts', a last reminder of the movement's desire to find negotiated solutions.

It also passed a resolution calling for strike action in the event of the *Sejm* giving the government emergency powers, and as a response to any 'obstruction of the union's elected representative bodies'. So there was no question of preparing for violent action or clandestine military resistance; no one behaved as though a police operation was imminent, despite all the signs pointing in that direction which began to appear in Gdańsk from about midday on Saturday 12 December. That night, most of the leaders in Gdańsk for the meeting of the Committee were arrested. To the bitter end, they had acted as members of a social movement which repudiated violence.

Quite unlike a revolutionary organisation, the workings of Solidarity were always based on a principle of transparence and open discussion. How could it have prepared illegal operations when its meetings were always held openly? In the face of a regime operating in the secrecy of 'democratic centralism' and basing its power on repression and the closed, centripetal structure of the apparatus, Solidarity, ten million strong and knowing its own moral strength, took its concern with the forms of legality almost to extremes. Faced with a totally undemocratic system, it lived within itself the democracy which it wanted for the whole of society. The movement's foundations were an ethic of conviction and a thirst for internal democracy, and it was incapable of military action. Incapable even of conceiving it, of thinking it possible: looking back, one is struck by the movement's inability, despite all the signs of imminent police intervention, to hear the sound of jackboots. When a movement does not think in terms of the seizure of state power, it does not imagine that those who hold that power might wish to destroy it, even if it is aware of their totalitarian ambition and has no confidence in them.

This is typically the behaviour of social actors whose motivations are fundamentally ethical and who take no precautions against the use of force by their enemies. A further dimension was the fact that the militants were convinced that the Polish army would never fire on the Polish people, and that, since many policemen wanted to join Solidarity, the police as a whole might be on their side. At Łódź, the vice-president of the union's regional organisation, Kropiwnicki, developed this idea in some detail, and the group agreed with him. He even added that, according to the union's calculations, the government simply did not have the means to impose a state of war. He has since received a heavy prison sentence. A movement for the liberation of society and a social movement, Solidarity was not prepared for what happened, and had no resistance ready. The first reaction of those who escaped the roundups and arrests was to organise a defence movement still dominated by the spirit of Solidarity. In a strike call issued by five of the movement's leaders on 14 December, they urged the movement to 'show discipline and strength, respect state property and avoid as much as possible any confrontation with the security forces. Our weapons are composure, honour, and organisation in the factories.' Before and after the coup, free or outlawed, in its strength and in its weaknesses, Solidarity stands for democracy.

DEMOCRATIC MOVEMENT OR REVOLUTIONARY STRUGGLE?

To the question whether Solidarity increasingly became a revolutionary movement, our answer has consistently been a negative one. A social movement, and more precisely a trade-union movement, Solidarity had a defensive side which, as we have seen, sometimes led to a more or less populist radicalism, and a more offensive side whose aim was the restoration of democratic institutions. In neither case did Solidarity seek to take over power within the state.

As a social movement, Solidarity did indeed go beyond the defence of workers' interests, fighting for the recognition of free trade unions and the acceptance by the Party of the legal and political conditions for their existence; but it never called on the working class to seize power. As a movement for the liberation of society, it sometimes sought to negotiate overall social change, and sometimes fell back on a rank-and-file, nationalist populism, charged with a desire for rupture but remaining more defensive than offensive. Again, in neither case were revolutionary proclamations heard. We certainly did encounter militants who were organising the independent distribution of consumer goods within the factory and others who were in favour of the active strike. More generally, in a country which was increasingly disorganised, a growing number of situations arose in which unofficial centres of power were established, and some leaders even let it be known that they were happy to encourage this. But this tendency was nearly always a result of the crisis rather than the product of political will. It was a response to the material needs of the moment or a means of forcing the authorities to undertake negotiations which everyone, or almost everyone, wanted to see succeed. Actions which seemed to imply a situation of dual authority or of rupture should be interpreted as crisis behaviour or a means of channelling the population's growing exasperation, and not as the beginnings of insurrection.

Immediately after the military takeover, some radical militants locked themselves in their factories or occupied their mines. They had known that confrontation was approaching, but they had done little to prepare for it. If the meaning of their action had been to seize power, they would have taken the initiative rather than waiting for it to come from others; at the very least, their reply would have been organised in advance, they would have planned a counter-offensive, prepared to occupy public buildings, and organised some kind of underground action. But after the declaration of martial law their manifest intention throughout the country was to define themselves as social actors in a movement which was the victim of repression, and not to situate themselves in the field of confrontation with the army or the police. Their strike was an act of unarmed resistance, not of insurrection. These workers were convinced that the terms of the social crisis in which they were involved were work and production, and that their opponents thought in the same terms; they did not know, or did not want to know, that a regime which exists through total domination of the state thinks first and foremost in terms of order and control.

But, some will say, Solidarity sought to liberate society. Under the cover of a new rhetoric replacing the outworn vocabulary, was this not still a revolutionary project? Once again, the reply must be categorically negative. Solidarity wanted to impose the democratisation of the country's social and political life, and a loosening of the state's grip on society; it never sought to take over the state. It wanted to see the opening up of areas of negotiation and social relation, and the emergence, especially through self-management, of social actors other than itself with whom it could negotiate, debate and, if necessary, enter into conflict.

The movement's strategy could have been to try to impose this liberation of society by means of immediate political action directed towards seizing control of the state. But what did it do? It consistently put all its efforts into the search for agreement with the authorities. More than that, it was prepared to accept a share of the responsibility for economic reforms, which, in exchange for political guarantees, would have meant that the workers faced a series of sacrifices and austerity measures.

Not only did Solidarity never take the slightest initiative in suggesting that its aim was the seizure of power; it constantly tried to restrain the political forces which from time to time seemed to be moving in that direction. How many times did the militants or the leaders of the movement take steps to channel protest which might have developed into insurrectional riots, or bring all their influence to bear in order to stop street demonstrations of a directly political character? At the same time, Solidarity consistently acted as a guarantor of freedom of expression, defending political prisoners whose beliefs were very different from its own, and doing so on a strictly legal basis. Moreover, the movement was always mistrustful of its own political militants. The KOR itself was often misunderstood, and its image within the movement was often a negative one: many militants believed that it was a political avant-garde trying to draw the workers into an alien political project.

Solidarity, then, was unable to define itself as an actor preparing to take over control of the state or to engage in military or political conflict with the state authorities, and was therefore constantly torn between the demands of strategy and those of its own democratic workings. Each time that authoritarian decisions were taken by Solidarity leaders in response to an emergency, whatever the justification of those decisions, the way in which they were taken met with violent criticism.

CONVICTIONS

The Polish nation, for so long denied a state of its own, and nowadays estranged from the regime which is maintained in the country by the international balance of power, is used to expressing its national destiny in more than purely political terms. It defines itself both by its culture and by the affirmation that the rights of the nation go beyond those of any state. Hence the constant distance in Solidarity between the movement and its action. It is true that Solidarity tended more and more to become a movement for the liberation of society fighting for self-management, against censorship and ultimately for free elections; but it is even more important to see that these aims did not absorb all the movement's energy. Solidarity was always more than these aims, however important they were. It represented hope and resistance; it never appealed to some notion of objective necessity, but always to a collective will based on justice and whose strength lay in the responsibility and sense of sacrifice of each of its members.

To articulate its opposition to an authoritarian state, such a movement may resort to notions of theocratic authority, or become the intolerant and terrorist expression of a sense of national community; or it may decide to recreate the foundations of democracy, that is to say of political representation. If Solidarity was democratic rather than traditionalist and theocratic, the reason is that it succeeded in defining the cultural stakes of a social struggle. It fought for modernisation and economic growth in a society which is fully engaged in the process of industrialisation, and its opponent is a government representing a ruling class, a political oligarchy and a foreign power, and whose programme of industrialisation has failed. The values to which Solidarity appealed were not a religious faith and a sense of community, but economic rationality, social justice and political freedom. There is a danger that the political and military dictatorship at present ruling Poland may succeed in forcing the popular movement to retreat to a traditionalist and religious defence of community values which up to now has been the position of only a very small minority. It is however a relatively minor danger. Thirty years of Communist rule have not prevented the Poles from creating a democratic movement, and have even encouraged them to do so: their opponent was a regime wishing to remain in exclusive and absolute control, with the result that in Poland the workers' social movement could not be separated from a struggle against totalitarianism seeking to establish the rights of individuals, social groups and the national society as a whole.

The people who organised the free trade unions and the self-management committees knew that they were carrying on, by different means, the work of the rebels of the past, primarily of those who fought and died in the Warsaw Rising of 1944, at the same time as they were avenging their comrades killed at Poznań in 1956 and at Szczecin, Gdynia and Gdańsk in 1970. Solidarity brought to life the collective memory of the nation: everywhere monuments were erected to remind Poland of its struggle and its glory. When a people is subject to the traditional masters of the land and of money, its will to act is symbolised by the creation of a state which will unify and liberate. When, on the other hand, it is dominated and exploited by a state which speaks in the name of science, history and even society, and which is a modernising as well as an authoritarian force, then the liberation movement fights for the survival of the national culture and national liberties. Far from identifying with a programme of political solutions, the people seeks to limit the hegemony of the authorities, and to expand the area, at present restricted to private life, in which convictions may operate. Solidarity was neither a party nor a revolutionary trade union: it was a movement for the liberation of a society and a culture dominated by a state,

185

omnipotent but incapable of ensuring the survival of the nation. It represented a call to responsibility, not to arms, and its hostility to the state was part of its desire to recreate public life. It did not seek power, and it cannot be destroyed by a coup, for its strength lies in its will and in its conviction that it represents the nation and the claims of justice.

Certain observers now believe that Solidarity is dead, and that the resistance networks which are now being organised have little in common with the movement as it was before Jaruzelski's coup. Their mistake is to see the movement as nothing more than an organisation with its offices, its officials, its newspapers and its systems of communication. Others see the events of 13 December as proof of the failure of a method of action, a defeat at the hands of a more skilful opponent. Such people reduce the movement to a political strategy, and it is only a slight exaggeration to say that in their opinion Polish intellectuals and the Church should return to the drawing board and work out a new set of plans to be handed down to the working and peasant masses. Both are wrong. Solidarity was much more than an organisation, and the stakes of the struggle were much more than purely political. The movement would have been unable to integrate the various elements of its action if it had not been inspired above all by its convictions. And these convictions, which amount to an ethic and a profound sense of responsibility, can clearly not have been destroyed simply by police and military repression; they lie within people's consciences, and it is hard to imagine that they will be dispelled by a few weeks, months or even years of dictatorship by the junta.

This sense of conviction means, first of all, that Solidarity is a non-violent actor, and comparisons with the movements inspired by Gandhi in India are tempting. Solidarity has constantly sought to avoid any risk of violent confrontation, and even in the disarray following 13 December 1981, it has continued to place an absolute priority on calls for passive resistance. But non-violence was never a theorised doctrine any more than it was a strategy or a means. It was inherent to the movement, and it proves not only that Solidarity had drawn the necessary conclusions from the bloody rebellion of 1970, but was also sure of the justice of its campaign.

This movement, although many of its members are Catholics, does not appeal to divine justice and bears no trace of mysticism. Its convictions are rooted in the culture of a community and of Christianity, but they are defined even more by opposition to totalitarianism.

This 'ethic of conviction', to use the expression of Max Weber, is socially situated: it is articulated by the working class. Other comparisons come to mind. Like the anarcho-syndicalists, the workers of Solidarity are convinced that a society only exists in and through its work. The workers only need to stop work and call a general strike: production will cease and the regime will fall. But the comparison must not be pushed too far. It is justified to the extent that it reminds us that the society which Solidarity seeks to liberate is one of workers and producers; it is misleading in the sense that the general strike was a reality and not a revolutionary myth.

Solidarity's struggle is responsible as well as just. Every member knows that he or she bears the whole weight of the movement, that personal commitment commits the whole movement, and if almost everyone wears a *Solidarność* badge, it is because they all, in the smallest acts and gestures, act as part of the whole. That is why they accept material shortages which everywhere else would be considered unacceptable: to accept them is to say that one shares in the collective destiny and that one assumes a general responsibility. It is also the reason for pride being one of the movement's dominant emotions. For sixteen months a large majority of the Polish people saw themselves as part of a just, responsible and proud movement. These were bright hours of unity and honour regained: how could repression ever wipe these convictions from people's consciences?

Conclusion: The end of Communist society

A military coup, police brutalities, the declaration of a state of war, the despondency of a whole people and workers' resistance in the factories: for those of us who believed that such an outcome could only happen in underdeveloped countries, the pain and indignation are so great that there is a temptation to mourn. Once more the uprising of a whole people has been crushed by brutal repression. Is Poland to go the way of Czechoslovakia, which has been living in silence and persecution for thirteen years now? Are Polish democrats about to join the Chilean and Argentinian exiles in Paris, London and Rome, with the year of freedom reduced to a memory and gradually losing their real understanding of what is happening in their country? The scale of protest, at least in France, seems to emphasise that a social movement has died.

But this must not be our conclusion.

We do not know what path the military government will decide to take, and it would be useless to speculate about the chances of repression being severe or limited.[1] We shall speak only of what has just disappeared. But, if the movement of the Polish people has been defeated, it is Communist society which has died, and with it the central principle on which it is built: the control and direction of social life by the ideology and political organisation of a Party which considers itself to be the representative of the workers and the voluntarist agent of modernisation. The Polish national identity has survived more than a century without a nation-state, and the Polish social and national movement will be no more easily destroyed by the present ban on Solidarity. The conflict between society and the regime, the Poles' consciousness of living under a regime which is alien to their values and needs, may not be openly expressed through public statements and meetings: but there will be hidden go-slows in industry, sabotage, passive resistance and non-cooperation. On the other side, the Party may re-form, but it is difficult to imagine its role as anything more than one of control and repression.

1 The book was published in France before the dissolution of Solidarity by the *Sejm*, 8 October 1982. (Tr.)

188

The rupture between the Party and society goes back a long way, and has perhaps always existed, but it would be a mistake to think that Communist domination has been nothing more than the rule of an occupying regime imposed by the Red Army in keeping with the spirit, if not the letter, of Yalta. Many who worked for the Polish liberation movement had in the past been convinced Communists: this is above all true of intellectual and political figures like Kołakowski, Pomian, Geremek, Kuroń, Modzelewski and Michnik, but is also the case with many worker militants.

Despite the brutality with which the non-Communist resistance was crushed at the end of the war, and the violence of the Stalin era, the Communist Party represented for many people the hopes of a mutilated nation which wanted to live, reconstruct, increase production and advance the education and wellbeing of the greatest number. After the uprising of Poznań and the popular movement of the autumn of 1956, these hopes were revived. The repression of intellectuals in 1968, reinforced by a campaign of anti-Semitism, destroyed the hopes of many intellectuals. The massacres which took place on the Baltic in December 1970 and the repression of the riots of 1976 finally severed the links between the working class and the Party. And yet, from August 1980 to December 1981, hopes for an agreement between the Polish people and the Party constantly came to the surface within Solidarity. Some people, although they were relatively scarce, still talked of returning to 'true' socialism. Others, and there were many more of them, insisted that the Party rank and file and the great mass of Solidarity members shared the same reactions and the same hopes, and that their only enemy was the ruling apparatus of the Party and the state. But the middle of 1981 marks the separation of the Party and the nation. The Party demanded of the leading figures in its various bodies that they leave the union, and Solidarity too finally expelled Party members from positions of importance. Workers belonging to the Party began to hand in their cards in massive numbers, and it is said that in December, when the miners had to leave the mine after their long strike in protest at the declaration of martial law, they threw their cards to the ground as they left the mine to its military occupiers.

For the first time in history, a Party First Secretary, in a solemn address to the Polish nation, made no mention of that office, introducing himself simply as an officer and the head of the government, as though he too, a general with an almost exclusively political career behind him, knew that the population had lost all confidence in the Party. Officers were appointed as military administrators to take over from the civil authorities. Does this mean that the Party became militarised? Yes, if we mean by that that power has not changed hands and that today the authority of Poland's rulers rests solely on the force of arms. But if we take a more precise definition of the Party, the answer must be no. It was not simply a ruling elite or a group of privileged individuals: at root, it was and remains a totalitarian force. It never accepted what Solidarity demanded: that it leave civil society and confine itself in the citadel of the state. The Party consistently rejected such a separation of society and state; it could not give up the popular and historical basis of its legitimacy. If it had just been a Prince, it would have combined tolerance and repression without for a moment seeking to maintain control of people's minds and of the whole social fabric. But the control of minds was even more important to it than its monopoly of structures of social advancement. It is impossible to imagine a Communist Party not presenting itself as the interpreter of the laws of history, the needs of society and the interests of the workers. It is too manifestly obvious that this claim did not correspond to the reality, that the Party was the regime but not the people. But the essential point is that the reason for its domination being so thorough was that this domination was not simply that of the state: even if it resorts to force or manipulation to obtain it, a totalitarian regime must enjoy the public support of a large part of the population.

But for more than a year, the great mass of the Polish population had been able to express itself openly and live freely outside the Party, and when this immense social and national movement was destroyed, the Party had to hide behind naked armed force, recognising its failure and its virtual destruction. A few weeks after the coup certain political observers, allies of the Party but neither members nor important officials within it, were even predicting that the army would intervene to put an end to the national crisis, imposing its decisions on the Party as well as on Solidarity, the two forces struggling for control of the same drifting ship. This prediction, which perhaps had something to do with wishful thinking, was not fulfilled. It is not true that the Army, like some impartial judge, dismissed the people and their rulers like two naughty children. It did not sever its links with the Party, and no one can seriously believe that the arrest of Gierek and a few others was a realistic counterbalance to the destruction of Solidarity. But it is true that the Party now has only force to rely on, and that it is therefore losing the basis of its totalitarian power.

Those who speak of a new fascism or national socialism in Poland today are entitled to express in that way their indignation at the military takeover, but they see the triumph of a totalitarian regime where we should see its defeat. National socialism mobilised the crowds, fired their nationalism, and promised economic recovery, at the same time as it persecuted scapegoats, denounced racial impurity and opened the concentration camps which were to become extermination camps. The Party subjected the whole society, and not just the state, to its ideology and the force of its arms. After the First World War and the changes and revolutions which it had entailed, totalitarian regimes covered a large part of Europe, from Italy to the Soviet Union, including Germany and later the regimes which it was to set up through conquest or domination.

Conclusion: The end of Communist society

Today, in Communist Central Europe, totalitarianism is dying. The Hungarian revolution, the Prague Spring and then Solidarity fuelled hopes, which lasted for a few days, a few months or more than a year, that it would be replaced by democracy. Everywhere, force of arms won the day: Hungary and Czechoslovakia were invaded by a foreign army, while in Poland a military and political ruler acted as the Soviet Union wished, so avoiding the heavy diplomatic price which would have been paid for open intervention. But popular movements and uprisings are not the only victim of this violence. From now on, the Communist regime can no longer claim to speak in the name of society and history: its only foundation is force, and it has lost the legitimacy on which it based its totalitarian ambitions.

In Czechoslovakia, the humiliation of the invaded country was only partly associated in world opinion with resistance by the vanquished social movement, for if the latter had fired public opinion in Czechoslovakia, it had not been massively followed throughout the world, and the workers' councils were only important as a means of resisting the Soviet invasion after the event. In Hungary, the result of the popular revolution of 1956 was that long afterwards, from 1968 onwards, Kadar was able successfully to carry out essential economic reforms: real autonomy was given to a ruling class of enterprise managers, and the totalitarian rule of the Party was abolished, to be replaced by a ruling group over which the Party maintained a hegemonic influence but within which the economic leadership was allowed to follow its own economic logic. This facilitated a sufficient increase in production and consumption levels for the opposition to be deprived of mass support. Hungary now is in no sense a democratic country and repression is still used, but the Party, while remaining the master of the state, can no longer claim to represent the whole of society, since it accepts an instrumental and pragmatic conception of economic management.

Solidarity wanted to achieve from below, through a popular movement and by democratic means, what Hungary had only realised from above, technocratically and shielded by political repression. It wanted to free the economy from the grip of the Party: it probably sought to go further, but the core of its action was still situated at that level in the autumn of 1981. The relative differentiation between centres of power which succeeded in Hungary failed in Poland, where the only possible outcome was democratic reform; and, in the light of an opinion poll published in *Paris-Match* at the time of the institution of martial law, showing that the Party would only receive 3% of the vote in free elections, it is clear that democracy meant the Party's complete loss of control over society. In none of the three countries has democracy triumphed. Czechoslovakia is governed by repression; the tolerance which prevails in Hungary cannot be taken for freedom; Poland now lives under absolute rule, but that rule is more counter-revolutionary than totalitarian in character. Franco or Pinochet would be more exact comparisons than Hitler or Stalin.

Conclusion: The end of Communist society

Is the regime which now rules Poland by force a Polish regime, or is it simply the local agent of Soviet omnipotence? The question is less easy than at first appears. It is self-evident that a military coup in a Communist country which remains faithful to its alliances cannot take place without the agreement and participation of the Soviet Union. Little is known about the precise extent to which the Soviet Union took a direct part in the coup, but it is a question of secondary importance. The Polish army is totally integrated with the armed forces of the Warsaw Pact, and its movements depend materially and politically on decisions taken in Moscow. The Soviet army itself is present on Polish soil and has its own communications network there. But the fact that Jaruzelski or Kadar cannot govern without obtaining the agreement or taking note of the directives of the Soviet leadership does not prevent their rule from being strongly marked by the particular conditions prevailing in their respective countries.

The military coup in Poland, just as much as the special forms which Communist rule takes in Rumania, indicates not the decline but the growing importance of these particular national conditions. The regimes in these countries tend more and more to be defined by their repressive role, the failure of their economic policies and the increasingly visible hostility of the workers in the main industries. The Soviet Union no longer acts as the leader of the socialist camp, but as the master of an empire, indifferent to the ideological problems of its vassals and above all concerned with its own power and security. It is incapable of directing economic and social change outside its own frontiers, being itself weakened by contradictions between its military and political action and the social and economic problems which it faces. It would be dangerous to maintain that the Polish people is more directly under the heel of the Soviet Union than it was before. On the contrary, the violence of the repression which was imposed with the collaboration or at the initiative of the Soviet Union only serves to emphasise the conflict between the nation and a state which governs against the nation's will and cannot manage the economy in the face of active hostility from all the nation's workers. The regime which the coup brought into being has to repress every manifestation of the social and national consciousness; and it can do nothing to prevent a situation in which Poland will be more marked than before by open rupture between the state and the nation. Repression can no longer bring Poland back within the bounds of Communist society, as it could under Stalinism.

As we witness Solidarity being destroyed, the only prediction that we can make is that the regime installed by the military coup will be unable to reconquer society. Perhaps it will be a purely repressive regime, and perhaps it will attempt some kind of accelerated 'kadarisation', using extremely authoritarian methods and imposing on the population a sudden decline in its standard of living in order to force through essential economic reform; alternatively, it may seek some form of concordat with the society which it rules. Whichever hypothesis is adopted, the rupture between state and nation will be just as complete as when a mutilated Poland was governed by foreign princes. At best, the Church will manage to interpose itself between the state and the nation in order to prevent the paralysis of the economy and of all social life. The role which the Church is trying to play, resisting the new regime but without urging the country to active resistance, indicates more clearly than anything else the state of cold war, of hostile coexistence, which is going to characterise relations between government and society in Poland.

All the signs are that as an illegal organisation Solidarity will maintain the strength and the convictions which it had when it could exist openly. Communist society with its totalitarian ambitions has disappeared; in the ruins there remains the dictatorship of arms and untruth, and underneath that the outlawed movement for the liberation of society.

Our whole century has been dominated by totalitarianism. Almost everywhere in the world, but especially to the East and South, on the continents which had been subjugated by capitalism and the armies of the trading and industrial West, new states undertook to liberate, build and govern societies which sought to shake off their dependency. Here in the West, the nations which emerged defeated from the First World War were mobilised by and subjected to the terror of totalitarian states. Has the retreat of the totalitarian state at last begun? Are economic forces and social movements coming into being, outside the control of the Party-state, and forcing it either to become a straightforward dictatorship, or to create a new ruling class? In both cases, if this were true, it would mean that the state ceased to identify itself with the whole of the society upon which it previously imposed its ideology and its forms of organisation.

Nowhere else has this desire for the liberation of society been as strong as in Poland. Once again the hope has been disappointed and force has won the day, but if force can silence social movements, it cannot make the Party-state once again able to act in the name of society.

This decline of totalitarianism is, however, not exclusively positive in its effects. The military dictatorship which succeeds it may choose to follow a policy even more directly geared to the search for power. As we near the end of the century the statue of revolution is crumbling, and in its place we are beginning to see the statue of war. After the death of Stalin, under Khrushchev, the Soviet Union made a partial and confused attempt to grant limited autonomy to social forces, or at least to the forces which managed the economy. Today, that attempted reform can be seen to have largely failed. The Soviet Union is ruled by the logic of military force, while part of the society has joined the ranks of dissidence. Between the state and the dissidents, managers and intellectuals lead an uncomfortable double life full of hidden motives and bad faith. In Poland, everything is much clearer. Never since the death of Stalin has the Party been able to impose its totalitarian rule on society; after 1956, certain sectors of society – religious life, agriculture and, in part, intellectual life – remained to some degree independent of the Party. Now that the Party is no more than the shadow of guns, how could it possibly win back the factories and working-class trade unionism?

Under attack from the military state, Solidarity reveals fully to the whole world what a social movement is. Until quite recently an idea inherited from the nineteenth century still held sway: it was widely believed that the only popular movements which could have any importance were those which went 'in the direction of history', which fought against an *ancien régime* in the name of progress. This notion reduced popular forces to an army commanded by political leaders and ideologists whose job it was to define the meaning of history. Popular demands and uprisings were inseparable from the creation of new centres of state power. The most important variety of totalitarian regime was a development of this idea: Communist leaders exercised absolute power in the name of the people, history and science. Their action was in the service of economic development, the liberation of productive forces which were to throw down the barriers erected by capitalist relations of production, and lead their country into the world of abundance and freedom.

This conception long ago ceased to correspond to reality, except for those whose faith was blindness. But never until the formation of Solidarity had the obsolescence of this old image of social movements been so clearly demonstrated. Never had the appeal to progress been so clearly replaced by an appeal to human rights and freedoms. Once a new, modernising, productivist regime has replaced the traditional forces of domination characteristic of an *ancien régime* as the main enemy of the popular movement, the latter, as long as it escapes the danger of community-oriented traditionalism, affirms the rights of individuals against a regime which claims to represent universal truth.

The social movements which before sought their legitimacy in history can today only find it in an inner appeal to freedom. Hence their alliance with morality, when the regime allies itself with science. Hence the desire of their members to live, in their relations with each other, here and now and in an exemplary way, the type of social relations which they wish to see established for all in the future. Previous social movements, on the other hand, saw themselves as the makers of a future which they themselves would never see; they organised their action according to a model of armed struggle, putting off until later the transformation of personal and collective behaviour. Solidarity was not concerned with the future reconstruction of Poland; its members lived it every day. Words such as 'base', 'mass' and even 'militants' did not correspond to their lived experience; it would be more appropriate to speak of workers, the people and volunteers. Such strengths of conviction, such faith in justice and in the rights which must be defended cannot be destroyed by persecution. Once again, but this time in a new way, the social and national consciousness of the Poles in their struggle against a dictatorship has taken refuge in private activity, whether personal or collective.

The Polish movement has been defeated and destroyed; it will continue to suffer repression, but it cannot disappear, not only because it corresponds to the deepest convictions of many people, but because it is impossible to uproot the free trade union Solidarity from the factories and from the minds of the workers. The Polish military coup is another victory for repressive state power; but we must look further, and understand that it is the most far-reaching and definitive failure of a totalitarian party, the end of Communist society, and a step forward to a more direct confrontation between regime and society, between state violence and social movements.

Chronology of events

BEFORE JULY 1980

17 June 1953: Workers' demonstrations in East Berlin.

28 June 1956: Workers riot at Poznań. Fifty killed.

19–20 October 1956: Gomułka coopted by the Central Committee. Khrushchev makes a surprise visit to Warsaw.

23 October 1956: Beginning of the Hungarian revolution.

13 November 1956: End of resistance to the Soviet occupation of Hungary.

October 1964: Open Letter to the Party by Jacek Kuroń and Karol Modzelewski.

January 1968: Dubcek appointed First Secretary of the Czechoslovak Communist Party.

8–9 March 1968: Student rising in Warsaw, followed by repression at the University. Many intellectuals, almost all Jewish, are forced into exile.

21 August 1968: Invasion of Czechoslovakia by Warsaw Pact troops.

December 1970: Strikes on the Baltic coast.

19 December 1970: Gomułka replaced by Gierek as First Secretary of the Party.

February 1971: Strike in the textile industry at Łódź.

1975: Campaign by the Party for the modification of the Constitution and the recognition of the 'leading role' of the Party and the 'inseparable link' between Poland and the Soviet Union. Protests by intellectuals.

April 1976: E. Lipiński, the economist, writes to Gierek predicting economic crisis.

25 June 1976: Riots at the Ursus factory, in Radom and several other towns.

September 1976: Foundation of the KOR.

November 1976: Foundation of DiP.

Spring 1977: Foundation of ROPCiO.

7 May 1977: A Kraków student, Pyjas, is murdered.

Summer 1977: Strikes and demonstrations by miners in Rumania.

Autumn 1977: First issue of *Robotnik.*

March 1978: Creation of free trade unions in Katowice.

September 1978: First issue of *The Baltic Worker (Robotnik Wybrzeża).*

16 October 1978: Cardinal Wojtyła is elected Pope John Paul II.

2–10 June 1979: John Paul II visits Poland.

18 December 1979: Mass demonstrations in Gdańsk in memory of the dead of 1970.

11–15 February 1980: Congress of the PUWP.

Chronology of events

1980

July
1. Food prices increased.
2–7. First wave of strikes.
10. Strikes in Łódź, Lublin, and at the Żerań car plant in Warsaw.

August
1. Demonstration in Warsaw in memory of the victims of the Katyń massacre.
14. Beginning of the strike at the Lenin shipyard in Gdańsk.
15. Start of negotiations at the Lenin shipyard; concessions on wages; the strikers decide to erect a monument to the dead of 1970.
16–17. The Gdańsk strike committee, MKS, is formed. Twenty-one demands are drawn up.
20. Arrest of eighteen members of the KOR. Strike begins at Nowa Huta. 62 Warsaw intellectuals express their support; their number will soon swell to 234.
21. Jagielski, Deputy Prime Minister, placed in charge of the negotiating team.
22. Negotiations begin at Szczecin.
23. First issue of the news-sheet *Solidarność*. Negotiations at the Lenin shipyard.
24. The 'committee of experts' is formed in Gdańsk. Cardinal Wyszyński calls for moderation.
28. First miners' strike in Silesia, at the Manifest Lipcowy mine at Katowice.
30. Szczecin Agreement signed.
31. Gdańsk Agreement signed.

September
1. Members of the political opposition released from prison.
4. Jastrzębie Agreement signed.
6. Kania replaces Gierek as Party First Secretary and promises to respect the agreements. Members of the *Sejm* call for the democratisation of institutions.
15. The Gdańsk Agreement extended to the whole country.
18. A government commission is set up to define a framework for economic reform.
28. Individual farmers demand the recognition of their union.

October
1. Creation of an independent students' union.
3. Protest in several areas at the non-implementation of the agreements. General strike of one hour to support the protest.
11. Miłosz receives the Nobel Prize for literature.
15. Kania declares that 'the process of change is irreversible'. 97% of the 43 000 workers at the Lenin steelworks have joined Solidarity, which now has six million members.
24. The Warsaw District Court registers Solidarity's statutes, but includes in them certain limits on the right to strike, and the recognition of the leading role of the Party. Solidarity calls a general strike for 12 November. Kania visits Moscow. A period of great tension.

197

November

10. The Supreme Court annuls the decision of the District Court. Withdrawal of the strike call.
11. Celebration at the Warsaw Opera in honour of Solidarity.
24. Arrest of Jan Narożniak, accused of disseminating a circular from the public prosecutor on ways of dealing with dissidents.
25. A general strike is threatened in Masovia; a strike begins at Ursus the next day.
27. Narożniak released and the strike called off.

December

2. The Central Committee eliminates Gierek's sympathisers from the Politburo, replacing them with Fiszbach, a liberal, Moczar, a nationalist, and Grabski, a hard-liner.
5. Kania visits Moscow; his policies are approved.
12. Monsignor Orszulik, spokesman for the Episcopate, attacks Kuroń and the KOR.
16. A Mass is held at the Gdańsk memorial.
29. Edmond Maire (leader of the French CFDT) visits Warsaw.
30. Kania visits the Gdańsk memorial.

1981

January

4. A Solidarity delegation visits the Primate of Poland.
7. Beginning of the movement in favour of the 'free Saturdays' promised in the Gdańsk Agreement. At the request of the union, no work is done Saturday 7 January.
13–19. Wałęsa in Rome. He has a meeting with the Pope.
24. Strikes at Bielsko-Biała directed against the local authorities.
27. Individual farmers occupy the headquarters of the official trade unions at Rzeszów, demanding the recognition of Rural Solidarity. Their demand is supported by strike action.
31. A compromise solution is reached on the five-day working week.

February

4. Renewed strikes at Bielsko-Biała.
6. Strikes continue in the Rzeszów area.
10. Jaruzelski, Minister of Defence, replaces Pinkowski as Prime Minister. Creation of a permanent negotiating committee under the chairmanship of Rakowski. Jaruzelski asks for a ninety-day truce, which is accepted by Solidarity.
20. The Supreme Court refuses to register Rural Solidarity on the basis that its members are not wage-earners.

March

4. Moscow hardens its line and demands that the 'course of events be reversed'.
5. Kuroń and Michnik, members of the KOR, are arrested.
8. Anti-Semitic and nationalist demonstration organised by the Grunwald Union.

10. Wałęsa and Jaruzelski meet to discuss the independent farmers' union.
13. *Pravda* accuses Solidarity of receiving financial support from the CIA.
16. Warsaw Pact forces begin manoeuvres.
19. Bydgoszcz incident in which three militants, including Jan Rulewski, the union's regional president, are beaten up by police.
27. General warning strike. National strike announced for 31 March.
28–30. Difficult negotiations with the government. Soviet threats, extreme tension.
30. On television, Wałęsa announces that next day's strike is off. This decision will later cause serious conflict within the union and the resignation of Modzelewski as the union's spokesman.

April
2. First issue of the weekly *Solidarność*.
7. Pacifying speech by Brezhnev.
15. Meeting of the 'horizontal structures' movement at Toruń.
17. The government promises to recognise Rural Solidarity.
29. Plenum of the Central Committee decides that elections to the Party Congress will take place by secret ballot. The maximum length of service in an elected post will be two periods of office.

May
3. In Warsaw, a considerable crowd commemorates the anniversary of the 1791 Constitution.
11. Recognition of Rural Solidarity, the union of individual farmers.
25. Student demonstrations in Warsaw.
26. Declaration by the 'hard-liners' of the Katowice Forum.
28. Death of Cardinal Wyszyński. Wajda's *Man of Iron* receives the grand prix of the Cannes film festival.
30. Popular demonstrations at the funeral of Cardinal Wyszyński. Thirty days' mourning is declared.

June
5. Solidarity takes part in the conference of the ILO at Geneva. Four leading members of the KPN are released. Threatening letter from the Soviet Party to its Polish counterpart.
9. Provisional agreement reached on the Bydgoszcz affair.
9–10. Kania remains First Secretary after Plenum of the Central Committee.
27. Big demonstration in Poznań in memory of the 1956 uprising.

July
3. Visit by Gromyko.
7. Monsignor Glemp becomes Primate of Poland.
8. Dockers' strike on the Baltic. Beginning of conflict within LOT, the state airline.
10–25. Hunger marches at Kutno.
14–20. Ninth Congress of the PUWP; 80% of the delegates are new, and 7 of the 11 members of the Politburo are replaced. Kania is elected First Secretary by secret ballot.

27 and 30. Hunger marches at Łódź.
31. Government reshuffle: four serving generals are appointed.

August
3. Buses block the streets of Warsaw. Demonstrations against the cost of living.
5. Members of the KPN arrested.
7. Strikes in Silesia. Hunger marches in Kraków.
12. Solidarity leadership asks the population to refrain from demonstrations.
15. Meeting between Kania, Jaruzelski and Brezhnev in the Crimea.
18–19. The print workers strike against censorship.
21. Confrontations between population and police in Silesia. Wałęsa calls for an end to strikes and for Saturday working.

September
5–10. First phase of Solidarity's Congress. Message to the free trade unions of the Eastern bloc and the Soviet Union. Call for free elections. 'An anti-socialist orgy', says Tass. The Soviet fleet conducts manoeuvres off Gdańsk.
10. Moscow demands 'radical measures'.
16. The PUWP attacks Solidarity's 'programme of political opposition'.
22. On television, Olszowski, a member of the Politburo, proposes the creation of a national front bringing together Party, Church and Solidarity.
25. Parliament signs an agreement with Solidarity on self-management.
26. Beginning of the second phase of Solidarity's Congress.
29. Congress passes a motion of censure on the leadership for accepting compromise on self-management without consulting the union.

October
2–7. The KOR announces its dissolution. The Congress sets out economic guidelines and a project for reform. Wałęsa is elected President with 55% of the votes.
18. Jaruzelski adds to his post of Prime Minister that of Party First Secretary, replacing Kania.
21. A wave of strikes throughout the country. Solidarity calls for 'an end to all strikes'.
28. General strike of one hour.

November
1. Strike at Żyrardów. Wałęsa intervenes to stop it.
4. Solidarity calls for an end to strikes for three months. Meeting between Monsignor Glemp, Jaruzelski and Wałęsa, with a view to setting up a 'Council for national consensus'.
11. Demonstration in Warsaw to mark the anniversary of national independence.
13. *Pravda* calls on Polish Communists to follow the path of 'ideological purity'.
18. Agreement reached on a negotiating procedure for the setting up of the Council for national consensus.
27–8. The Sixth Plenum of the Central Committee gives discretionary powers to Jaruzelski.

December

2. The Warsaw Fire Officers School, occupied since 18 November, is evacuated by militia. Solidarity declares that 'the authorities are destroying any chance of reaching national agreement'.
7. Parliament refuses to approve emergency laws after a letter from Monsignor Glemp to every deputy.
11. Tass accuses Solidarity of preparing to 'seize power'.
12. Solidarity demands 'a referendum at national level, or within the union, on the authorities' methods of government'.
13. Declaration of martial law and constitution of a National Military Council under the chairmanship of General Jaruzelski. Mass arrests of workers and intellectuals.

Bibliography

Arendt, Hannah *The Origins of Totalitarianism*, 3rd edn, London, George Allen and
Unwin, 1966

Babeau, André *Les Conseils ouvriers en Pologne*, Cahiers de la Fondation Nationale des
Sciences Politiques, No. 110, Paris, Colin, 1960

Bethell, Nicholas *Gomulka: his Poland and his Communism*, Revised edn, Harmondsworth, Penguin, 1972

Bromke, Adam *Poland's Politics: Idealism versus Realism*, Cambridge, Mass., Harvard
University Press, 1967

Broué, P., Marie, J. J. & Nagy, L. *Pologne, Hongrie, 1956*, Paris, EDI, 1966

Dziewanowski, M. K. *The Communist Party of Poland*, 2nd edn, Cambridge, Mass.,
Harvard University Press, 1976

   Poland in the Twentieth Century, New York, Columbia University Press, 1977

Esprit, Special issues, January 1977 and January 1981

Faye, J.-P. & Fišera, W. C. *Prague. La Révolution des conseils ouvriers*, Paris, Seghers-
Laffont, 1977

Fejtö, Ferenc *Histoire des démocraties populaires*, 2 vols, Paris, Le Seuil, 1969; trans. as
A History of the People's Democracies: Eastern Europe since Stalin, 2nd edn,
Harmondsworth, Penguin, 1974

Hegedus, Zsuzsa *Reforma economica e conflitto sociale. Il caso hungarese*, Milan, Angeli,
1981

Kecskemeti, Paul *The Unexpected Revolution*, Stanford, Calif., Stanford University
Press, 1961

Kende, P. & Pomian, K. (eds) *1956. Varsovie–Budapest. La deuxième révolution
d'octobre*, Paris, Le Seuil, 1978

Kołakowski, L. 'Hope and hopelessness', *Survey*, summer 1971

Kuroń, J. and Modzelewski, K. *List otwarty do partii*, Paris, Instytut Literacki, 1966;
trans. as *An Open Letter to the Party*, London, International Socialism, n.d.

Lefort, Claude *L'Invention démocratique*, Paris, Fayard, 1981

Matejko, Alexander *Social Change and Stratification in Eastern Europe*, New York,
Praeger, 1974

Miłosz, Czesław *The Captive Mind* (1st edn in English 1953), Harmondsworth,
Penguin, 1980

Mlynar, Zdenek *Le Froid vient de Moscou* (1st edn, Prague 1968), Paris, Gallimard,
1981

Bibliography

Molnar, Miklos *Victoire d'une défaite, Budapest 1956*, Paris, Fayard, 1968
and Nagy, L. *Imre Nagy, réformateur ou révolutionnaire*, Geneva, Droz, 1959
Nowak, Stefan 'Values and attitudes of the Polish people', *Scientific American*, Vol. 245, No. 1, July 1981, pp. 23–31
Pomian, Krzysztof 'Miracle en Pologne', *Le Débat*. No. 9, February 1981, pp. 3–18
Pologne: défi à l'impossible? De la révolte de Poznań à Solidarité, Paris, Editions ouvrières, 1982
Raina, Peter *Political opposition in Poland 1954–1977*, London, Poetry and Painters Press, 1978
Rakovski, Marc *Le Marxisme face aux pays de l'Est*, Paris, Savelli, 1977; trans. as *Towards an East European Marxism*, London, Allison and Busby, 1978
Smolar, Alexander (ed) *La Pologne, une société en dissidence*, Paris, Maspero, 1977
Strmiska, Zdenek 'Programme socialiste et rapports sociaux en URSS et dans les pays socialistes', *Revue des études comparatives Est–Ouest*, Vol. 7, No. 3, September 1976, pp. 101–233
Szczepański, Jan *Polish Society*, New York, Random House, 1970
Les Temps modernes, 'Le socialisme polonais', Special issue, February–March 1957
Tigrid, Paveł *Le Printemps de Prague*, Paris, Le Seuil, 1968

The translator has referred in notes to the following additional works:

Ascherson, Neal *The Polish August*, Harmondsworth, Penguin, 1981
Macshane, Denis *Solidarity: Poland's Independent Trade Union*, Nottingham, Spokesman, 1981
Touraine, Alain *La Voix et le regard*, Paris, Le Seuil, 1978; trans. as *The Voice and the Eye*, Cambridge, Cambridge University Press, 1981